The BEING Zone

"*Drawing on the wisdom she gleaned from an illness that could not be healed through conventional methods, Marla Williams generously shares how we can heal ourselves. Her methods are both practical and mystical, giving all of us the opportunity to embrace our own abilities through her methods.*"

~Brenda Michaels, Host of Conscious Talk Radio; Founder of Intentional Healing; Emotional and Spiritual Healer and Coach

"*This book is different than anything out there. Instead of just sharing the knowledge, Marla is teaching you how to make it a reality in your life and providing you with options so that it works for you.*

Life situations, limiting beliefs, and subconscious programing can set wheels in motion that leave you feeling stuck, living a life you are not in alignment with. This fact can lead to disharmony, disease and dysfunction.

As you read this amazing book, you will gently follow a path Marla has laid out stone by stone. With the applied understanding of the latest mind-body-spirit health and healing modalities as arrows in your quiver, you will unite all of the mental, physical, and spiritual fragmentation that keeps you stuck, unhealthy, and unhappy. This is a powerful tool for remembering your authentic self, aligning with Source, and BEING who you really are, DOING what you really want, and HAVING the life you truly deserve.

I have complete faith that anyone who opens themselves to the journey to The BEING Zone will find the best version of their true, authentic self, right there under their own un-DOING."

~Jeff Granville, Founder of Mindful Presents

"Sharing her own story of transformation and over 100 journaling exercises to empower readers, Marla Williams' heartfelt *The BEING Zone* is a sensitive guidebook that will take you on a journey of personal healing and discovery."

~Theresa Nicassio PhD, Psychologist, Wellness Educator, Radio Host, and Award-Winning Author of *YUM: Plant-Based Recipes for a Gluten-Free Diet*

"In front of you, you have a power-packed, insight-rich guide designed to help you transform and transition from *The DOING Zone* to *The BEING Zone*. This is a must-read for anyone looking to make this critical leap! As you explore the pages of this book, you'll be met with ideas, stories, and tools that will save you years of your life, bringing you to a place that feels like your true home!"

~David Morelli, Host of the Enwaken Podcast, CEO of OwlHub, Inc., and Creator of Peak Performance Week

"The tools in this book are invaluable with clients who are stressed, depressed, anxious, or suffering from other mental health issues. Marla Williams' SHIFT Tool is the most powerful tool in my toolbox."

~Jann Finley, LMHC, CCHT

"For years, I was unhappy. No matter what goals I set and accomplished, I felt like something was always off. I had worked with various counselors and coaches, but nothing seemed to help. Then I started working with Marla and read *The BEING Zone*. It turned my life around, and I started to feel happy inside for the first time ever.

I enjoyed the examples given in the book, and the exercises provided in each chapter were of tremendous use. Since no two people are alike, the fact that there are options for how to resolve my issues was a welcome oasis. I highly recommend reading *The BEING Zone* or working with Marla if you are ready to find happiness and take your life to a higher level."

~Trudie German, Online Personal Trainer, Health and Fitness Speaker, Corporate Wellness Specialist, Owner of Body Envy

THE
BEING ZONE

A Transformational Experience for
Rediscovery, Reconnection, and Healing

Marla Williams

Foreword by Moorea Seal

© 2020 by Marla Williams

Published by PS Zone

All rights reserved. No part of this publication may be reproduced, distributed, or transmitted in any form or by any means, including photocopying, recording, or other electronic or mechanical methods, without the prior written permission of the publisher, except in the case of brief quotations embodied in critical reviews and certain other noncommercial uses permitted by copyright law. For permission requests, please contact:

Support@TheBEINGZone.com
www.TheBEINGZone.com
The BEING Zone™

Ordering Information:
Quantity sales. Special discounts are available on quantity purchases by non-profits. For details, contact the publisher at the address above.

Printed in the United States of America

Marla Williams
The BEING Zone : A Transformational Experience for Rediscovery, Reconnection, and Healing

Cover Design by John Browning
Illustrations by Amanda Stovall
Interior Design by Colleen Sheehan

The names and identifying details in the client stories that follow have been changed to protect the privacy of individuals. Except for a few clients who wanted their story told.

The information contained in this book does not constitute medical advice. It is meant as a source of valuable information for the reader but is not a substitute for direct expert assistance. Please consult with your physician or medical professional to determine what may be best for your individual needs.

Print ISBN 978-1-7349253-0-2
Ebook ISBN 978-1-7349253-1-9
Journal ISBN 978-1-7349253-2-6

First Edition

I dedicate this book to anyone who is struggling in life and the practitioners who dedicate their lives to helping them. I know it takes an open mind and heart to have the courage to take this journey of transformation. I am grateful for my husband Mark, my two sons, Brady and Bryan, and all my friends, family and clients who have graciously supported me through this process. I am so very blessed to have all of you in my life.

TABLE OF

Contents

by Moorea Seal

I DON'T SAY THIS sort of thing often or really ever: the change, or rather, the realignment with my authentic self that I have experienced since meeting Marla Williams and integrating her practices into my life has been profound.

Within this book, she shares a wholistic view of what it truly means to seek and experience wellness, and something even greater than the healing itself, a guide towards *BEING*. You are destined as a reader of this book to uncover a version of yourself that has been quieted within you for a long time. Imagine each page that you turn being a new layer of excavating what was once thought to be lost or intangible within you. Whether you are looking to heal a physical manifestation of your suffering or hoping to become a more empowered version of yourself, hungry for happiness, or just needing a spark of clarity, direction will be found here.

I first met Marla through a collaboration with a local business here in Seattle, but during the process, amidst the many career and life projects I had become accustomed to piling on my plate, I found myself and my health suffering. I briefly mentioned a bit of what I was experiencing to Marla and she offered to provide me with life and business coaching. I turned the opportunity down, thinking, "This is just how my life is. If you work hard, you just get sick a lot and depression is inevitable and I am used to this, I just need to power through." As the year passed by since chatting with her via email, my life began to fall apart and my health issues worsened.

In the Fall of 2019, I was at one of my lowest points in some time. It was becoming clear that my romantic partner of ten years and I had grown in different directions, my business partnerships were splintering because retail was crushing our spirits, I was questioning the choices I had made in my various careers and doubting I was on the right, or rather, truest path for myself. Over the course of a few years, I had accumulated a variety of undiagnosable physical ailments. It was like fires were alight in every area of my life and I had no idea where to focus first. I fought hard to stay positive, but everything felt like it was caving in.

In what felt like a moment of clarity, I remembered that Marla had offered life/business coaching to me almost a year earlier, and I hoped with all my heart that the opportunity was still on the table. As soon as I reached out, it was like a trajectory to healing and finding my true state of *BEING* was set. I came to her asking for business guidance, and within one coaching session, she empowered me to see that I needed to start at a deeper level of healing from within, to truly gain clarity in my work and in my personal life. I took a risk to trust and learn, and from that moment on, every challenge that has been present in my life over the last few months has felt like a gift, a stepping stone towards the me I have been missing.

What I discovered through asking myself the questions that Marla lays out in each chapter of the book ahead—and through practicing the tools she provides for clearing emotional blocks and false narratives—was that, to lay the stepping stones to my freedom from cycles of pain and suffering was to see the earth upon which I lay my stones. What does this mean? It means, I didn't just feel empowerment to face the challenges that lay ahead of me in the new path I needed to create. But even more so, I was able to have greater clarity into the complex and dynamic life I had lived thus far, the beauty and the mess of all I had been *DOING* in trying to protect the sensitive yet powerful me I hoped could just *BE* someday.

I had felt like my life was out of my control in so many ways, and Marla's words and insights made it clear in an instant that at 33, I had yet to truly step into my own power. I always felt I was on the precipice of my truth, my power, yet so far away. I piled so much on my plate for years in hopes it would get me to the clarity of my power faster. But with Marla's wisdom, I was able to see it's not in the adding that my truth would be illuminated, it's through finding peace with myself in the present that the authentic me could rise up.

Just a few months after applying the teachings found in this book to my life, I find myself here, a woman who can say for certain *BEING* is the state in which I flow more and more each day with positivity and light. Each challenge I have faced over the last few months, I have approached with grace and true wellness of *BEING* because of Marla Williams' teachings, guidance, and practices.

As I write this, I am now a woman no longer in a marriage that was suffering, and I was able to navigate uncoupling with consciousness and kindness. I am no longer in a business partnership that felt emotionally draining; rather I am now in a lifelong friendship. And I find myself blissfully unattached from the unhealthy relationships that once haunted my past and made me feel trapped. I finally feel free. There are challenges ahead of me, as there are for all of us. I write this while in an Airbnb during COVID-19, living alone for the first time in my life. I had to shut down my storefront and online retail site because of this pandemic. I, like many, am in a state of experiencing loss, but what I know for sure is that I myself am not lost. While the world changes around me, I sit in calm, centered observation, seeking to love myself and love others, trusting I am capable of anything I set my heart and mind to as long as I seek *BEING* rather *DOING*. Marla's insights on living and healing have transformed me, and I know they can do the same for you if you are willing.

Commit. Commit to showing up to yourself before all else. Seek *BEING* rather than *DOING*. Let the challenges you face be the things that unlock the you that you have been waiting to see, feel, experience, and know, the you who is meant to live in wholeness. As the things we lose fall to the wayside, turning into fertilizer for the ground we stand tall upon, may your setting of the stone path of your life ahead be easier with each lifting and placement. You're getting stronger each day.

The pages ahead are your guides for lighting the path ahead. Marla isn't the one saving you, YOU are—one page, one practice, one moment of contemplation and devotion to the self at a time. May you find as much profound inspiration to *BE* you as I have found through the clarity Marla provides.

Thank you, Marla, for *BEING* so wholly you, sharing your wisdom and research, inner knowledge, and experience with the world so we all may find our joyful and free state of *BEING*.

—Moorea Seal

Best-Selling Author of the Wellness Series:
The 52 Lists Project, 52 Lists for Happiness,
52 Lists for Calm, and 52 Lists for Togetherness

Introduction

"Silence is a source of great strength."
—Lao Tzu

THE DAY MY doctor said, "You will die if you don't stop" was the day I realized I had to find a way to change my life permanently. After years and years of existing in high stress and pushing myself too much, resulting in multiple autoimmune illnesses which were breaking down my ability to function, it was time to listen. I was struggling each day and no longer happy. I had to stop doing what I had always done to regain my health and my happiness. I had to learn how to operate differently in this busy world of ours. Over the next few years of my healing journey I learned my most valuable life lesson yet: "The art of happiness is in the pause."

I had been in survival mode, a state of "fight or flight," and did not even realize it. So many of us think tension, headaches, inflammation, digestive issues, rashes, and other stress-related symptoms are a normal part of life. Now I know they aren't normal and are actually an indicator of deeper issues or high stress. It turns out stress is more rampant in our world than I realized. According to the World Health Organization, stress is the health epidemic of the 21st century.[1] When you are in the middle of it, it is hard to see it. The day I had my wake-up call was the beginning of me understanding the severity of this epidemic and what we can do about it.

After successfully healing myself from living in stress, I have helped over 1,000 clients reboot their lives and have created a system that works called *The BEING Zone™ System,* and I am sharing a large number of my tips and tools in this book.

Are you running in a continual state of exhaustion, stress, anxiety, or overwhelm? Or are you often feeling unhappy or depressed and feel there is more to life than what you are experiencing? If so, you are in the right place if you are looking for a proven system to help you find long-lasting happiness and health. With so much chaos and dysfunction in our world, people are faced with a myriad of problems that can feel overwhelming. I know as I have been there. I am happy to say this book will help you rediscover and reconnect with yourself while navigating many of the issues or problems you are facing. My story tells it all and will help you understand why I share what I do in this book.

I was a successful corporate leader, had a beautiful home, a vacation property, a loving husband, two young sons, a dog, and a cat. My life looked perfect from the outside, but I was crumbling on the inside because I wasn't listening to my body. I thought I was happy until I kept getting stress-related illnesses and realized that happiness and health were not what I was experiencing. Over time, it became clear to me that old, ingrained belief systems were the underlying reason I lived in a state of stress, unhappiness and overwhelm. Through many years of self-study, trial, and error, I cleared past issues and healed myself, transforming my life. I learned to quiet my mind, listen to my body, love myself unconditionally, and found true happiness. Now my mission and purpose are to help others transform their lives.

According to a Gallup survey of more than 2.5 million people, happiness is in sharp decline across the United States.[2] I wasn't surprised by this because I hear over and over from clients, "I am physically, mentally, and emotionally exhausted at the end of each day." "I worry too much." "I can't sleep." "I'm not happy." Most of us are going strong 24/7, 365 days per year. Our bodies were not designed to be in perpetual stress. Over time, when that stress is constant in us, we are working ourselves into burnout and illness.

When we are exhausted and stressed all the time, our bodies respond to our thoughts by elevating our emotions, which releases the stress hormones of adrenaline and cortisol into our system and prepares our bodies for "fight or flight" response, putting our bodies in emergency mode.[3] Best-selling author Dr. Joe Dispenza indicates in his books *Evolve Your Brain* and *Breaking the Habit of Being Yourself* that we become addicted to these emotions, and when we live in that elevated survival state, our immune system is compromised.[4] We are draining our own life force, which results in illness. That is where I existed for many years.

I transformed my life and currently thrive in health, happiness, and well-being, following my heart and doing what I love. As a result of my personal success, I used the same practical tools with my clients with great success, leading me to create *The BEING Zone System* that I am now sharing with you in this book. Earlier in my life, I wasn't ready—it took three bouts of stress-related illnesses before I was able to create a life I love.

Let's start at the beginning. My favorite memories during my early teenage years are mostly of sitting by myself on the shores of Lake Meridian in Kent, Washington, where I grew up. I would genuinely connect with my surroundings and put myself in what I now call my personal *"BEING Zone."* In this space, I would journal, reflect on quotes about nature and life's meaning, and write my own quotes, thoughts, and poems. I would tune in to my surroundings of the lake, trees, and wildlife. Those were some of my first introductions to feeling the calming energy of the earth and bringing that energy into myself. They were also the first steps on my path to a career I love, helping people and businesses find peace, purpose, and prosperity.

Though my reflective sessions at the lake were a start, it would take many more years before I was ready to help myself and others. I come from a long line of overachievers who believe a person must go to school to gain credentials, so they can get a respectable job that brings in good money. I inherited my workaholic nature from my father, a C.P.A. who owned his firm and worked long hours. I basically didn't see him from January through April and not a lot during the rest of the year. My dad was lots of fun on those few weekends he was home, leading my sister, brothers, and me on outings like waterskiing or long drives in the countryside. Yet he always conveyed a strong message that life was not about fun except on short breaks.

Like my father, I believed that I had to work hard and put in long hours to get what I wanted. I knew from a very young age that I would go to college. As a driven, high-energy person, I found the stress of college life put me on an emotional roller coaster of highs and lows. To get off that roller coaster, I would occasionally head to the beach to walk and relax by tuning into the calming energy of the waves, rediscovering my personal *BEING Zone* that I had discovered on the dock as a young teen.

One day when I was on the beach, I heard a voice in my head, and it was not the urgent, do what it takes voice I usually heard. This different voice told me to slow down, to stop and just "*BE*," and to allow life to unfold instead of pushing. That made sense to me, as I knew Newton's law of motion basically tell us that what we push will push back. I share this thought because surrendering to what is and allowing what will be is a key part of what keeps me healthy and happy.

Even though I was in the midst of my frenzied college life, I remembered that during my formative years, I journaled a lot and it calmed my mind, so I made the decision to start journaling again. I would go to the beach and journal, getting all my emotions, fears, stresses, and feelings written out on paper. Writing about how I was feeling provided me with the ability to reflect on situations instead of reacting, which resulted in better decisions because they were made in a calm state of *BEING*. As a result of adding these small conscious steps to my life, I found I was better at leveling out my emotions, which helped my focus in school.

After graduation, though, I reverted to living full-time in more of a stress-state when I started my corporate career. I felt I had to prove myself as the only woman leader in a male-dominated industry, so I worked my tail off around the clock, and on weekends, too. I thrived in the company's fast-paced environment, where I was instrumental in developing the company's vision and strategies while helping to create a corporate culture that included powerful guiding principles and a model human resources department. The company thrived, growing from a $12 million company into a $2.3 billion global company.

I loved my high-powered, challenging position and was excited to be making such profound differences in the company, but I'd lost the ability to turn off. I was "on" or in the "doing" mode all the time. I took care of everyone else more than myself. I was the queen of multi-tasking—I worked too much, overcommitted, and rarely said "no," even though I was exhausted and was not sleeping well.

One morning when I woke up, I could barely crawl out of bed. My body ached all over. I had no energy at all. I thought I had the flu, but the flu never went away.

I grew up using conventional medicine, so I turned to doctors, expecting them to fix me. It took months but a doctor finally diagnosed me with Epstein-Barr Virus (later called Chronic Fatigue Syndrome). This was in the mid-1980s and at that time not much was known about autoimmune diseases. In a 2016 *Newsweek magazine* article, they referred to Chronic Fatigue Syndrome as the Yuppie Flu, which was a derogatory name they gave the illness that implied it was simply a case of burnout and a fashionable form of hypochondria.[5] It is still a very real ailment today that traditional doctors struggle with because the causes aren't fully understood yet and the known cures are found in natural herbs, Chinese medicine, and energy work,[6] which is what I learned on my own over the years. I would have extreme fatigue for days, joint paint, headaches, loss of memory, sleeping but waking feeling not rested at all. My doctors offered no solutions other than that I should slow down and rest more. How could I rest more when all I was doing when I wasn't working was sleeping? I had no energy for anything else.

My doctor told me that my illness was all in my head, which didn't sit well with me. I have always been a positive thinker with a can-do attitude, but no matter how hard I tried, I couldn't *will* myself to have more energy. What was he talking about? As it turns out, I now understand my doctor was right. A high percentage of autoimmune illnesses do start in the head because body, mind, and spirit are connected, and a person's thoughts become their reality.[7] I believed that I had to work hard to be successful, so I couldn't let up. My constant thoughts were, "I'm stressed. I have too much to do and not enough time. How can I get all I need to do done?" That constant litany of negative thinking while pushing myself to do more gave my body the wrong messages; it is no wonder that my body started breaking down.

One day when I was driving home from work, I heard an ad on the radio about a free yoga class that would give me energy. Energy was all I wanted at that point in my life. I knew I needed to try it (I was finally starting to listen to my intuition), but I was too exhausted to drive myself to the after-work class. I convinced my husband to take me. That yoga class turned out to be a breakthrough. For the first time in months, my body felt lighter and I actually felt what I would call a flow of energy moving through my body. It was like a heavy lead blanket had been weighing me down making arms and legs feel numb, and that feeling began to dissipate. After the class, I could walk across the room and pick up my feet to walk instead of dragging my feet because they felt like lead weights. My overall body felt lighter and in time, I was no longer needing to fall into bed as soon as I got home. I started to have energy to do things. Elated, I started integrating more yoga classes into my life. I felt my body's energy returning and staying.

Those yoga classes became a crucial part of my healing process, and yoga is still a big part of my life today. I started realizing I was receiving health benefits from doing yoga, which inspired me to explore more natural healing solutions. Afraid to make the full jump to all natural, I found a new doctor who was both a naturopath and a medical doctor. He referred me to a psychologist whose recommendations changed my perspective and became a key part of my healing journey.

The reason it was so powerful is that my psychologist encouraged me to meditate, write, journal, and do art projects—activities where I could lose track of time and find peace within, as I did on that dock when I was a child. I realized that my reflective, meditative time was the constant in my early life that kept me sane, happy, and healthy, and that I got into trouble when I stopped giving myself the gift of downtime.

Reincorporating meditative time, along with the right supplements and my yoga practice, enabled my body to heal, and I returned to work full-time. Unfortunately, I went right back into the workaholic lifestyle that had led to my stress-related illness. My new yoga practice kept me healthy for a few years, but our bodies aren't meant to be in the "on" state all the time.

I got sick again. I started having daily headaches, never-ending sinus infections, and insomnia. I treated myself with over-the-counter medicines. I just kept popping those pills and saying everything was great though I was barely hanging on. It wasn't until I got to my third breaking point that my new naturopathic doctor explained to me that the medications that I was taking were masking my illness and even making me sicker because they were not allowing my body to heal. I was only covering the pain up. He explained that my body has a natural ability to heal. He indicated that I needed to remove the obstacles preventing my body from healing naturally. His advice was to stop taking medications that were hiding my symptoms, to decrease the excessive stress I was under, and spend more time in a relaxed state or, in other words, more self-care and rest.

About that same time, our family's beloved nanny, who had been with us since my first son was six months old, left to have a baby of her own. I put my one-year-old son in childcare. He started getting very high fevers every time he went. I would take days off to help him heal, but the fever would come back again whenever he went to daycare. We tried multiple caregivers and locations and got the same results. Between my demanding job and my son's needs, I was in a state of exhaustion. I asked my employer if I could work three 12-hour days per week so I could stay at home with my son for two days. My husband, my mom, and his mom would cover the other three days. The company agreed but said they would have to move me out of overseeing large teams.

My new job was not very exciting and not very interactive. Instead of managing and inspiring teams, I was sitting by myself in an office, analyzing proposals and working with people to vet projects. I did not love the work and it became an effort to drag myself in. In addition, working 12-hour days was difficult. One more time, my body was talking to me, but I tuned it out. When a person does things they don't love, it affects their mind, body, and spirit. As a result, I got sick again, and this time, I was told my adrenal glands were shutting down. My doctor called it adrenal fatigue, which is a term applied to a collection of symptoms, such as body aches, fatigue, sleep disturbances, and digestive problems, and I had all of them. I was also suffering from a loss of appetite, muscle weakness, and depression. My adrenal glands were not making enough of the hormone cortisol and were in a crisis mode, which is a serious condition.

The day my doctor told me I could die; I knew I had to make major changes in my life. I had to learn to listen to my body and the wisdom it kept offering.

It had taken years to listen to my body, but I finally retired to raise my family full-time and to begin my real healing journey. When I made the decision, I felt an overall lightness in my heart, mind, body, and soul. It was as if a weight was removed that had been holding me down.

After focusing on healing for an extended time and learning to love and nurture myself—ideas we will talk about more in the chapters to come—I started a consulting business. I was in a much healthier and happier state, with healthy daily habits that kept me in good health. My former company, which had been bought out by a Fortune 500 company, heard I was consulting and recruited me to come back, which I did. I loved my job, made a difference, and still managed to maintain self-care, but I kept having this feeling that to be truly fulfilled, there was something more I needed to do in this world.

In 2008, the economy tanked. The new owners of my long-term employer decided they wanted to run the company with a different philosophy and laid off most of the long-term leaders, including me. After many years helping make the company what it was, and feeling highly valued, it was a shock to be laid off. I felt alone and lost. It was painful. It also turned out to be one of the greatest gifts of my life. Because I didn't have a job, I was forced to figure out what I wanted to do next. That led me to (finally) create an authentic life. The Universe had opened worlds of possibility for me. I just had to listen.

I learned about a free event in Colorado called "Everything is Energy." The goal of the event was to teach participants how to tune into their own energy and intuition. Everything in me said I needed to go to this event.

In the first hour, the event leader, David Morelli, announced he was going to teach us how to "read" others energetically. He asked us to stand up and look around the room, and we would know when we saw the right person to read. I rolled my eyes, thinking he was a little off. How would I know who I was meant to talk with? It was almost embarrassing to look around, trying to pick someone; it felt fake.

Then my eyes connected with a young woman across the room, and I had zero doubt that she was the one. It was like some unknown power was pulling us together and we each turned and walked to each other and introduced ourselves.

David told us to face each other, close our eyes, and read each other for one minute. Again, I rolled my eyes, thinking I had no idea how to "read" someone. However, when I closed my eyes and followed the instructions from David, I was shocked that I could see little black dots on the woman's lungs. How was I going to tell her that? When the minute was up, I reluctantly told her she was going to think I was crazy, but all I could see were little black dots on her lungs. She started crying and shared that she had been diagnosed with cysts on her lungs the week before. She had just started treatment.

It was almost scary to fathom that I could have seen that. Similar experiences that seemed like magic continued through the weekend, so often that many participants asked if I was a psychic or channeler by training. I didn't even really know what that meant. All I knew was I felt connected to something much more significant than me, and it was the same feeling I had experienced in my youth sitting on the dock.

For the first time in my life, I realized how intuitive and spiritual I am (and everyone is), and it changed my life forever. I immediately enrolled in the coaches' training course. Everything came so naturally to me that I knew without a doubt that I was meant to teach and guide others on their healing and self-discovery journeys so they could make permanent changes in their lives just as I was doing.

The energy modalities I started learning at that first event are game-changers that give all of us the ability to tap into the energetic Universe that connects us all to what I call our superpowers, and quantum physicists call the "Field." I incorporate my connection with Source and energy healing into my coaching, as it helps me get to the core of issues quickly and identify precisely what is blocking my clients so we can work together to overcome those challenges. I teach my clients these same skills so they understand that they, too, are intuitive, and can tap into Source and use their intuition to learn, grow, and heal their lives.

Many of you may connect with my story and many of you may not, and that is not important. What is important is that I believe everyone has the ability to create a life they love by learning to operate in *The BEING Zone*. You just need to understand how to make that possible, which I will outline in this book. You will learn to identify and clear ingrained blocks and barriers, get out of your head, and tune into your energy, intuition, and the natural wisdom of your body. By the end of this book, you'll know how to slow down, listen to your heart, recognize what makes you feel happy inside, and begin to love yourself, perhaps for the first time, so you can begin to live the authentic, happy life you were meant to.

I also believe there's no one-size-fits-all solution for becoming happier and healthier. This is why I provide options throughout the book. You know yourself and can decide what works for you.

You might be asking what it looks like to have a life you love. When you are happy and love living life, you:

· Have cleared old belief systems and blocks that are holding you back.

- Live every day in *The BEING Zone*, where you have an inner knowing from being tuned in to your body, its energy, and its messages.
- Understand the power of your thoughts and focus on what you want.
- Wake up happy and healthy, looking forward to the day and living life to the fullest.
- Feel a deep sense of interconnectedness and seek guidance from a Universal Source.
- Are heart-based and use your intuition to recognize and take advantage of abundant opportunities that show up in your life (that previously you failed to notice).
- View challenges and struggles as a gift, embracing and learning from them.
- Love yourself, spend time with people you love, and do things you love to do.
- Spend your time being YOU, doing and being what you are meant to.

Creating a life that you love starts with reading this book, being diligent about journaling, and applying the tools, techniques, and exercises that are provided. *The BEING Zone System* is laid out in this book as a step by step process through each chapter with activities and exercises. You might be living in a state of exhaustion or leery about trying new things so it will take a leap of faith to trust that *The BEING Zone System* will help. Just know, we are creatures of habit and when you change these habits, you can transform your life into one you love.

When my clients go through *The BEING Zone System* and then commit to the deceptively simple yet remarkably effective 5 Daily B.E.I.N.G. Steps for at least 10 minutes a day (which I will explain in detail in Chapter 10), they can't help but change. In this book, I'll tell some of my clients' inspiring stories of transformation. I'll also mention a few clients who changed only a little or not at all—it takes practice, discipline, and commitment to go through change and then adhere to a daily practice. Some people are not ready to make even the minimal commitment of 10 minutes a day.

I am so grateful for the clients I have had the opportunity to work with over the years and when they quiet their minds and tune into their hearts, they begin to experience self-love, which is a vital part of their healing and finding happiness within. You have the exact same opportunity. Your natural state is health, happiness, friends, laughter, and abundance. My goal is to get you back to that state of *BEING*. You will discover as I did that your happiness is in the pause.

PART I

Why We Are the Way
We Are and What We
Can Do About It

CHAPTER 1

Our Disconnected World

"These pains you feel are messengers. Listen to them."
—Rumi

ARE YOU STRUGGLING to figure out why you aren't happy? It can feel daunting. Worry no longer—this book will help you discover the issues affecting you the most.

Have you ever felt alone in your own home even when surrounded by family? I know I have. When everyone is so busy and focused on what they need to get done, or are buried in media, there is very little conversation or personal bonding. Even when you try to have a conversation, you might feel like you are interrupting or are in the way. Or possibly you have observed your own group or others in a restaurant where no one is talking because their heads are buried in their phones. Or your experience may be that everyone is running in so many different directions that your conversations only center around what you need to do and where you need to be. As a result, you might lack connection even in your own home and workplace. A research organization called Study Finds shares that the average adult spends up to three hours a day on social media but only 37 minutes of quality time with their family on weekdays.[8]

My clients come to me saying "Something is wrong with me, I feel empty." I hear statements like "I have no joy or happiness inside anymore." "I feel alone with no one to talk to about my dreams and desires." "I am surrounded by family, friends, and coworkers but I don't feel connected." "I feel exhausted and burned out with no downtime to just enjoy others and have real conversations." Have you ever felt this way?

If so, I imagine that you might want to be part of the solution for change within yourself and for the greater good. That is why you picked up this book. That is my dream, too, to be a part of bringing people back together, to reconnect with themselves and others. This starts with cultivating self-love, which you will learn about in this book, as it leads to stronger bonds and connections.

Beyond feeling alone in our own homes, we have watched the dysfunction in our government, our systems, and our society worsen over the years, and it can be challenging to wake up with hope of a better and more fulfilling future.

There are many theories out there as to why we are so disconnected and what causes the loneliness, health problems, and unhappiness that people face in their lives. Everyone has their own opinions, but after hearing many stories and helping guide people to heal, I have turned my focus to two primary areas: psychological trauma and technology, which I believe have the biggest impact on human suffering and loneliness. When you exist in these places, you may not be able to experience the level of unconditional self-love and connection you are meant to. Even if you felt love in your family, most likely these factors played a role in how you think, feel, and operate in the world today.

Psychological Trauma

In my own experience as well as the opinion of National Center of Biotechnology Information (NCBI), psychological trauma is the main culprit of debilitating emotional issues, stress-related illnesses, depression, loneliness, and inability to make sound judgments and decisions.[9] Survivors' immediate reactions after trauma are varied and impacted by their own life experiences as well as dependent on how much support they receive, their innate coping skills, and the responses of the larger community in which they live. Think about your own life or the life of your friends or family. Did you experience unfair treatment, psychological abuse or trauma in any way or were you a witness to others suffering from psychological trauma? Did you ever hear anyone say to you, "You are stupid"? Or "You will never get it"? "Don't be a crybaby"? Or "I wish you were never born"? Those statements are all examples of psychological abuse whether it was intended or not.

It is heartbreaking to see how many of us were raised in dysfunctional environments where we felt incompetent, not good enough, unworthy of affection, and were emotionally, verbally, or physically abused or neglected and felt powerless to change our situation. Some situations were more benign but still painful. Simple statements can have a profound effect. For instance, a young girl may end up with self-esteem or weight issues if her mother tells her she looks heavy or needs to lose weight. My clients have shared story after story of adverse experiences from their child-hood. Others experienced abuses that were so hurtful that they blocked them from their memories.

We can block these memories and keep them repressed. Repression of memories is a defense mechanism where a person unconsciously pushes away painful or traumatic memories allowing them to have what appears as a normal life where they seem to be unaware of the memory. Several stories below will demonstrate this. It is important to identify and clear any repressed memories as part of your healing process because the feelings you retain from these memories reside in your cellular body and can result in illness or physical issues in your body. There are many studies that have proven the connection between emotional stress or trauma and physical issues and pain.[10] [11] This book will help you uncover the issues that are affecting your life so you can use the tools to let go of them and move on.

You will be asked to journal, which will become a key part of your healing and happiness journey. It will help you recognize issues that are keeping you stuck, overwhelmed, or unhappy. You will begin to identify when your thoughts and actions put you in conflict with your true self. Journaling allows you the opportunity to discover and document old and new issues that you need to release, so they don't impact your life or your happiness moving forward.

You will find that journaling is a very big part of your whole healing process. Expect to journal a lot to get the results that you desire. Without journaling, this book is informational but with journaling, this book is transformational. Journaling is key to discovering what to fix, where to go, and what to do. I recommend handwriting your journal using a notebook or *The BEING*

Journal, a companion journal that was developed to complement *The BEING Zone* book for the following reasons:

- According to a study at Indiana University, handwriting has been proven to increase neural activity in the brain, similar to meditation.[12]
- Dr. Claudia Aguirre, a neuroscientist and mind-body expert, indicates that handwriting can quiet or rest the mind.[13] She indicates the very act of handwriting causes you to focus on what's important, moving you into a moment of mindfulness.

The most important thing in this process is that you do take the time to journal. If handwriting isn't your favorite, then by all means use what works for you, whether it is a digital device or recording.

Journaling Time

PSYCHOLOGICAL ABUSE OR TRAUMA JOURNALING EXERCISE #1:
It is time to journal. Grab a pen and your notebook or *BEING Journal* and start.
- What are the things that were said to you as a child that affected your happiness, your confidence, your well-being or belief system?
- What things did you hear growing up that made you feel small or incapable or not enough?
- Take yourself back to those early years and brainstorm all the innocuous comments that may have caused you to feel inadequate, dis-

missed, or unimportant. It is important to capture all that you can so we can clear them from your psyche when you learn the tools in Chapter 3.

Client Story: John, age 62, was outgoing and excited about life as a young child and would often try to share his excitement with his family. His father would criticize him, saying, "quit showing off" or "don't be a grandstander; people don't like grandstanders." John didn't even know what a grandstander was, but he knew he couldn't voice his excitement and fell in line with the family expectation to be seen and not heard. He experienced a second verbal abuse event when his first-grade teacher punished him for speaking out when he wasn't asked to speak. These seemingly ordinary life events manifested in him an inability to speak out in business meetings when he had a unique or creative idea. He would hesitate just long enough for someone else to suggest the same thing he was thinking and get all the glory. He would be angry at himself each time, but his belief system that he should be quiet kept him from speaking up. The physical symptoms that showed up in his life from not speaking up included tightness in his throat and ringing in his ears. We used the tools provided in this book and cleared the old painful memories, which eliminated the physical manifestations.

Studies Showing Impact of Abuse

It is unbelievable to me how rampant abuse is, how much it impacts every single one of us, and how little we talk about it.

Many of us unknowingly carry feelings or memories from childhood experiences into our adult years that show up as pain, anger,
or resentment. Below I will share some statistics on how prevalent abuse is in our world.

Adverse Childhood Experiences (A.C.E.) Study

This study is one of the most significant investigations of how
childhood abuse, neglect, and household challenges affect later-life
health and well-being. The original A.C.E. Study was conducted
at Kaiser Permanente from 1995 to 1997.[14] Over 17,000 Health
Maintenance Organization members from Southern California
receiving physical exams completed confidential surveys regarding
their childhood experiences and current health status and behaviors. Of those, 4,906 (28.3%) of the individuals had been physically abused, and 3,589 (20.7%) had been sexually abused per the
study. On average, 1 in 4 people suffered from abuse.

A.C.E. CATEGORIES	THE CDC-KAISER PERMANENTE ADVERSE CHILDHOOD EXPERIENCES (A.C.E.) STUDY		
ABUSE	Women (9,367)	Men (7,970)	Total in Study (17,337)
Emotional Abuse	13%	7.6%	10.6%
Physical Abuse	27%	29.9%	28.3%
Sexual Abuse	24.7%	16%	20.7%

HOUSEHOLD CHALLENGES	WOMEN (9,367)	MEN (7,970)	TOTAL IN STUDY (17,337)
Mother Treated Violently	13.7%	11.50%	12.70%
Substance Abuse	29.5%	23.80%	26.90%
Mental Illness	23.3%	14.80%	19.40%
Parental Separation or Divorce	24.5%	21.80%	23.30%
Incarcerated Household Member	5.2%	4.10%	4.70%

NEGLECT	WOMEN (9,367)	MEN (7,970)	TOTAL IN STUDY (17,337)
Emotional Neglect	16.7%	12.40%	14.80%
Physical Neglect	9.2%	10.70%	9.90%

This wide range of stressful or neglectful events in a young person's life can shatter their sense of security, making them feel helpless, overwhelmed, or isolated in a dangerously disconnected world. It is not about how traumatic the life event may have been but how the person reacted to it emotionally. The more frightened, alone, or helpless they felt, the more likely they still hold that trauma inside, or if they pushed the feelings down or tuned them out, it still resides in them.

What people don't realize is that these traumatic events are buried in their subconscious memory, and when they face a similar situation, it can cause the same intense reaction. These emotional traumas left uncleared can also be manifested in the body as ongoing illness or pain.

I have found that clients who experienced the most traumatic abuse have a more difficult time functioning in their day-to-day lives. The scary part is that studies below are showing that violent abuse is more rampant than I ever could have imagined.

The A.C.E. Study Journaling Exercise #2:

Grab a pen and your notebook or *BEING Journal* and begin documenting.

- Review the A.C.E. Study Chart and identify anything from their list that may have impacted you.
- Write out as much as you can about each of the different types of abuse or trauma you may have faced throughout your life.
- Make enough notes so that you can gain clarity about how it has impacted you so you can come back and clear these issues after learning the tools.

Hamby and Taggart Studies

In 2011, two separate studies done by Hamby et al. and another by Taggart, a high percentage of people have been exposed to physical violence or psychological aggression during their lifetimes. The findings show:

· **26%** (approximately 18 million) were exposed to family violence during their lifetimes.
· **35.6%, or 42.4 million,** women have experienced rape, physical violence, and/or stalking by an intimate partner at some point in their lifetime.
· **More than 1 in 4 men** (28.5%) has experienced rape, physical violence, and/or stalking by an intimate partner at some point in their lifetime.
· **Nearly half of all women** (approximately 57.6 million) and 48.8% of men, or 55.2 million, have experienced at least one form of psychological aggression by an intimate partner.
· **Approximately 4 in 10** (40.3%) reported some form of expressive aggression (e.g., their partner acted angry in a way that seemed dangerous, told them they were a loser or a failure, insulted or humiliated them, etc.).[15]

RAINN Statistics

The statistics from RAINN—the Rape, Abuse, and Incest National Network—are even more shocking:

· **Every 73 seconds** another American is sexually assaulted.
· **One out of every 6 American women** has been the victim of an attempted or completed rape.
· **About 3% of American men** (1 in 33) have experienced an attempted or completed rape.

· **From 2009-2013,** Child Protective Services agencies substantiated, or found strong evidence to indicate, that 63,000 children a year were victims of sexual abuse.[16]

According to a Justice Department analysis of violent crime in 2016, 80% of rapes and sexual assaults go unreported.[17]

Journaling Time

REVIEW DATA ON VIOLENCE AND RAPE JOURNALING EXERCISE #3:
Grab a pen and your notebook or *BEING Journal* and start capturing your memories.

· First, review the above studies and facts and identify anything from the above statistics that may have impacted you.

· Then write out as much as you can about each of the different types of violence you may have faced throughout your life. Get clarity about how it has impacted you so can clear the issues when you learn the tools.

Whether it reaches the extreme of physical abuse or rape, or seems harmless, such as being quieted down, these events have a profound impact on our souls, happiness, and health. I have had many clients see the emotional or verbal abuse they suffered as simply a way of life, not realizing the impact. There are some with repressed memories or others who may not have realized they were victims of abuse or recognize how it affected their happiness and well-being.

I was stunned when I recently discovered I had a repressed memory to clear. I realized it was there when I was coaching someone else who had a similar experience. My client was raped in college by someone she knew. Her friends told her not to report it, and she was still struggling with fear. As she told me her story, my right hand and arm went numb. They hurt so badly I could hardly use them, and the pain remained through the day and into the night. At the time, I thought I was feeling her pain, but the next morning I was still hurting while doing my daily practice. As I connected with a higher Source in my morning work, all of a sudden, I clearly remembered that I had been raped in college. It was almost like a movie playing in front of me, but I knew deep down it was real. As I allowed that memory to surface, I clearly remembered the room, the event, and the perpetrator. At the time of the rape, I numbed up and disconnected from reality. Afterward, I told no one and pushed it out of mind. I felt demeaned and dirty. This individual was a leader in his fraternity, and I felt if I said anything I would be scoffed at or blamed.

My entire right side, from my toes to my jaw, hurt as I went through the memory to release it. I used my powerful *SHIFT* Tool, which I'll tell you more about in Chapter 3, and replaced the memory with a better feeling. Once I *SHIFTED* the memory, my entire right side went back to normal.

I learned a precious lesson from this situation: repressed memories are real. I also have discovered that it is possible to fabricate memories, believing they are repressed, as you will see in the next story. Later, my husband asked me, "How could you not remember that until now?" I believe that I genuinely wanted to forget it at the time. I never talked about it to anyone and pushed it way down, out of my conscious memory. I honestly thought I had gone in and cleared all of my old issues, so it was a surprise to me when my body reacted so strongly, and those memories came back.

Client Story: A client of mine, Joe, was accused of molesting a relative. The accuser filed a lawsuit, saying his beliefs came from repressed memories, but Joe swore he never touched the individual inappropriately. Joe's rage was intense, and it cost him hundreds of thousands of dollars to get through this bogus suit. When I was coaching Joe to clear some physical ailments (back and leg issues that were crippling him), he suddenly had a very clear repressed memory of playing whiffle ball with this relative when they were both very young. The child was uncoordinated and could not hit the ball, devastated and embarrassed, he ran into the house crying. When his mom and my client's mom asked him what happened, the child didn't say, "I couldn't hit the ball." Instead, he told them that Joe had hit him with the bat even though nothing of the sort had happened. Joe's mom came out and yelled at Joe and hit him with the plastic bat "so he would know how it felt." Joe believes it was one of his accuser's first successful experience of fabricating a story and accusing Joe of something he didn't do, which is precisely what later happened in the lawsuit. Both times, Joe felt he had no voice, wasn't heard, and that became an ongoing theme in his life. We have now cleared that belief so Joe will be able to move forward, speaking his truth and standing in his power.

Other Trauma

Beyond the traumatic events listed in the A.C.E. Study chart within this chapter, emotional and psychological trauma can also be the result of what might seem incidental, unavoidable, or even benign. They may include general and specific incidents, as demonstrated below:

General Events

- **Previous traumatic events,** such as an accident or injury, especially if it was unexpected or during childhood.
- **Ongoing stress,** like living in an unsafe neighborhood, battling a life-threatening illness, or experiencing repeating events such as neglect, bullying, including cyberbullying.
- **Humiliating or disappointing experiences,** especially if someone was deliberately cruel saying things like you aren't good enough or smart enough or you won't amount to anything. Even simple statements like John's father about not grandstanding can be damaging.
- **Coping with the trauma of a natural or human-made disaster** affects a person's psyche. Even if they were not a direct victim of an earthquake, terrorist attack, plane crash, or mass shooting, rioting or a pandemic, just watching horrific images on social media or the news can result in a traumatic stress response.

Specific Events

- **Surgery** is traumatic to the mind, body, and spirit. When it happens during early childhood, it can have a significant long-term effect on a child.
- **The sudden death** of someone close or the breakup of a significant relationship can weigh in a person's psyche for a long time and affects them in daily life.
- **A child left on their own** as a result of disconnected, stressed, overwhelmed, or absentee parents.

Journaling Time

GENERAL OR SPECIFIC EVENTS JOURNALING EXERCISE #4:
Grab a pen and your notebook or *BEING Journal* and start writing.

- First, review the above list of events and identify any that may have impacted you.
- Then write out as much as you can about your memories in each area. Make enough notes so that you can gain clarity about how it has impacted you. If you experienced none of these, keep reading.

Client Story: One of my clients, 42-year-old Sally, had a seventh-grade teacher who was disrespectful and demeaning to her in front of the entire classroom on more than one occasion. Those incidents left a lasting mark on Sally. She became defensive and angry if someone spoke to her or anyone else disrespectfully. Sally worked with me, and we identified how disrespectful words directed at her felt in her body and did some *SHIFTS* on early memories. As a result, she doesn't get triggered any longer by disrespect. Instead, when faced with a triggering situation, she breathes deeply, does not take it personally and lets the offender know that their behavior is not acceptable.

Personal Reactions

If you have experienced a childhood trauma or difficult life event, your personal reactions may be wide-ranging. You may struggle with memories or anxiety that never leave you. You may feel numb, disconnected, unworthy and unable to trust other people. You might react with resentment, anger, or defensiveness. You might suppress old feelings and think you are fine, but when bad things happen that trigger those old feelings, you may find yourself reacting in a way that surprises you. If you were neglected, you might find that you take care of everyone but yourself because you never had self-love or self-care role-modeled for you. Like many of my clients, you may have no idea how much some of these childhood events impacted you. You may think you have moved on until you find something triggers an old reaction.

Client Story: Sue, age 52, saw her father beat her mother repeatedly. She has never been able to have a healthy, honest relationship with a man because she was holding fearful beliefs inside her that impacted her ability to love and trust herself or others fully. She has a healthy life and works a good job, but she tends to accept emotional mistreatment and disrespect from men, which we still haven't curbed completely. She still has unhealthy boundaries because she hasn't fully dealt with her past and can get triggered.

Journaling Time

TRIGGERS JOURNALING EXERCISE #5:

Grab your notebook or *BEING Journal* and pen and start writing about what triggers you.

- What types of things trigger you?
- Who are people who trigger you?
- What are you struggling with in life as a result of how you were treated in childhood?
- What memories and struggles have you pushed under the carpet because they feel so painful?

In Chapter 3, you will learn tools to help you clear these triggers and struggles. You will be able to go back to these notes at that time to clear each one that you wrote about in your journaling.

How Childhood Trauma Can Result in Future Trauma

Experiencing trauma in childhood can result in severe and long-lasting effects. While traumatic events can happen to anyone, you're more likely to be traumatized by a current event if you're already under a heavy stress load, if you have suffered a series of losses, or you have been traumatized before—especially during childhood. When childhood trauma is not dealt with and resolved, a sense of fear and helplessness is more likely to show up in adulthood, setting the stage for further trauma.

The good news is, even if your trauma happened many years ago, there are steps you can take to overcome the pain, learn to trust and connect to others again, and, most importantly, learn to love and trust yourself.

Client Story: Liz, age 45, had parents who worked all the time to make ends meet, leaving her in the care of her older sister. Her sister didn't want to deal with Liz, so she would lock her in a room with the lights out. Liz would sit there for hours and was not big enough to reach the light switch or open the door. Her sister threatened her, saying that it would be worse if she said anything to their parents. Liz has worked through her fear of being left alone and in the dark with the healing tools in this book. Liz is now able to live her life with more joy and much less fear.

We all react to past or current trauma in different ways. There are a wide range of physical and emotional reactions. There is no "right" or "wrong" way to think, feel, or respond. So, don't judge how you feel. Know that your response, no matter what it looks like, is a normal reaction to the unhappy, unusual, disturbing, or disruptive event(s) in your life.

Below are examples of how you might respond because of past trauma:

EMOTIONAL & PSYCHOLOGICAL SYMPTOMS	PHYSICAL SYMPTOMS
Confusion, difficulty concentrating	Insomnia or nightmares
Anxiety and fear	Fatigue
Withdrawing from others	Being startled easily
Feeling disconnected or numb	Difficulty concentrating

Shock, denial, or disbelief	Racing heartbeat
Anger, irritability, mood swings	Edginess and agitation
Guilt, shame, self-blame	Aches and pains
Feeling sad or hopeless	Muscle tension

SYMPTOMS JOURNALING EXERCISE #6:

Pull out your notebook or *BEING Journal* and make notes based on the above list.

· List the different symptoms or beliefs from the examples listed above that are currently a part of you and your life.

· Make a note of which of these you experience a lot and how it impacts you. This will assist you in identifying what to clear when you get to Chapter 3.

Simple Activities for Clearing Trauma

· **Get Moving!** Trauma disrupts your body's equilibrium and can put you into an immobile state. Getting out and moving, especially outside where you are connecting with the natural and powerful energy of the earth, can help you calm your nervous system.

- **Walking, running, hiking, or dancing**—rhythmic activities swinging arms and moving legs—helps. Focus on the rhythm of your breath to help release anxiety.
- **Energy-based movements** such as yoga or Qigong are very beneficial practices.
- **Surround Yourself with People Who Fill You Up.** Do not isolate yourself. Find a friend or family member you like and plan to spend time with them doing something fun. You do not have to talk about the trauma. The comfort will come from engaging in things with someone you like.
- **Volunteer:** Doing something that makes a difference for someone else and makes you happy is an excellent way to overcome the sense of helplessness you may feel.
- **Join a Support Group:** Find the right group for your issue. Connecting with others with the same pain can reduce your sense of isolation and help you discover new ideas that could work for you.
- **Listen to Music that Picks You Up:** Just listening to music is uplifting; however, when you sing at the top of your lungs the vocal part of this is healing to your system. I sing with the radio a lot when I am in my car driving. It makes me smile and revitalizes my soul.
- **Get a Pet:** Dogs and cats love you unconditionally, and that feels good.

Journaling Time

SIMPLE ACTIVITIES FOR CLEARING TRAUMA

JOURNALING EXERCISE #7:

Pull out your *BEING Journal* or notebook to document your thoughts.

· Create a list of any of the above activities that would be useful in your life right now.

· Make notes on how these new activities might help and what you are ready to commit to.

Client Story: Raeann grew up in a dysfunctional home where her father sexually abused her. She was terrified to go to sleep as a child and has experienced sleep issues, including nightmares and trouble falling asleep, since that time. She tried all kinds of meditations and sleep medications, but nothing helped. When we were able to use the tools, you will learn in this book to remove her old memories and fears, Raeann began to sleep through the night for the first time she could remember.

Post-Traumatic Stress Disorder (PTSD)

Numerous people in the world today suffer from some level of trauma or PTSD.[18] Different events impact people in different ways. If you find that your fears or symptoms, both psychological or physical, don't disappear after processing or trying to deal with a traumatic event, you may have PTSD.

Many people will be fine most of the time and then get triggered by certain things causing them to go back into the fear place. The *SHIFT* Tool and tapping are known to be effective tools for PTSD. If the fears or symptoms don't ease up after tapping or using the *SHIFT* Tool on your own, you may want to work with a skilled *BEING Zone* practitioner or therapist. Coaching or therapy provides a safe place for trauma survivors to share their fears so it can be *SHIFTED* out of their psyche.

Journaling Time

POTENTIAL PTSD ISSUES JOURNALING EXERCISE #8:

Pull out your *BEING Journal* or notebook and start writing.

- Write about events in your life that you can't let go of and are continuing to impact you years later.
- Make a note of which of these you experience a lot and describe how. This will assist you on your healing journey, when you use the tools shared in Chapter 3 to help clear these issues.

The Impact of Technology on Disconnection

One of the most beautiful things about technology is its ability to connect us to family and friends all over the world, at any time for anything. Technology was a lifesaver during the coronavirus pandemic, allowing people to work and visit during quarantine.

There are many pluses to having access to the internet, but technology is also changing the way people interact. Most of us have witnessed an increase in screen time and a decrease in one-to-one conversations. The surge in use of personal technology has flooded us with endless amounts of information which has been proven to impact us psychologically—increasing our anxiety, stress, concentration, and sleep.[19] Have you noticed the increased use of technology impacting you? Think about how it affects your daily life. I have included a few facts below that demonstrate the severity of the problem.

- Americans check their phone on average once every 12 minutes—burying their heads in their phones 80 times a day, according to new research by global tech protection and support company Asurion.[20]
- They found the average person struggles to go more than 10 minutes without checking their phone.
- Of the 2,000 people surveyed, 1 in 10 check their phones on average once every 4 minutes.
- Four hours is the longest time the average person studied was prepared to go before the need to check their phone becomes overwhelming.
- The survey showed that 31% of phone users feel anxiety at any point when separated from their phones.

In my opinion, that is an addiction. A high percentage of people in the world today are so connected to technology and feel that they must be timely with their responses,[21] [22] that I believe they quit enjoying life as much as they could.

The technological age started with personal computers and has increased with smartphones. It may be more difficult for some of you to walk away from work at the end of the day, because you are carrying your work with you via technology.

Many of us are more connected to technology than we are to our feelings, desires, or others. Our well-being is dependent on real connection with others, and that is an underlying need we all have. Many of us feel more lost and alone.[23] The International Society for Neurofeedback and Research found students who have high usage of their phones experience significantly higher levels of isolation, loneliness, depression and anxiety.[24] Anxiety and isolation both contribute to feelings of disconnection, which can lead to further emotional and eventually other stress-related issues. Disconnection to yourself and others can turn into a breakdown of your meaningful relationships, leaving you feeling unloved and not good enough.

Nearly half of Americans (47%) report sometimes or always feeling alone despite the advances in technology that are intended to connect us.[25] We may not be as happy or have as many close nurturing relationships where we feel loved and connected because we spend more time on smartphones or with online connections instead of with people.[26] Having online relationships may lack the same substance as we would have in person where we can physically feel connected to the person we are with.

It can be challenging to form meaningful relationships over social media.[27] An issue with online friendships is when there is an argument, or something is misinterpreted, one person can just unfriend the other. No discussion or exploration. Friendship over. In person we have a chance to work things out, especially if we see them at school or work.

In a study by University of Michigan they examined how Facebook use influences the two components of subjective well-being:

how people feel moment-to-moment and how satisfied they are with their lives.[28] The results indicate that Facebook use predicts negative shifts on both of these variables over time. The more the participants used Facebook over two-weeks, the more their life satisfaction levels declined over that time. What was meant to be a fun, all-inclusive place for people to go online and connect is now more of a facade about posting where you have been, your latest meal, or accomplishment. It is also a place where people can be mean or disrespectful.

As a result, our relationships have grown more superficial. In a study titled, "My life has become a major distraction from my cell phone," Meredith David and James Roberts suggest that what they call phubbing (ignoring someone in favor of using our phone) can lead to a decline in our most important relationships. In the study of 145 adults the scientists found that phubbing lowered satisfaction levels in relationships and contributed to depression levels.[29] A follow-up study by Chinese scientists assessed 243 married adults with similar results: Partner phubbing contributed to greater feelings of depression.[30] How many times have you prioritized your electronic device over a conversation lately or have had that happen to you? It doesn't feel good, and it can have a huge effect your relationships.

On top of that, technology is a distraction that makes it hard for us to want to be alone with ourselves or our thoughts. It fills our lives with noise and leaves many people uncomfortable in silence and downtime without distractions.[31] When things are quiet, we have to face issues or concerns and problems. When we drown feelings out by watching television, spending time on social media, watching online videos, podcasts and or playing video games, we numb ourselves. Our phones put us in a place where we can avoid feeling and talking about sensitive subjects.

Science Magazine refers to 11 studies where they found participants typically did not enjoy spending 6 to 15 minutes in a room by themselves with nothing to do but think. They enjoyed doing mundane activities much more. Many preferred to administer electric shocks to themselves instead of being left alone with their thoughts. Most people seem to prefer to be doing something rather than having to be present with themselves even if that something is negative.[32]

If you have a difficult time being present with your thoughts, it may result in more screen time. The more screen time you have, the less time you have to socialize in person. In person you use your emotional intelligence which is your ability to identify your own feelings and the feelings of others.

Dr. Daniel Goleman in his book *Emotional Intelligence (E.I.)* says there are five key qualities of E.I.; self-awareness, self-regulation, social skills, empathy, and motivation.[33] Yes, you use your E.I. online but it's more challenging and limited. It's not as easy to be aware of other people's feelings and have empathy online. When we as a society spend more hours on technology than we do quality time with our friends, coworkers, family, and spouse we are not cultivating our E.I which is our gateway to meaningful relationships.

Spending time on technology can affect relationships. For instance, *Computers in Human Behavior* in 2016 concluded that "how individuals use cellphones in the presence of a romantic partner impacts the partner's satisfaction with their relationship, which in turn can negatively impact their well-being."[34] Studies have shown cellphones can be also be addictive and infiltrates your life force while not providing real connections. They say it is a distraction that fills your valuable time up, but not you and that can result in depression, loneliness, more stress among other things.[35]

Journaling Time

TECHNOLOGY ADDICTIONS JOURNALING EXERCISE #9:

Take time to write in your notebook or *BEING Journal* about how you or others use technology, phones, computers, television, etc. in ways that impact you and your life. There are prompts below to help.

- Think about the last time you witnessed a family or group of friends sitting with their faces in their phones instead of having conversations. What were they missing out on?
- Have you experienced someone who disrupts your conversation by responding to a text message or email when you're in mid-sentence? How does that make you feel?
- Has there been a time you wanted to have a serious conversation with someone, but they couldn't stay focused because of technical distractions? How did you feel or respond?
- How often are you on your phone or technology where it impacts others? What can you do about that?
- How often do you bring your work home? Does your work ever make it difficult to enjoy your life at home? Have you seen this in your family or friends?
- What would you like to change about the role technology plays in your relationships?

It has been documented that many managers routinely overload their subordinates and make last-minute requests outside of work hours. To satisfy those demands, employees remain tied to their electronic devices 24/7. [36]I personally coach many people who feel they have to be connected to their work 24/7 whether it be their self-imposed expectations or the perceived perceptions of what their bosses expect. Dr. Goldstein, assistant professor of psychiatry and behavioral sciences at the University of Oklahoma Health Sciences Center believes technology today makes that overcommitment to work easier than ever.[37] You take driven people who believe they have to work hard and provide them with 24/7 access to work issues, and you open up the door to workaholic tendencies.[38] As a result, when people start being "on call" all the time, they begin to operate in what I call the *DOING Zone* where they are "on" all the time. They begin to not turn off anymore, and they have a difficult time just *BEING*. Their health often suffers as they don't take time out to self-nurture, which was my story.

Client Story: 38-year-old Leanne is a highly paid Operations leader in a Fortune 500 company. She is a perfectionist and workaholic by nature and works around the clock, partially because technology allows her to do that and partially because she is so driven. She oversees a high-volume operational department that has a direct impact on the bottom line, so she finds it difficult to turn off her phone at night or on the weekends. She is chronically stressed and overwhelmed from not turning off from work. Her family wants more attention from her when she is with them, but she can't always give them focused time. She tells me she wants to make her family her priority in evenings and on weekends but has a difficult time making that a reality. She gets upset with herself as she feels she is always quieting her children so she can concentrate on her work. As a result, they act out, and that stresses her more. Leanne had tried exercise and massages to relax herself, but her life was still in a state of stress. Leanne came to me to help her figure out how to better manage her workload, decrease her stress and have more quality family time. She has made progress by clearing old belief systems, setting limits, taking mini breaks to walk and breathe deeply to rejuvenate herself. She has prioritized evenings for fun with her family and is now feeling the benefits and value of more work-life balance.

Having technology available means we can avoid our current surroundings at any point, which means we can basically be absent from where our body is and tuned out from our surroundings and the people we are with. Have you ever had someone not be able to get your attention because you were too focused on your phone? I know I have. You may even feel like it takes extra effort to spend "quality time" with those you are with. I remember growing up when there were no cell phones or computers and my family would spend our evenings doing puzzles or talking about the day or watching shows together, laughing together and discussing them. If there was a silver lining of the coronavirus pandemic, it allowed people to slow down and have more family time, play games, enjoy the outdoors, and spend more quality time together. The quarantine forced many of us to reprioritize our lives in a good way.

Journaling Time

TECHNOLOGY USE JOURNALING EXERCISE #10:
Grab your pen and notebook or *BEING Journal*, to increase your awareness of how technology is impacting your life so you can manage it.

· How many total hours do you spend in an average day using technology?

- How much time do you spend on each of the following? Gaming? Researching things on the internet? Is it primarily for fun or for educational purposes? Working? Social media?
- How many hours a week do you spend watching TV or streaming videos on average?
- How many hours a week do you spend in person socializing with friends or family?
- If you are in a relationship, how many hours a week do you spend in quality time with your significant other, where you are in person and having an actual conversation?
- How many hours do you spend in-person extracurricular activities with others, such as exercise, sports, volunteering, group activities, spiritual worship, or at specific events?
- Are all your activities balanced in your life? If not, what changes can you make?

The Outcome of Abuse and Technology

When you spend all your time buried in technology or are living in the emotional aftermath of abuse or trauma, you may feel tired, disconnected, lonely, and unhappy. The reason is you exist in your auto-programmed subconscious brain or feel detached as a result of your addiction to technology, or both.

When you exist in either of these places, you are not refilling your energy reserves; you are draining them. And the amount of energy you have impacts how you feel and your health. The topic of energy and how to capitalize on it is discussed in more detail in Chapter 7. For now, it will suffice for you to understand that you have energy circuits running through your body. If your energy circuits are aligned and healthy, then so is your body. If you are buried in your smartphone, are stressed or anxious, or have unresolved emotions, or you are living in the DOING *Zone* without being able to shut off, your energy circuits become blocked in your system.

When this is the state you exist in day after day, your body starts failing. It cannot function as it is meant to. You feel more alone and separate, which results in feeling worse emotionally, physically, and energetically. This drained, tired state is a big piece of feeling disconnected. You know how it is when a car isn't maintained and isn't running well? The same is true with the human body if something is blocked or not working right. Your body starts to react, and you may feel more alienated, alone, or disconnected when you are in pain or suffering. Your lack of energy is often a result of the disconnection from trauma or abuse in your life or the emptiness from your addiction to technology. When you understand this, you can begin to address your specific issues and heal.

Another scary statistic is that the death rate from heart failure has risen over 20% between 2011 and 2017, and according to the Kaiser Permanente study, it is likely to continue to grow. The researchers believe there are many reasons for this, including lifestyle issues like poor diet, lack of exercise, and long-term blood pressure issues.[39] Featured as one of the "Best Doctors in America," Kavitha Chinnaiyan, MD, is an integrative cardiologist and associate professor of medicine in the greater Detroit area, with training and expertise in both western medicine and Ayurveda. Dr. Chinnaiyan talks about the importance of addressing emotional issues that sit in the heart chakra.[40] She indicates that the accumulation of guilt, shame, resentment, hatred, anger, hostility, anxiety, and similar qualities results in "closing off" the heart. It causes a constriction of energy flow and results in heartache—both emotionally as well as in the form of heart disease.

I agree with Dr. Chinnaiyan. When I look at this from a spiritual standpoint, I see a direct correlation between heart disease and loneliness and disconnection in the clients that I work with. According to the National Institute of Health, when a person feels the perception of social isolation (loneliness) they are at higher risk for cardiovascular disease as lonely individuals have increased peripheral vascular resistance and elevated blood pressure.[41] The American Hospital Association concurs, showing data that proves psychosocial factors contribute significantly to the likelihood of coronary artery disease.[42] I believe when a person does not feel connected, does not feel loved, or feels let down, they experience painful or negative emotions, which cause an imbalance or blockage in their heart center. When there is this energetic blockage, it can lead to the manifestation of physical disease and illness (primarily heart disease) if not addressed, cleared, and healed.

It's Not Easy!

I have just gone through a lot of depressing facts that may feel very overwhelming, especially if any of it applies to you. When you are sick, stressed, or feel stuck, you can become depressed, and then it is hard to see how to get out. It's not easy, and I know that as I have been there. That said, I want you to know you can move beyond feeling stuck to find happiness within and joy in your life. It does take work and commitment, but you can get there if you genuinely want to.

I was very depressed when I kept getting sick and could no longer work. Everything inside me wanted to be able to keep working at the pace I always had. I didn't know how just to *BE* present, I wanted to be doing something, and my subconscious thoughts controlled me. I would worry about things or think about what I had to do by when. It was extremely difficult for me to turn off the thoughts and learn to exist in, and be happy in, silence.

Some people never stop doing. They keep giving and doing even when they no longer have any energy or reserves. I did. It was like having an addiction. The Merriam Webster definition of an addiction is a compulsive, chronic, physiological, or psychological need for a habit-forming substance, behavior, or activity having harmful effects. I was addicted to doing. This is no different than people who are addicted to their smartphones, gaming, or technology who have a difficult time putting them down. They are always in the mode of doing something with their technology. They tell me they feel like they can't function without them.

In reality, this is also no different than people whose addictions might be drugs or alcohol. When your Ego mind is always going a mile a minute thinking about the drug or alcohol, that is existing in a doing state. It could be an addiction to sugar or salty foods. It is a need where you can't stop thinking about it, you feel like you have to do it.

What is important to understand is, it doesn't matter what your addiction is or which type of situation you are facing; the tools are the same. I have helped overachievers, stressed executives, drug addicts, overeaters, gaming addicts, etc., with the tools I share. You have to replace these deep-seated needs with something else. You have to learn to be completely present, which you will learn more about in Chapter 5. It is how you begin to heal.

Releasing

When you are releasing old issues, you may cry and feel angry or a lot of pain as you uncover these things. I did, and most of my clients do, and that is perfectly normal. Crying is a sign that we have hit the core issue, and that is when we make the most significant gains. These pains and memories you uncover are what needs to be healed so you can feel less burdened or weighed down. You will start to see and understand that the greatest pains that you uncover will end up being your most significant gains. Not that I wish pain on anyone, but it is a reality and the stepping-stones to recovery or healing. Once you identify the pains and issues, there are a variety of tools offered in Chapter 3 to help you let go of these issues so you can begin to regain happiness.

There is a light at the end of the tunnel. I have learned that some of you may not want to see that because it means you will have to make a choice and that might not feel safe or possible. I know that if you take one step at a time, you will eventually find your way. You now know what traumas and technology impacted you. When you understand the what, your healing can begin.

Key Messages

· Trauma and technology play critical roles in the disconnection of our world and ourselves.
· Past trauma or abuse can lead to future trauma and trigger automatic responses. The trauma may be as simple as an injury, illness, a breakup, or absentee parents.
· Everyone has different reactions and symptoms in response to trauma and often do not know that they can improve their happiness dramatically by clearing old issues.
· Technology is an addiction that decreases social aptitude, has negative effects on happiness and relationships and increases disconnection and loneliness.

- The issues you uncover are your opportunity for your greatest gains.
- Journaling will help you discover what is holding you back from living the life you dreamed of.
- It's not easy to go through your past to transform your life, but it is possible when you are ready to learn and commit to the processes explained in this book.

This Chapter's Gift: You will gain a greater understanding of the correlation between abuse, trauma, and technology and your health and well-being, which will allow you to identify anything that decreases your happiness or feeling of connectedness.

CHAPTER 2

*Ingrained Beliefs
And Blocks*

"Every adversity, every failure, every heartache carries
with it the seed of an equal or greater benefit."
—Napoleon Hill

*Y*OU NOW HAVE a deeper understanding of how trauma and
technology has impacted your life. This chapter will show you
how the evolution of your brain has been impacted by your role
models and why this forms how you respond to specific stimuli
in the world today. Knowing the why makes it easier to change.

Your Brain is Like a Sponge

Between the ages of six months and seven years, you existed in
the Theta brainwave state with a frequency between 4 and 8 Hz.

Brainwaves refer to the electrical activity of the brain and are measured by an electroencephalogram (EEG) which is an electrophysiological monitoring method that records the wave activity and are fairly common in scientific and medical circles.[43] The Theta brainwave state is known as the hypnosis, or suggestive state and everything you experienced, heard, or saw during these years became part of your subconscious belief system.

Your parent's belief system, based on their families' belief system, was programmed into your psyche (or subconscious) from birth. It didn't matter if they were your birth or adopted parents. Even relatives or primary caregivers impacted your belief system. Their ways of being or responding to situations were ingrained into your subconscious and began to form how you think and react to the world.

What is important to understand is this is not the real you. Numerous cognitive neuroscientists have conducted studies that have revealed that only 5% of our cognitive activities (decisions, emotions, actions, behavior) are conscious, whereas the remaining 95% are subconscious. In simple terms, your auto-programmed past is your subconscious and impacts most of your thoughts, beliefs, and actions. With awareness and practice, you can change your thoughts, release those self-limiting beliefs, and learn to create the beliefs and thoughts you choose. A key part of this is learning to exist in *The BEING Zone* state where your energy is calm, and that state allows you to change your state of *BEING* and how you respond to the world.

The Real You

From birth, you naturally followed your heart and occupied yourself with toys or activities that filled you up (if you lived in a loving, supportive environment). Without any thought about it, you instinctively existed in *The BEING Zone*, which is a present, calm state where your heart is full of joy.

In the very early years, your natural reaction was not about pleasing others. It was about doing what felt right to you at the moment. If you loved what you were doing, you would become so immersed in the time and space of that activity that you might not notice what was happening in the world around you. This was the real you. You were naturally connected with the earth and universal energy, tuned into your body and your intuition.

The BEING Zone is where most of us existed as young children, where we lived in the present moment. This *BEING Zone* is the state where you want to learn to exist again, where you can learn to know and feel what is right and learn to follow that. It is about learning to "just *BE*." When you live in this *BEING* space, you will begin to feel deeply happy inside your heart, every moment of every day.

As you grew up, there were situations and events that impacted how you perceive and respond to the world today. You may have been raised in a loving home or a home of chaos and trauma. Everyone's story is different, even for two people raised in the same household.

My younger brother and I remember having phenomenal childhoods. My older brother and sister, not so much. Mom and Dad were stricter with them and expected them to "toe the line." By the time my younger brother and I were born, they'd relaxed a lot. They were more at ease with us, allowing us to make more decisions and do more things. As a result, my younger brother and I have much happier childhood memories. What about you?

Even if you grew up in a loving home, there might have been situations where friends or family members were inappropriate or mean to you, or times when your parents fought or yelled at you or each other, and it felt awful. All the situations you experienced in these early years when your brain was developing in the Theta state, absorbing all the stimuli around you, impacts who you are as a person today, and how you respond to the world.

Client Story: Diana, age 47, never experienced *The BEING Zone* or felt safe or loved as a young child. Her mother wasn't a happy person. She was often highly anxious, never nurturing, and she expected perfection. Diana was fearful when they went to significant events like weddings because her mom would lose control, drink too much, and yell at her on the way home. She also intuitively knew that her father was having an affair, and she couldn't say anything for fear of reprisal. As a result of this traumatic childhood, Diana has never had a real boyfriend, drives herself too hard trying to be perfect, and tends to have throat issues when trying to speak her truth. She continues to work through these issues, but because she is a driven perfectionist, she often works too many hours to take the time to change at the level she is capable of.

Journaling Time

BIRTH TO AGE 5 JOURNALING EXERCISE #11:
Take out your *BEING Journal* or notebook and think about your years between birth and age five. You may not have a clear memory of yourself

at that age, and that's OK. If you remember stories that you have been told, you can use that information too. If you don't remember, ask someone who knew you then (your mom or dad, your grandparents, older siblings, caretakers, etc.). If no one knew you at this age and you have no memories, move onto the next section.

- What do you remember from those years? What stories have you heard from family members or friends?
- Describe any memories of being yelled at, scolded, spanked, or struck.
- Explain any memories of being reprimanded for doing things you loved.
- Write about things you were told such as: You are not enough or not smart enough, etc.
- Write down any memories about being locked in your room or sent to bed without dinner and how that felt to you.
- Detail out any memories you have around having tantrums or wetting your bed.
- Identify and describe any negative beliefs or blocks that may have come from one of the above incidences.

Age five is when most children start kindergarten in the United States, and for many of us, it started the transition from *The BEING Zone*, doing what we love most of the time, to pleasing others. We learned very quickly that if we listened to our teachers and did what they said, our parents and teachers were happier. So, most of us fell in line and followed the rules. Children who didn't were viewed as disruptive, even if, in reality, they were rebelling because they could no longer follow their instincts or spend time doing what they loved. The good news at this age was that there wasn't much homework and we still had recess, so we were able to spend a reasonable amount of time following our hearts and enjoying life...unless you also faced a crushing blow, as explained in the next story.

I was a happy-go-lucky child full of confidence and joy. I loved school, and my teachers in my early years believed in me and encouraged me to be me. We moved in December of my third-grade year to a new city and a new school. On my first day, my new teacher, Mrs. McCrae, told me to stand up and introduce myself. I stood up, said my name, talked about where I came from, and explained why we moved. Mrs. McCrae berated me in front of the class, saying, "I didn't ask you to tell your life story. I just asked you to introduce yourself." I was stunned. I felt small, stupid, and embarrassed, and that feeling didn't go away for years. She cut deep into my core, and it took a lot of self-reflection work to realize that I didn't have the problem; it was her. I was so confident and happy, and she wasn't, and she couldn't handle seeing a joyful, self-assured little girl in her midst, so she tried to destroy my buoyant personality. Once I cleared the painful memories and feelings, I was able to speak my truth and shine my light again!

You may have turned off your ability to grow and express yourself during those early years because of issues inside or outside of school, like dealing with abuse, neglect, control, or lack of support from your family. Situations like this may have taken you away from heart-based living because coping with day-to-day functions in a chaotic household meant you sometimes had to turn your wants and needs off just to get by. For some, dealing with family issues and having what felt like no foundation at home, while also dealing with the mounting pressures to fit in during school and get decent grades, may have been enormous. If this was your reality, you may have started to put up protection and walls to get through these times. Alternatively, you might find some of the early activities you enjoyed as a young child point out natural skills and desires that you still have today. You may also discover that you are not using these organic talents today because they did not fit the mold of success passed down to you or the reality of the survival state in which you exist today.

Journaling Time

Grade School Journaling Exercise #12:

Grab your *BEING Journal* or notebook and think about each year you were in grade school. Try to remember and document them all.

- What are your hardest or most painful memories from those years?
- Were there teachers or others in positions of authority who embarrassed or belittled you? Describe how you were—or still are—influenced by those situations.
- Were there kids who bullied you? If so, how did that make you feel?
- Describe situations where teachers, peers, or family members were mean or rude to you and how it felt.
- Did you ever get left out and feel hurt deep inside? Describe the memory.
- Did you feel supported by your family? Explain why or why not.
- Can you identify any negative beliefs or blocks you have today that may have come from one or more of these experiences?
- What activities did you enjoy doing at this age? Where did you get lost in the moment? Do you still enjoy any of these today?

As a young child, I loved being outdoors. One of my earliest childhood memories is building homes in the woods with soft moss for a bed. I would lie on that soft moss, look up at the blue sky, and watch the clouds through the canopies of the trees. I had no idea that just sitting on the earth was making me feel good, but now I understand the powerful energy of the earth in our health and well-being.

I also loved playing with my dolls, talking, listening, nurturing, and caring for them. My mother called me empathetic from a very young age, but I had no idea what she meant by that. Now I understand she saw that I showed an ability to understand and share the feelings of others. This is a trait that is crucial for the work I love as a Life Coach. I put on shows or performances with the neighborhood kids, followed by participating in plays at school, revealing a craving for the stage that serves me well when I speak to audiences about the messages and passions that arise from my work.

Your Middle Years

If you were fortunate enough to have experienced a healthy childhood where you could tune into what made you happy, you most likely found that the amount of time for heart-based activities continued to decrease as you aged. When you reached fifth or sixth grade, peer pressure may have started to kick in, and most likely continued through eighth or ninth grade. These are challenging years for anyone, when many of us learned to ignore our intuition and true happiness in favor of choices that made us part of the "in" group. That shirt you loved and wore all summer landed on the floor of the closet when the cool kids called it dumb. The instruments you enjoyed playing have been put away.

Of course, there are exceptions. Some children, especially those with parents who urged them to focus on what they loved to do, had enough confidence in themselves to stick to their guns and follow their hearts. I had a friend in junior high who never got sucked into what was popular. He loved playing the violin and never wavered from doing what he loved, even though most violinists don't make a lot of money. Instead of veering off into a life in the *DOING Zone*, he followed his heart and now makes a good living playing violin and bass guitar with rock bands around the world.

Journaling Time

MIDDLE SCHOOL YEARS JOURNALING EXERCISE #13:

Find your notebook or *BEING Journal* and think about ages 12 to 15 and begin writing. These years may have been full of insecurities because you were moving from listening to your intuitive heart to listening to that voice in your head that just wanted to fit in. These were critical years in your development and had a significant impact on your belief system.

- What were your greatest insecurities at the time?
- What are your greatest regrets now, looking back?
- How important was it to you to be cool or accepted by the popular kids?
- Were there things you did, or risks you took, that looking back you wish you hadn't done? If so, explain.
- Were you telling your parents—or maybe yourself—lies about what you were doing or how you felt?
- Write about any specific times when you didn't stand up for yourself or say no.
- Can you identify and explain any beliefs or blocks that came from a childhood experience?

· What activities did you enjoy doing at this age? Where did you get lost in the moment? Do you still enjoy any of these today?

Client Story: One of my clients, Louise, had a boyfriend throughout her middle school years who was always cheating on her with other girls. Instead of standing up for herself or breaking up with him, she would turn a blind eye and pretend she didn't know, even though it was killing her inside. She ended up in two marriages where her husbands cheated on her. She has worked through most her issues by releasing old beliefs systems that she wasn't good enough. She has learned to love herself, speak her truth, and is now in a healthy relationship for the first time.

Doing the Right Thing

In high school, the pressure to conform intensifies for many kids, with the pressure to take the "right" classes, get the "right" grades and get into the "right" colleges. If college isn't a priority, there might be the pressure of getting the "right" work experience or building the "right" skills to find the "right" job after high school. You may fall into the category of people who didn't have any options for the right college or perfect career because you were already working to take care of yourself or your family. Instead, you may have experienced immense pressure to do things "right" on behalf of other people, always trying to fulfill someone else's needs and wants. Many of you try to do what is considered "right," or exist in the *DOING Zone*, focused on success and achievement or survival instead of what makes you happy or fills you up. You also may have been lucky and been encouraged to follow your heart and ended up working in a field you love.

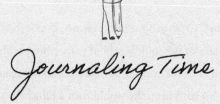

Journaling Time

HIGH SCHOOL YEARS JOURNALING EXERCISE #14:

Grab your notebook or *BEING Journal* and think about your high school years. These are the years where grades, achievements, and popularity might drive your decisions. This exercise is to help you discover and clear old feelings.

- What are your worst memories or regrets? List them and write what you remember.
- Do you remember anything said or done to you that made you hurt or feel left out? Take time to write about those times.
- Were there times you were in situations you knew were wrong, but you didn't have the confidence, strength, or power to walk away? Explain.
- Can you identify any negative beliefs or blocks you have today that may have come from one or more of these experiences? What are they?
- Did you feel confident, loved, supported, and encouraged to follow your heart? If not, explain.
- Do you still feel like you are living your dream? If no, why not?
- What activities did you enjoy doing at this age? Where did you get lost in the moment? Do you still enjoy any of these today?

For some of you that went to college, it may have still been about fitting into the "right" social groups and getting the "right" grades, so you could get into the right program so you could make money. If this was your situation, after graduation you might have strived for the top name companies and the most lucrative starting salaries and have stuck with it even if you didn't like it because you'd invested so much time and money into getting where you were. For some, the focus became on buying stuff: new cars, the first house, exciting vacations—doing all you can to impress your friends and neighbors. If you got married and had children, the pressure increased to stay in your job to pay bills.

There are a group of you who followed your passion and earned degrees that weren't about money, and gathering stuff wasn't a priority, and you may still feel authentically happy in life today. Or you may have been a stay-at-home spouse or parent. You may have left the workplace to travel, be self-employed, or to do things that made you happy. Some of you may love your life just the way it is and some of you may feel stuck.

If you didn't go to college but started working to support yourself and others, you may be in a dead-end job that doesn't make your heart sing. You are good at it; you like who you work with, and it pays the bills. No matter what your background was, what your goals were, what school you went to—or didn't go to—we usually all have some degree of wanting something more. For reasons very personal to each of us, we can get stuck where we are.

I have covered a lot of scenarios, as I know we are all leading very different lives. However, as different as we may be, we all have the potential of facing similar challenges at different times in our lives.

Journaling Time

College Years to Now Journaling Exercise #15:

Grab your *BEING Journal* or notebook and think about your years between college and now. Your goal is to identify the issues from this time in your life to clear as well as what might inspire you.

- Are the decisions you've made based on ensuring your safety or security or do they consider what makes you happy and fills you up? Describe.
- Looking back, what were your worst memories or pains during your adult years? Why are these memories so hurtful?
- Did you ever get fired from a job or laid off? How did that make you feel?
- Were you ever treated disrespectfully or incorrectly in a work environment? How did it feel?
- Were you ever treated as if you weren't good enough or not smart enough? Or passed over for a promotion when you were the best candidate? Describe how that felt.
- Can you identify and describe any negative beliefs or blocks you have today that may have come from one or more of these experiences?
- What other memories do you have that you would like to clear?
- What activities did you enjoy doing at this age? Where did you get lost in the moment? Do you still enjoy any of these today?

Happiness First

I meet a lot of 40- and 50-something clients who come to me looking to transition to a new career. Later in life, they've begun to understand that happiness is more important than status or money. They listened to their parents and went after a career to make money instead of following their passion and are now unhappy. Others love their job and company, but they worked so much they burned themselves out, which is what I did. I was looking for external happiness and accolades instead of internal joy.

Unhappiness Looms

When you add up the auto-programming we accepted—any traumas we experienced as children (living in the Theta state) that

CURRENT LIFE OBSERVATIONS JOURNALING EXERCISE #16:

Grab your *BEING Journal* or notebook and think about your current life. The point of this exercise is to help you discover and clear what may not work for you while tuning into what will inspire you moving forward.

- Do you love your life? Are you fulfilled? Describe what, why, and how.
- If you were to stop and tune into what you really wanted your life to be like, what would you see or hear?

- What would you like to do differently now that you are increasing your awareness?
- What beliefs in your life are stopping you from stepping into your power?

formed our belief systems, and the pressures of our culture and society put on us to go after money and success—you can see how many of us began to create lives we don't love. Income often prevents people from leaving their jobs even when they are unhappy, or the environment is toxic. I coach so many people who are miserable or stuck in life and many who are unhappy in their profession because they went after money instead of following their interests. Their friends or parents may have told them they couldn't make money doing what they love, and it was more important to follow money over passion. They opted to listen to their parents, or other influencers in their life, to do what they were told was the right thing. Their focus became getting a good-paying job to support themselves and their family to the best of their ability, sometimes at the expense of losing who they are. The real wants, needs, and desires of their hearts easily got lost in dollar signs and trying to keep up with the cost of living and social status. I have clients who feel stuck because they believe the money they make is too good to leave, and they don't realize it's not too late to create a happier existence.

Client Story: 55-year-old Keith is a very creative person by nature. When he was younger, he was passionate about writing, film production, and documentaries and wanted to go to school for that. Instead, his friends and family told him he couldn't make money doing that. He ended up with a degree in business and fell into the trademark and intellectual property world, which he has never loved. He spent 25 years doing work that wasn't filling him up. He called me when he was getting physically ill each day before going to work. He knew it was job-related when he had a two-week vacation and wasn't sick at all, but immediately got ill the day he returned to work. Keith didn't feel he could quit his day job, so we channeled his energy into doing what he loved in his free time. Keith is now writing a book, and his scripts are winning awards. He also writes articles for a newsletter and helped create a documentary for a global nonprofit. He is no longer getting sick from his day job as he knows he is making progress toward his dream in his free time.

Journaling Time

LIFE HAPPINESS JOURNALING EXERCISE #17:
Grab your notebook or *BEING Journal* and think about your current life and journal about your happiness.

· Is money or happiness more important to you? Why?

· How many people do you know who live in the survival state and just get by? Are you one of those? Describe how your life feels if you are operating in this way.

· How many people do you know who don't love their life or their job? How about you? Describe your situation.

· What do you love about your life and job? What do you dislike?

Are You Happy?

In the introduction, you learned that happiness is deteriorating across the nation. Even if you are supposedly "successful" with a beautiful home and toys, you may be miserable on the inside. You might feel stuck in a thankless job that does not fulfill you, but you just keep going because you think you have to, or you don't want to let others down. You may be stuck in the *DOING Zone*, where you go through the motions daily and then fall into bed exhausted and drained, only to repeat the same thing the next day. Are you deeply unhappy and have this inner knowing, feeling or sense that there *must* be more to life?

Client Story: Wendy, a 30-something mother, lawyer, and business leader, had been working long hours in a company that did not appreciate her value or the time she put into doing the job right. She earned good money but was burned out, not feeling well, and no longer happy. She looked happy and smiled when anyone asked how she was, but inside she was dying. She was close to a breakdown and didn't even know it. We worked together and she made the decision to move to part-time hours and work from home. After four months at home, she told me she was still recovering and had had no idea of how sick she was. She is utilizing the tools in this book and incorporating essential oils and daily work into her life to create more balance. Next up, she has done a lot of work on her True North (which will be explained in Chapter 6) and is planning to move into doing something more fulfilling where she can keep balance and make a difference in this world.

Why Do We Do This to Ourselves?

Many of us grew up in a time where we were expected to line up and comply and behave. The belief system was there was no time for "dilly-dallying," there was work that needed to be done. You might have heard, "quit being lazy" or "quit wasting your time, be responsible." In addition, by nature, many of us are pleasers. We try our best to line up with expectations that come from our innate desire to make others happy.

With the pressures of work, family, and the American Dream, there were high expectations, schedules, and responsibilities that moved us out of self-care and focusing on what made us happy into more of a driven state. When we operate full-time in the *DOING Zone* and don't take time to play or just *BE* present in the moment, it can lead to unhappiness, an increased stress response in our bodies where it is hard to turn off and relax, and ultimately illness.

Family Belief Systems

Another major factor in why we end up unhappy or sick is based on ancestral beliefs which were passed down the family line. Science has proven that our thoughts become our reality. We hear things growing up and those become our beliefs, which often send us into anxiety and stress and can result in the creation of the health issues we are terrified of.

How many times have you heard "cancer runs in my family"? Or "depression is in our family"? We learned in science classes that our genes dictated our likelihood of obtaining diseases. I am happy to say, scientists have proven that is not true.

Best-selling author, scientist, and biologist Bruce Lipton, PhD, was ahead of his time in the 1970s when he discovered that a person's genes do not control their health as previously believed in the scientific and medical world. He found the environment (including thoughts) has a major influence on a person's cells, which impacts their health. He did a stem cell study and put genetically identical cells put into three different Petri dishes, each with their own culture medium so each identical cell lived a different environment. Cells are like fish; they live in a fluid environment, so a culture medium is a liquid environment designed to support the growth of cells. Dr. Lipton found the identical cells developed different traits based on which culture medium (environment) they were put into. The most important insight is that the genetically identical cells didn't decide their fate; the environment controlled their outcome.

· **Petri Dish A:** Muscle formed.
· **Petri Dish B:** Bone formed.
· **Petri Dish C:** Fat formed.

What that means to you is that your genes do not control your health—your environment does.[44] Your environment includes your physical and chemical make-up, where you live, what you put into or on your body, as well as all your thoughts. You may have heard family members say, "we are predisposed to this illness because our parents or relatives have it." This is not true for the majority of diseases. The illness will not develop if the environment isn't right for that. But if you create a belief that you are likely to get it, those thoughts can create the environment that may cause the disease to blossom.

Dr. Lipton explains two terms that make this understandable.

· **Causation:** An act causes an effect.
· **Correlation:** There is a relationship between.

Dr. Lipton goes on to explain that having the cancer gene does not cause cancer. The gene must be engaged by the environment in which the cells live in and your thoughts and beliefs impact or can change that environment. Your thoughts become your reality. Your thoughts produce neurochemicals which go into your cells and cause a reaction or change in the environment. In other words, when we believe something, those thoughts or beliefs help make it come true.

Dr. Lipton uses Angelina Jolie as an example. She had both breasts removed because she believed she would get cancer as she had the same gene as her mother and grandmother who died from it, yet 50% of the people with that gene never get cancer because future gene mutations need to happen that may not.

There is also scientific evidence that is proving your thoughts and mental state impact your results based on a study by the Carlson Group , they found meditating cancer patients are able to affect the makeup of their DNA, which could change their outcome.[45] The internal thoughts (environment) caused the expression of the gene. Dr. Lipton says if you believe the gene causes cancer those thoughts may help cause the cancer to form and you may become a victim of cancer as a result of your thoughts. There is scientific proof of depression resulting in a later onset of cancer, which shows how powerful your thoughts are in impacting the onset of disease.[46]

We often feel like victims when we get sick—what I didn't realize is all the unconscious choices we make impact our health greatly. Pay attention to your thoughts, the food you eat, and your environment at the onset of illness to determine what might be a contribution source that you can change. Sometimes it is family belief systems as demonstrated in Angelina's story. If this is the case, you may need to work on clearing and eliminating belief systems that do not serve you. I had to do this. My grandfather died from bone cancer, and I used to fear that I was suscepti-ble to having the same cancer until my doctor set me straight. My thoughts, beliefs, and fears were the problem, and there was no reason for me to worry. My fear was built up by the medical questionnaire I had to fill out every time I went to the doctor as well—it made me feel there was a correlation.

As you learned, your ingrained belief systems, the environment you live in, including the people you surround yourself with, and thoughts can impact your happiness and health. The trick is to recognize these tendencies and stop them in their tracks.

Journaling Time

Health Beliefs Journaling Exercise #18:

Time to write in your notebook or *BEING Journal* on your health beliefs based on your family's health or beliefs that were passed down.

- If your parents were (or are) overweight, do you believe that will be your reality? Describe how that has impacted you and your life.
- If any of your family members have heart disease, is that your destiny? Explain the impact this type of belief has had on you.
- If people in your family had cancer, do you expect you will also? Describe your current fears and how you can change these beliefs.

· What other illnesses or diseases do you feel you are predisposed to as a result of family beliefs? Now do some online research asking what diseases are genetic. The list is short. You will be able to eliminate many fears.

· It is essential to clear these old beliefs as part of your healing process. Make a list of what you need to clear.

 ## Tool #1: The 5 Whys to Get to The Root Cause of Your Unhappiness

The "5 Whys" is a powerful way to get to the root cause of your unhappiness. The "5 Whys" is an analytical technique that helps to explore cause-and-effect relationships when you encounter a problem. I have discovered that this technique can be used to get to the core reason you may be having struggles in your life or happiness. The basic idea is to repeat the question "**why?**" until you find the root cause. That most often requires asking the question of **why** at least **five** times.

Below is an example of how you can apply the "5 Whys" to a problem in your personal life.

The Problem: I Am Unhappy

1. **Why?** – I feel stuck in life and have no energy.
2. **Why?** – I am not doing what I love to do.
3. **Why?** – I got a good-paying job out of college and stayed on that career path.
4. **Why?** – I went after money instead of passion.
5. **Why?** – I was taught that money and earning a good living was the responsible thing to do (the fifth why, a root cause).

So now you are at the root cause of your unhappiness. You may have believed that to be responsible you must make good money, so you went after that. You chased wealth instead of happiness. So, what you can do about that? *SHIFT* your belief system using some of the tools in the next chapter.

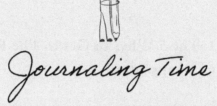

Journaling Time

5 WHYS ON EACH NEGATIVE BELIEF OR BLOCK JOURNALING EXERCISE #19:

Grab your pen and notebook or *BEING Journal* and begin writing.

· Ask yourself and document the "5 Whys" on each negative belief or block you identified or on why you feel like you do in your life.

· See if you can identify the root cause of your unhappiness through the "5 Whys" process. Then make notes on what you can change to improve how you feel. When you understand it, you'll be ready to *SHIFT* or clear it from your life.

You are in an excellent position to begin the healing process if you have taken advantage of the journaling exercises in Chapters 1 and 2. You have started excavating your life's journey by going back to your childhood to discover what caused you pain or made you feel bad. Identifying your greatest pains is empowering. These are the memories that are holding you back and when discovered, you can clear them to begin to create the authentic life you desire.

Journaling Time

SUMMARY OF KEY LEARNINGS JOURNALING EXERCISE #20:
Take the time to review and highlight all the memories you journaled about in your *BEING Journal* or notebook.

· Document where you feel the most pain, have negative beliefs or blocks, as those are the ones you should target with the healing tools offered in Chapter 3.

Key Messages

· When you were a young child, you naturally followed your intuition and immersed yourself in activities that made you happy; you lived in your personal *BEING Zone.*

· You also operated in the Theta brainwave state, where your brain was like a sponge, downloading the beliefs and messages of adults. Their views became your ingrained belief system which resides in your subconscious and is what holds you back in life.

· As you got older, you began to care about fitting in and doing what you felt your peers and adults would see as successful instead of following your instincts on what would make you happy. This is when you began to live more in your subconscious and personal *DOING Zone.*

· Identifying and releasing the beliefs, messages, pain, and false stories that are holding you back or making you sick enables you to start building an authentic life.

· Your thoughts, feelings, and environment impact your health and happiness directly, so learning to focus on what you do want and stop doing what you don't want is imperative in your healing process.

This Chapter's Gifts: The opportunity to identify blocks and ingrained beliefs that are holding you back, keeping you stuck, and preventing you from living an authentic life in your personal *BEING Zone*.

CHAPTER 3

Tools For Clearing Blocks, And Beliefs

"Courage is knowing what not to fear."
—Plato

*Y*OU HAVE SPENT the first two chapters understanding why you are the way you are. Now it is time to *SHIFT* or release previous trauma and eliminate your underlying beliefs, blocks, and pains, allowing you to move on in your life. You are unique, and you should utilize the tools that will be most effective for you, your style, and your temperament. Utilizing the right potent tools will heal your soul.

It's time to find and open up your *BEING Journal* to identify what issues you want to clear using these tools. Review your notes from Journaling exercise #20 and see what you prioritized. You will find that when you are using the tools to clear the actual situations or incidents that you have journaled about, you will begin to experience the magic of the tools. Using real life struggles is the most effective way to learn the tools and know that they actually work. Try different tools on the issues that bother you the most as those more extreme issues often take more work.

Once you experiment with and experience each tool, you will intuitively know what works best for you. I personally use different tools for different issues, depending on what I hear or feel when my clients are telling me their stories. It is a deep knowing I get inside. That said, I have provided stories or examples on when I might use these different tools to make it easier for you to connect with them and try them out.

The first six tools listed provide detailed instructions so you can implement them on your own. Tool #8 requires listening to a recording on *The BEING Zone* website. The final four tools are the most powerful and capable of providing exceptional results and are best done by a skilled practitioner in the beginning.

The Foundational Tools

We are going to start with a variety of breathing exercises as they will calm your mind and body, opening you up to being able to operate in *The BEING Zone*. Breathing increases the supply of oxygen to your brain and stimulates your parasympathetic nervous system, which brings you into a state of calmness. Breathing techniques help you feel connected to your body by taking your awareness away from the worries in your head while quieting your mind.

Tool #2: Three-Part Breathing

It is called Three-Part Breathing because there are three steps. You count in three second intervals, and you repeat the three steps three times.

· Take a very deep breath in through your nose on a count of three, breathing in love.
· Hold it for a count of three.
· Release it through your mouth on a count of three, releasing all that doesn't serve you.

Repeat these two more times for a total of three deep breaths. Once you have completed this breathing sequence, you should feel much more grounded, centered, and relaxed.

When to Use This Tool

This is my favorite and I use it daily. I start every daily practice with this breathing and teach my clients to do the same. It has become a very natural response I use when I am facing a stressful situation. Listen to the three-part breathing recording at www. TheBEINGZone.com/tools.

Journaling Time

THREE-PART BREATHING JOURNALING EXERCISE #21:
Grab your notebook or *BEING Journal* and make notes.

> · Write about how well the Three-Part Breathing exercise worked
>   for you.
> · Did you feel more centered and calmer? If so, explain how you felt.
> · If not, how did you feel?
> · Is this an exercise you will most likely use moving forward?

Tool #3: Mindful Breathing

What makes it mindful is the fact that you are aware of your breathing. The goal should be to become a natural at tuning to your breath to increase your calmness, help you center, and relax while decreasing your stress or anxiety.

· Find a relaxed, comfortable position. You could be seated on a chair or on a cushion on the floor. Keep your back upright, but not too tight. Rest your hands wherever they're comfortable. Press your tongue on the roof of your mouth if that's comfortable, as that helps turn off your active mind.
· Be mindful of and relax any areas of tightness or tension in your body by visualizing breathing directly into those specific areas.
· Tune into your breath. When you are tuned in and mindful, you will feel the natural flow of it in and out. You don't need to do anything to change your breath—do not try to make it long or short, just breathe naturally. Notice where you feel your breath in your body. It might be in your abdomen. It may be in your chest or throat or nostrils. See if you can feel the sensations, one breath at a time. When one breath ends, the next breath begins.
· If and when your mind starts to wander, know this is very natural. Just notice that your mind has wandered and say "think-

ing" or "wandering" in your head softly. Then gently redirect your attention right back to the breathing.

· Stay here for up to five minutes. Notice your breath in silence. From time to time, you'll get lost in thought, then return to your breath.

When to Use This Tool

This tool is a tool of awareness, or mindfulness, and is most powerful when you are stressed and tense. You will find the more you mindfully focus on your breathing into the area of tenseness, the less stressed you will feel. Listen to the Mindful Breathing recording at www.TheBEINGZone.com/tools.

Journaling Time

MINDFUL BREATHING JOURNALING EXERCISE #22:
Grab your notebook or *BEING Journal* to start writing.

· Make notes on how well the Mindful Breathing exercise worked for you.
· How did it make you feel? Do you feel more peaceful or tranquil?
· Do you feel this is an exercise you will most likely use moving forward?

Tool #4: Breathe into It and Surrender

When you identify a pain in your body that is not extreme, breathing into it is the perfect tool to use to help release it and to understand why it showed up in your life. What were you meant to learn?

Here is what often happens when people have physical pain. They focus on it, worry about it, and make it worse. For example, one of my clients was having abdominal pain and immediately believed that she had cancer. She went into a state of panic. You might have shooting pains in your head and worry that it's a brain aneurysm. If you're having chest pain, it might be hard to believe it could be anything but a heart attack, even if you've been given the all-clear and you know your heart is fine.

If you become aware of your tendencies, you can release those beliefs, which will help lessen the mental agony you are creating. The next time those pains show up, you can breathe into them and release the tension or stuck energy. The breath is a wonderful tool for dealing with discomfort. Give it a try and see what happens.

Breathe into It and Surrender Process

- When there is a pain in your body, bring your attention to the area of muscular tension.
- Do some slow, deep, smooth belly breathing, with a prolonged exhalation to lessen the stress and tension in your body.
- Once you are calm, direct your breath, like a laser, into the area of pain. By visualizing that you are breathing directly into the pain, you allow that area to relax. It will lessen your pain.
- Continue to breathe into the area for as long as there is a pain.

When to Use This Tool

This Breathe into It and Surrender tool is most powerful when
you are holding pain or anger in your body that comes from stress,
mistreatment, harsh words, exhaustion, or an accident. When you
learn to pay attention when an area starts hurting, you'll recognize
when it's time to focus on it and start breathing into it. Listen
to the Breathe Into It and Surrender recording at www.TheBE-
INGZone.com/tools.

> Note: If there is a deeper underlying issue (like my
> repression of rape, described earlier), it won't clear by
> breathing alone. You will learn additional tools later in
> this chapter.

Client Story: Jeanne had a lot of stress at work, which
built tension in her shoulders that then developed into
regular migraines. She'd usually take ibuprofen and go to
bed and that gave some relief, but the migraines would always
return. I had her stop and breathe to relax until she was able to
pinpoint where in her head she felt the pain. Then I had her visualize breathing directly into that point, filling it with loving energy
while allowing the pain or tension to release. She was amazed that
the migraine disappeared so quickly. She now uses this technique
regularly whenever anxiety shows up in her body to stop the headache before it develops.

Journaling Time

BREATHE INTO IT AND SURRENDER JOURNALING EXERCISE #23:
Grab your notebook or *BEING Journal* and make notes.

- Write about how well the Breathe into It and Surrender exercise worked for you.
- Describe how it felt in your body.
- Did you feel a release of pain or anger? Describe the feeling of that release.
- Is this an exercise you will most likely use moving forward? Explain how.

Tool #5: Emotional Freedom Technique (EFT), Also Called Tapping

This tool is so useful that an estimated 10 million people around the world use it.[47] It works with your body's meridians, the channels that transport energy (chi) throughout the body.

You start by focusing on a negative emotion like fear, anxiety, an unresolved problem, or whatever is bothering you. Then you tap on your meridians while verbalizing the issue and releasing it, replacing it with love and acceptance for yourself.

Tapping is fast, it doesn't have to cost a penny, and it gives you the power to heal yourself! There have been multiple studies showing that EFT is an effective tool for healing memories from Post-Traumatic Stress Disorder (PTSD),[48] which I believe most of us have in one form or another. Tapping is also being accepted by mainstream medicine as a viable healing technique and is being taught to medical doctors at medical conferences and conventions. A 2014 paper published in the *Review of General Psychology* examined 51 peer reviewed reports or studies on EFT published in scientific journals. In those studies, one group received tapping, and the other received a different intervention, or none, and results were compared. All 51 studies demonstrated a positive outcome, ranging from slightly to vastly improved, with conditions ranging from anxiety, depression, physical pain, tension headaches, Fibromyalgia Syndrome (FMS), PTSD, and more.[49]

Emotional Freedom Technique (Tapping) Process

Before you begin, choose a specific "target" using issues you identified through your journaling or an issue that is bothering you right now (it could be an emotion, belief, symptom, or event). Identify three ways to verbalize the issue. For example, you might say "I feel stressed. I am completely overwhelmed. I have too much to do and too little time."

Start by very lightly tapping on the karate chop point on the left hand (see left-hand visual below) with the tips of your fingers of your right hand. Stay on the karate chop point while you state the target issue three different ways, followed by an affirmation of self-love. Repeat three times.

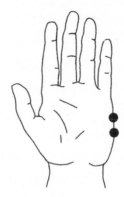

- Even though I feel all this stress, I totally and completely love and accept myself.
- Even though I am overwhelmed, I totally and completely love and accept myself.
- Even though I have too much to do and too little time, I totally and completely love and accept myself.

EFT Facial and Body Tapping Points

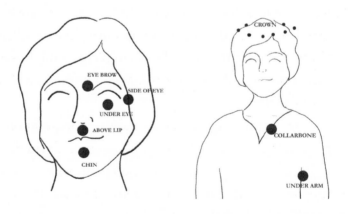

Go through the tapping process on various Acupressure points (see diagram above), **lightly tapping the points while rotating through the statements:**

- **Eyebrow:** Even though I feel stressed...
- **Bone on the side of the eye:** Even though I am often over-whelmed...
- **The bone under eye:** Even though I have too much to do and too little time...
- **Above lip and under nose:** I totally and completely love and accept myself...
- **On chin:** Even though I am often stressed...
- **On soft spot outside collarbone:** And I am usually feeling over-whelmed...
- **Under your arm:** And have too much to do and too little time...
- **On top of your head** (in a circle like where a crown of daisies would sit): I totally and completely love and accept myself...

In addition to these instructions, listen to the EFT audio on my website at www.TheBEINGZone.com/tools to help you easily practice tapping.

When to Use This Tool

This tool is most useful for current or recent upset, trauma, or disruption that is impacting how you are feeling. For example, if someone just had a car accident and was shaken up, I would use this tool to help calm their system. I use it with clients if someone yelled at them or they feel stressed or emotional. To measure success, I often ask my client to rate the level of pain or upset on a scale of 1 to 10 prior to starting and again at the end.

Client Story: Dani worked hard and was building phe-nomenal relationships with regular customers at the restau-rant where she worked as a server. They always requested her section and were excited to see her. Dani's supervisor, who is more head-based and disconnected, felt left out. As a result, she started riding Dani and saying disrespectful things to her and tried to erode the connection Dani had created with the customers. Dani began to feel tension in her shoulders and would get headaches. We used the tapping technique to *SHIFT* how she was reacting, and it gave Dani immediate relief. In the long run, Dani realized her supervisor was dysfunctional and wasn't going to change without help, so Dani decided to leave the job, which was the right thing to do.

Journaling Time

TAPPING OR EFT JOURNALING EXERCISE #24:

Grab your notebook or *BEING Journal* to write.

- Write about how well the tapping exercise worked for you.
- Did you feel lighter overall from the experience? Describe how that felt.
- Did you feel a release? If so, how would you describe it?
- Will you use this tool? Make notes on the types of situations where this tool may be most useful to you.

Tool #6: The Healing Codes

This tool was developed by psychologist and naturopath Dr. Alexander Loyd, who presented this tool at the Enwaken Coaches' training in Colorado that changed my life. For this self-healing technique, you use the fingertips of both hands to point to one or more of the four different healing centers in the body: directly over your Adam's apple, temples, the bridge of your nose, and your jaw. I have provided visuals of the hand positions and basic instructions below, and there are many videos on YouTube. For many people, this will be enough to get started using the healing codes. If you are struggling in figuring it out, please set up a session with me or seek out a trained coach at www.dralexanderloyd.com/coaching

Healing Code Process

The graphics below illustrates the four hand positions for the healing centers. Pinch all fingers together with thumb in tight to the sides of the fingers.

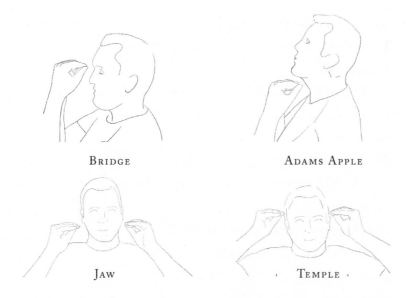

BRIDGE

ADAMS APPLE

JAW

TEMPLE

· Hold your fingers about one inch from the designated locations.
· Visualize energy flowing from your fingers to the body positions.
· Hold your fingers at each location for approximately 30 seconds.

You want to start with a healing prayer followed by specific steps in a specific order as shown below.

Healing Code Prayer

"I pray (or request) that all known and unknown negative images, unhealthy beliefs, destructive cellular memories, and all physical issues related to (Define your issue) will be found, opened and healed by filling me with the light, life, and love of God (or Source, Universe, Spirit). I also pray that the effectiveness of this healing be increased by 100 times or more." (This tells the body to make the healing a priority.)

Code #1: For the Issue Bothering you Most in your Life

- Left hand temple, right hand jaw
- Both hands bridge
- Both hands jaw
- Left hand Adam's apple, right hand bridge
- Left hand jaw, right hand temple
- Both hands Adam's apple
- Both hands bridge
- Left hand bridge, right hand Adam's apple
- Both hands jaw
- Left hand jaw, right hand bridge
- Left hand Adam's apple, right hand jaw
- Left hand jaw, right hand temple
- Both hands Adam's apple
- Both hands bridge

Repeat daily for at least 10 days and up to 2 weeks. Rotate hand positions every 30 seconds OR when it feels best to you.

When to Use This Tool

This tool is helpful when you are feeling frustrated, defeated, a loss of control, or it can be used for the most significant issue you are facing right now in life.

What do I mean by significant issue? It might be the loss of a loved one, getting let go from your job, a relationship breaking up, dealing with a challenging child or parent, etc. It works on painful memories (with repetitive use) and for self-control related to overspending, trying to find a love substitute, or needing people to see you in a certain way. There are many other uses also, in which a trained practitioner would be able to help. Go to www. TheBEINGZone.com/tools to hear the recording of a Healing Code practice.

Client Story: Randy and his wife own a house cleaning business. Some months they have more business than they can handle, and some months it is hard to make ends meet. One morning, Randy heard a noise when it was still dark outside. When he got up later in the morning, he realized his car had been stolen. He had a full day of clients, and his transportation was gone. He went into a depression, feeling frustrated and defeated. I had him use the healing codes for the feeling of defeat, and he immediately felt better and found temporary solutions to get through the day.

Journaling Time

HEALING CODE JOURNALING EXERCISE #25:

Grab your *BEING Journal* or notebook to document your experience.

· Write about how well the Healing Codes exercise worked for you.

· Did you feel different afterwards? Describe how.

· Did you feel less frustrated or defeated? Describe what you were
able to release.

· Is this an exercise you will most likely use moving forward? Explain
how.

 ## Tool #7: Subconscious Suggestion Before Sleep

"Never go to sleep without a
request to your subconscious."
—Thomas Edison

It's been widely known for many years that our subconscious is
always running in the background whether we are awake or asleep.
It's still making our hearts beat and digesting our food, among
many other things.

Your subconscious directs what happens in your conscious life,
so this tool is used to influence your subconscious mind deliberately. You will find that the more regularly you do this activity,
the more likely you will get consistent results, attracting what you
want into your life by deliberately suggesting it each night and
not thinking about what you don't want.

Subconscious Suggestion Process

· Five or ten minutes before you go to bed, start thinking about
  things you want to get done or cultivate while you sleep, to set
  yourself up for the next day.
· Take a few deep breaths, settle down into your space, and write
  down what you want. You can also state the phrases in your
  mind if you cannot write them down.
· Be very specific and always use the present tense. For example:
· I will wake up feeling energetic and refreshed so I can get to
  the gym with ease.
· I will have a therapeutic dream tonight to help release stress
  about work.
· I am healthy and active and feel good about who I am.
· I feel joy and notice the abundance around me all the time.
· As you write these suggestions down or state them in your
  mind, also visualize them the best you can and feel them as
  much as possible. This helps you tap into your subconscious.

When to Use This Tool

This is the perfect tool to use when you want to change how you
think, from a negative or defeatist viewpoint into a positive, what-
you-want point of view.

Client Story: Amanda had issues expressing herself,
which left her resentful and angry about the times she
should have spoken up. Before she went to sleep one night,
she suggested to herself, "I will have a therapeutic dream to release
stress about not sticking up for myself." She later reported she had

a dream where she was arguing with a past partner. She yelled and got to say everything she had needed to say but never did. She felt a release when waking and had movement in her frustration and shame. She has done this several more times and continues to make suggestions to herself before sleep.

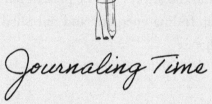

Journaling Time

SUBCONSCIOUS SUGGESTION PROCESS JOURNALING EXERCISE #26: Grab your notebook or *BEING Journal* and make some notes. This is a good one to write in the morning after trying the process.

· Write about how well the Subconscious Suggestion Process exercise worked for you.

· Did you sleep well? Did you have any dreams? Did you wake up feeling different? Write about your experience.

· Do you think this is a useful tool moving forward?

 ## Tool #8: Pond Visualization to Reconnect with Inner Child and Release

This Pond Visualization process takes you through the process of extending love, compassion, and forgiveness to all who have harmed you. The important part of this exercise is to understand how powerful forgiveness is. In her book, *The Law of Forgiveness*, author Connie Domino devotes a chapter to the scientific evidence for the power of forgiveness.[50] Additionally, Dr. Fred

Luskin, director and cofounder of the Stanford University Forgiveness Project, conducted research and found that people who were taught to forgive became less angry and more optimistic, compassionate, and self-confident.[51] One study from the *Journal of Behavioral Medicine* associated forgiveness with lower heart rates, lower blood pressure, and stress relief.[52] Another from the University of Tennessee and University of Wisconsin, Madison, attributed forgiveness to fewer medically diagnosed chronic conditions and fewer physical symptoms from illness.[53]

Start this process by visualizing all the people in your current life who have judged you or hurt you in any way. Imagine sitting on the edge of a pond as you work your way back through your entire life in reverse chronological order, visualizing each person who caused you harm through judgement or actions. You look at each person in your mind's eye, forgive them, and offer them love and compassion. When you have revisited all those who you need to forgive, you will reconnect with the real you and you will begin to feel free and whole.

When to Use This Tool

This is a good tool to use when you need to forgive someone and let go of the anger or hurt you feel inside. No matter what happened in your life or by whom, it will benefit you greatly when you can forgive them. When you send compassion and unconditional love, it opens up your heart to more love and releases your pain. It is difficult in the beginning because of the anger you may have from people hurting you, but when you are ready, it is hugely healing in the long run. You will find this process of listening to the recorded visualization very powerful. Please go to www.TheBEINGZone.com/tools to access the recording.

Journaling Time

POND EXERCISE TO RECONNECT WITH INNER CHILD

AND RELEASE JOURNALING EXERCISE #27:

Grab your *BEING Journal* or notebook and start documenting your experience.

- Make notes on how well the Pond Exercise to Reconnect with Inner Child and Release exercise worked for you.
- Do you feel you were able to let go of old issues? Write about what you feel different about.
- Did you feel lighter afterwards? Describe what that feels like in your body.
- Do you feel you have more people to forgive or were you able to address most issues in your life?
- Is this an exercise you will most likely use again?

Client Story: Bob had anger and rage inside of him from a variety of situations where he was told what to do and how to feel. His parents were very controlling, and he married a woman who had similar tendencies. He felt like he had no control over his life as he was always adhering to the expectations of others instead of doing what made him happy. After *SHIFTING* old beliefs, we worked through several other tools in the book, and Bob realized what he needed was to forgive all of those who he felt wronged him in any way. I took Bob through the Pond Exercise, and he felt lighter and better than he had in a long time. Over time he began to stand up for himself and do more things that made him happy instead of pleasing everyone else.

Tool #9: The Mind-Body Connection

John E. Sarno, MD, is best known as a pioneer who developed groundbreaking research and processes on Tension Myositis Syndrome (TMS), also known as mind-body syndrome, to help people to heal from pain and different ailments without drugs, surgery, or exercise. Dr. Sarno's was a Professor of Rehabilitation Medicine at the New York University School of Medicine and wrote four books about a variety of pain disorders between 1984 to 2006.

Dr. Sarno was a specialist in rehabilitation for back pain but found over the years that his discoveries applied to all types of pain. He became aware that most of his patients with back pain were not healing through conventional methods utilizing surgery and medications. Over time, he came to realize that much of their pain was due to psychological issues, and it changed his practice for good. Dr. Sarno discovered that his patient's pain decreased markedly after talking candidly with him about painful lifetime experiences, matters they had never fully disclosed to anyone. In his book *Healing Back Pain: The Mind-Body Connection*, Dr. Sarno describes how he realized that people have the ability to improve their well-being and some physical pains just by acknowledging and addressing their underlying psychological issues.[54]

When he talked to his patients further, he found that most were perfectionists who put themselves under unreasonable pressure. When Dr. Sarno suggested the connection between their emotions, their tendency to put themselves under such pressure, and their pain, most patients rapidly improved. He came to understand that their unconscious minds were activating their auto-nomic nervous system. In his last book, *The Divided Mind*, Dr. Sarno expanded this observation to conclude that the interaction between the generally reasonable, rational, ethical, moral conscious mind, and the repressed feelings of emotional pain, hurt, sadness, and anger characteristic of the subconscious mind appeared to be the basis for mind-body disorders. He believed that chronic pain served as a distraction from the suppressed feelings, therefore keeping the person safe from having to deal with emotional pains.[55]

Dr. Sarno discovered that the subconscious mind does this by withholding oxygen to some regions of the body, and this creates pain.[56] A person might get an X-ray of their spine due to pain, and the X-ray shows only typical abnormalities due to age and activity. Still, they are having pain and they want it fixed. Conventional medicine might try to address this pain through medications, adjustments, back braces, surgery, physical therapy, etc. However, Dr. Sarno found that the pain would persist or, if it went away, it would come back again. Sound familiar?

The Process of Eliminating Pain Through the Mind-Body System

Dr. Sarno recommends individuals address their unconscious anger first, since the pain they are experiencing is psychological and then they should resume all regular physical activity as soon as possible.

Here is an example of what that looks like:

· Just knowing and accepting that your pain could be psycholog-ical and not structural is a massive step in itself. Say to yourself,

"I am ready to identify and release the underlying unconscious, psychological reasons for my pain."

· For the pain to stop, you must be able to say, "I have a normal and healthy body (or back, or identify a specific area that hurts), and I know the pain was initiated by my brain to serve a purpose. What am I meant to learn and release?"

· Taking it a step further, depending on your situation, state truths such as, "I know the MRI, C.T. scans, or X-rays show normal changes for aging and activity, which means I can heal."

By speaking these truths to yourself, you become a wedge in your brain's plan to keep diverting and protecting you by giving you pain in certain areas of your body. You begin to stop the cycle of pain.

Client Story: Jack had been having severe back pain for years and could no longer ski, which is one of his passions. He had almost given up, resigned that that was his life sentence, until he read Dr. Sarno's book. He felt an immediate release of his back pain. Jack felt so good that he was able to go skiing that afternoon. He has done additional work on his anger over the years, releasing other pains. Jack continues to enjoy a full life, skiing in the winter.

I shared earlier the story of how I worked to release old anger that I didn't even know I had. When I discovered it and released it, my hip pain disappeared. For some individuals, however, this is not enough. They require psychotherapy with a psychotherapist experienced in the treatment of mind-body disorders. Whatever your situation, Dr. Sarno's life-changing book, *Healing Back Pain: The Mind-Body Connection,* will help you understand the power of this process. Several of my clients, as well as Dr. Sarno's patients, have reported instantaneous healing after reading this book. He has two other books that are helpful also: *The Mind-body Prescription* and *The Divided Mind*. Decide which resonates the most with you. *All the Rage* is a feature film about Dr. Sarno and others who are pioneering mind-body approaches to treating chronic illness. You will see in the documentary that Howard Stern, Larry David, John Stossel, Senator Tom Harkin, and pro-golfer Ben Crane all suffered from debilitating pain until they met Dr. John Sarno.[57]

Journaling Time

THE MIND-BODY CONNECTION JOURNALING EXERCISE #28:
Grab your notebook or *BEING Journal* to make notes.

· Do you have any chronic aches or pains in your body? Describe what those are.

· Do you have any untold stories or traumatic memories that you can share that will help release those chronic aches or pains?

· Follow the example above and write about how well the Mind-Body Connection exercise worked for you.

· Were you able to let go of any old pains or aches? Describe those.

· Did you feel better or lighter afterwards? Describe the difference you felt.

· Do you feel that this will a valuable tool in your toolbox?

Tool #10: The *SHIFT* Tool

The most potent tool in the tool kit, and my favorite tool to help my clients move past old beliefs and clear blocks or pains, is the *SHIFT* Tool. This will literally *SHIFT* the early programming or negative beliefs and feelings out of your body and replace them with other, more supportive feelings.

It is a tool that is best done by a certified practitioner in the beginning. Once you learn the technique and understand how it works, you will be able to practice the method on your own, although you are more likely to get to your root issues faster when you work with an Intuitive Life Coach like one of my certified *BEING Zone System* practitioners or me. Go to www.TheBEING-Zone.com/grow/ to find a practitioner and schedule a session.

In preparation for the practitioner, identify the issue, pain, or anger you would like to address. It might be something like "my mother was controlling," or "my husband was lying," or "I was traumatized by my boss," or "I got lost and couldn't find my way." It can be almost anything in your life that has created fear, pain, or problems.

When to Use This Tool

The *SHIFT* Tool is beneficial for all people clearing trauma, abuse, or even PTSD or deep childhood pains. It often takes more than one *SHIFT*—it is like peeling the layers off an onion until you get to the core issue. I have had many clients try to *SHIFT* their worst memories on their own without success, so I recommend you work with a trained practitioner on the deepest issues. The tool will *SHIFT* early programming or negative beliefs and feelings out of your body and replace them with another, more supportive self-loving feeling. The tool itself engages you because you choose the words that result in the transformation. My clients tell me all the time that this tool changed their lives. I have had a few clients who only need one *SHIFT* and they were able to move on and live the life they had dreamed of. Listen to an example of the *SHIFT* Tool at www.TheBEINGZone.com/tools.

Client Story: Fifty-four-year-old Steve appeared hugely successful on the outside, playing sports on the world stage and owning many successful companies. However, he was one of the most unhappy people I ever coached. Steve had grown up trying and failing to please his autocratic, sports and success obsessed father, and he had lost touch with what gave him satisfaction. He kept doing the same things (buying more companies) and expecting different results, and things only got worse. Using the *SHIFT* Tool, Steve revisited and released the traumas of his childhood, which changed his belief system and how he responded to life. He lost his need to please his father, sold off a few companies, and started a nonprofit that was meaningful to him. He started to feel happy and began to love living life for the first time.

Journaling Time

THE *SHIFT* TOOL JOURNALING EXERCISE #29:
Grab your notebook or *BEING Journal* and make notes on how well the *SHIFT* Tool worked for you.

· Did you feel completely different after going through the process where you felt you had let go of whatever it was that was holding you back in life? Write about your experience.
· Did you feel better or lighter afterwards? Describe the differences you feel.

Please take the time to experience this tool as it is one of the most powerful tools in this book. It is one that I highly recommend you have in your toolbox

Tool #11: The PSYCH-K Method

This effective tool was developed by Rob Williams and utilizes muscle testing to determine what issues to address and whether or not the technique worked. I have used muscle testing for years to help people learn to listen to their body's response or natural intuition. You will learn more about muscle testing in Chapter 4.

PSYCH-K allows for a change of subconscious beliefs that are limiting you by addressing your mental, emotional, physical, and spiritual well-being. PSYCH-K requires practitioners who are trained and certified to utilize this technique on clients. You can also use this tool on yourself once you are trained. You can learn more or find a certified practitioner at https://psych-k.com/.

When to Use This Tool

I have found PSYCH-K to be most useful for people who have a lot of emotional distress, anger, or depression. You can quickly and easily communicate directly with your subconscious mind, and while using whole-brain integration techniques, change old self-sabotaging beliefs into new positive ones that support you in just minutes. The greatest gift you can give yourself is that of self-transformation.

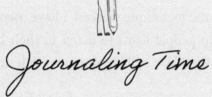

Client Story: One of my clients, Jeff, used to struggle with depression. He tried many different therapists, but nothing worked. He went for one PSYCH-K treatment with a certified PSYCH-K practitioner, and his depression lifted immediately. Between the PSYCH-K session and working with me, he has been able to move forward without falling back in the hole.

Journaling Time

THE PSYCH-K JOURNALING EXERCISE #30:

Grab your notebook or *BEING Journal* and start writing.

· Were you able to find a PSYCH-K practitioner to help you with this? If so, write about how well the PSYCH-K tool worked for you.

· If you experienced the tool, did you feel a change in how you felt?

· Is this an exercise you will most likely use moving forward?

· If you didn't experience this process, move onto the next journaling exercise.

Tool #12: ThetaHealing™

This tool is a series of techniques that allow you to change life patterns held in place by core, genetic, historical, and soul beliefs, either self-imposed or externally imposed. These changes happen in the relaxed Theta brainwave state.

This practice can quickly replace limiting beliefs or feelings with positive ones through Source, called the Creator of All that Is. The ThetaHealing™ technique can be learned by going through basic courses, or you can schedule a call with me or Amanda at www.TheBEINGZone.com or another certified ThetaHealing practitioner at www.Thetahealing.com to take you through the process. The technique will help you change the underlying limiting core programs and beliefs held in your subconscious, thereby transforming you to increase your health, happiness, and personal growth, allowing you to create the life you have always wanted.

When to Use This Tool

If you believe in God or the Creator or Source, this is a powerful tool for you. It is most effective when you are trying to do one of two things:

· To replace current thoughts and beliefs that you don't like with thoughts and feelings that you do want.
· To ask for guidance.

Client Story: Lori grew up praying and feeling very connected to Source. She lost that connection when she fell into a life where she never felt loved or supported, which resulted in fibromyalgia. She recently took the ThetaHealing course and discovered that it was the perfect tool for her. She was able to reconnect with Source and it became a safe place she can turn to when she is struggling or needs clarity. She no longer needs fibro-myalgia as an excuse because she now can speak her truth. Lori is coming into her own, utilizing the ThetaHealing tool.

Journaling Time

THE THETAHEALING JOURNALING EXERCISE #31:

Grab your *BEING Journal* or notebook and start writing.

- Were you able to find a ThetaHealing practitioner to help you with this? If so, make notes on how well the ThetaHealing process worked for you.
- If you experienced the process, did you feel a change in how you felt and is this an exercise you will most likely use moving forward?
- If you didn't experience this process, move onto the next journaling exercise.

You just learned a lot of new tools in this chapter. To clear the issues, events, pains, beliefs, and blocks you identified in Chapters 1 and 2, you will want to use these tools over and over to release them. This will assist you in getting used to the tools, have clarity on what works for you, and also begin your healing process. You will learn many more tools as you go through the book and you will want to identify all your favorites. You will make great progress by using any of the tools included in this book.

Key Messages

- You CAN *SHIFT* previous traumas, underlying beliefs, and blocks with these tools. You should experiment with all the different tools to find the ones that best suit you.
- Utilize a variety of breathing and grounding exercises to create calm in your life.
- EFT or tapping has been proven to positively impact anxiety, depression, pain, and PTSD.
- Forgiveness for yourself and others is a critical step in your healing process.
- Capitalizing on the mind-body connection can eliminate pain and improve your well-being.
- The *SHIFT* Tool is the most powerful tool in your new tool box, but you may want to utilize a variety of tools to completely clear an old issue.
- Take your experience to a higher level by visiting www.The-BEINGZone.com to access recordings and visuals or choose to schedule a session with a coach for extra help.

This Chapter's Gifts: There are many tools provided that you can use to clear out old belief systems, trauma, and blocks in your life. You are unique and need to choose the tools that work best for you, knowing that could change over time, so never hesitate to go back and revisit all the tools. Some people do well on their own and some do best with guidance or coaching. Do what feels right to you.

PART II

Steps to Transformation

CHAPTER 4

A Heart-Based Life

"The best and most beautiful things in the world cannot be
seen or even touched—they must be felt with the heart."
—Helen Keller

O NCE YOU HAVE cleared your issues using the tools in
Chapter 3, it is time to move forward. It may be overwhelming to learn how much your past and Ego mind has controlled your life. Do not fear, you will begin to transform when
you learn to listen to the whispers in your heart.

Let's start by talking about your thoughts. The universal law
of attraction says that we will attract into our lives the things we
think about and what we focus on. That is because our thoughts,
feelings, emotions, and words create our daily reality.

Mike Dooley is famous for his book, *Choose Them Wisely:
Thoughts Become Things*, that says we create what we think about.[58]
The more we think about it, the more it expands. And our thoughts
are repetitive. According to a published article by the *National*

Science Foundation in 2005, the average person has about 12,000 to 60,000 thoughts per day. Of those, 95% are the same repetitive thoughts as the day before, and about 80% are negative. I was not able to locate the original source of these numbers and percentages about thoughts per day, even though articles are flooded with this information online. However, I did find scientific studies showing a direct correlation between negative thoughts and depression.[59] What this means to us is that the quality of our existence is dependent on the quality of our internal thoughts.

You may believe you are a positive thinker in general, but are there negative thoughts, ingrained beliefs, or doubts that permeate your thinking that are outside your conscious mind or your control? I would have put myself in that category before I started this journey. I always saw my glass as half full, but there were belief systems ingrained in me that have affected how I operated in the world. For instance, I believed I had to work hard to make money. Thus, I worked long hours because I believed that I had to in order to earn good money.

Journaling Time

THOUGHTS BECOME THINGS JOURNALING EXERCISE #32:
Get your *BEING Journal* or notebook out and then take a minute to think about your thoughts and then start writing.
- What thoughts do you have day after day?
- Note which are positive and which are harmful or draining.
- How do your harmful or negative thoughts impact your life?

· What do you want your reality to be without thinking about current
  limitations?

· What tools can you use to change your thoughts?

Your Neural Pathways

Scientists have proven that our thoughts become our lives, our reality, and our beliefs, especially when those thoughts are repetitive.[60] Your outcome is dependent on whether those repetitive thoughts are constructive or destructive. Think about what that means to you. When you have a thought like, "I am not good enough," you feel that in your body and then you become that belief. Or if you say, "I am stressed," you will be stressed. Multiple studies have identified that people who are experiencing depression are more prone to rumination and repetitive thoughts of shame, anger, regret, and sorrow.[61]

Your neural pathways are like a super-highway of nerve cells, and their function is to transmit messages. Just like walking a track into the grass, the more you walk back and forth over the same area, the more trodden and apparent it becomes. The same thing happens when you think specific thoughts over and over again. They become your reality. According to scientists and psychologists, for a thought to become a belief, it must be recurring. It's this repetition that creates a neural pathway. And even more powerful is the fact that studies have shown you can use your imagination to overcome fearful situations or anxiety. [62]

If you don't like what is happening in your life, you can begin to change it by simply changing your thoughts. How easy is it to change your thoughts? You will learn tools in this chapter to help.

Tool #13: Change Your Thoughts!

Take out your *BEING Journal* or notebook and draw a line down the middle of the page. On the left side, list all of the complaints you have in your life right now. What are all the things that bother you? These negative, repetitive thoughts that run through your head all day are considered your subconscious ingrained beliefs that you learned about in Chapter 2.

**EXAMPLES OF
SUBCONSCIOUS THOUGHTS**

My son leaves a mess in the kitchen every day.

I weigh too much.

My husband is always finding what I do wrong.

Hatred and violence break my heart.

Your goal is to turn your subconscious into conscious thoughts. On the right side of your paper, I want you to change your statements into a list of being thankful for what you do want, as shown below.

EXAMPLES OF SUBCONSCIOUS THOUGHTS	EXAMPLE OF CONSCIOUS THOUGHTS TO FOCUS ON
My son leaves a mess in the kitchen every day.	I am thankful my son has begun to leave a clean kitchen each day.
I weigh too much.	I am grateful I will soon be at my ideal weight.
My husband is always finding what I do wrong.	I am blessed every time my husband focuses on what I do right.
Hatred and violence break my heart.	I am grateful when I see love and peace in the world.

The way to think about these lists on the left is your unconscious thoughts that are unintentionally creating a life you don't want. On the right is the conscious list, creating intentions for the life you do want. When you are optimistically thankful for what you do want, it makes it even more powerful. We tend to live more in our unconscious than our conscious, which is why an exercise like this is valuable when you would like to attract more positive results and abundance into your life. When you are unhappy or having negative consequences or pain in your life, take the time to do this exercise and start the process of turning your life around.

Journaling Time

CHANGE SUBCONSCIOUS THOUGHTS TO CONSCIOUS THOUGHTS JOURNALING EXERCISE #33:

Find your *BEING Journal* or notebook and take a minute to think about your thoughts.

· Write about what you seem to complain about. Things you feel are unjust or unfair. Who do you blame?

· What negative thoughts do you consistently have? List these in the left column.

· In the right column, replace the negative thoughts with thankfulness for a new Conscious thought of what you do want to focus on instead.

· Will you use this tool again? When might it be helpful to you?

The Voice in Your Head

What is your belief system? On top of creating our reality with our thoughts, most of us exist in the subconscious belief system (Ego) that was passed down the ancestral line and programmed into us at a very young age when we were in a Theta brainwave state. If you heard you weren't smart enough, you most likely still believe that today. Or if you heard "our family isn't good at math," that is your belief.

Client Story: When Michelle was growing up, she heard her parents say things like, "you have to work hard to get ahead." She heard it a lot, so now she holds the belief (without realizing it) that she, too, has to work hard to make money. Michelle has worked long hours for as long as she has been working. It has affected her marriage, family, and health. She started having issues sleeping because she was not doing self-care. Her belief of working hard to make money is her reality. She has tried to cut back hours but always failed in the past. Since we have been working together, she is now better controlling her hours, building in time for workouts, focusing on self-care, plus trying to be more present when she is with her family.

The words and messages many of us received and heard growing up resulted in programming ourselves for an unsatisfying, head-based life. We became victims of the voice that tells us we aren't good enough/smart enough/rich enough, etc. If this is your story, you might feel stuck, or those beliefs might drive you to push your way through life to achieve success. Learning to quiet your Ego and listen to your heart is much more effective. Let's learn more about this concept of Ego and what you can do about it.

That voice in your head that rarely stops is your subconscious mind, also called your Ego. Most people think of the Ego as being a boastful place, but that isn't what I am talking about. Most people live in their Ego mind. We were brought up that way. One of the oldest ideas in psychology is that we each have a subconscious mind that, despite our best conscious intentions, is the real controlling force in our lives. It leads us to sabotage ourselves or make poor decisions.

Client Story: Sixty-year-old JT is a genius and very talented, but he is also a perfectionist who lives in his Ego mind 100% of the time. His family had very high expectations when he was young, and they were successful in all they did. JT believes he has to live up to that standard. He doesn't know how to turn off; he is always trying to find solutions to everything and keeps pushing his way through life trying to find the perfect answers instead of following his heart's desires and his intuition. I know JT can learn to move out of his Ego and develop a life he is excited about as he is making progress on this. He has all the brains and talent. That said, he is very independent, so he wants to figure this out on his own as he believes he needs to achieve based on his own talents and has a hard time accepting help. I coached him a couple of times, and he is now reading books I recommended and trying to transform on his own into *The BEING Zone.*

Your Belief System

Your thinking and the content of your mind is conditioned by your past upbringing, culture, family background, etc. Many legacies and stories are passed along without a lot of reflection. An idea may not be as valid in today's world or your life, but previous generations saw it as truth and reality, and so that is what you heard and experienced. Now it is ingrained in your subconscious memory.

You probably identify with your "story" and the habitual roles you play within it. Most, if not all, of your long-standing opinions, resentments, grievances, judgments, fears, and self-concept started here. They show up in your belief system. It is who you think you are.

When we are living in our Ego mind and we experience a setback, our Ego goads us on, sometimes pushing us further into our Ego where we might get angry or frustrated and lash out, or move into fear and defensiveness. Our Ego wants to be right. When we fall into a blaming or complaining place, we often push back at others. This will get us nowhere. As you read in the introduction, Newton's laws say, when you push at something or someone, it or they will push back at you. This creates a back and forth cycle, and you will find forcing or pushing your way through life does not work.

Learning to recognize or identify the underlying reason your Ego or subconscious mind is blaming, complaining, or pushing is the key to letting go. I may be reacting a certain way because of always having to defend myself as a child. When I recognize this, I clear it, so I no longer need to push back. When someone starts to pick on me or blame me, it causes less of a response in my psyche, so I don't have to push back. It is about learning to adapt and flow.

Journaling Time

BELIEF SYSTEMS JOURNALING EXERCISE #34:

Think about your family's belief systems and your repetitive thoughts and start writing in your *BEING Journal* or notebook. Take a few minutes to journal what you heard growing up.

- What beliefs do you feel were passed down to you? They may be religious beliefs or beliefs about how to treat people or a feeling that your family always struggles.
- What stories did you hear or do you tell yourself that built up these beliefs?
- Do your beliefs impact how you show up in life? Do you flow more through life or push your way through life because of your beliefs?
- What beliefs do you want to change?
- Was this a useful exercise for you?

Client Story: Melinda came from a line of beautiful women. She inherited her dad's build, so she heard from a young age that she was too heavy or not taking care of herself enough. Melinda's mother encouraged her to diet and to dress differently. She felt she was not pretty enough, not trim enough, not cultured enough, not good enough. These feelings were ingrained in her and became her unconscious belief system. Instead of trying to change her beauty, she went after accomplishments and has been successful in her career but never confident

in relationships. It has taken a lot of work to get her to the point
that she loves herself and her life. Next step, I know she will find
a life partner.

The key is to understand that the Ego plays an essential role in
your life, and it shows up for a reason. It will still show up from
time to time after you release your old ideas, but your job is to
stop and ask, "what am I meant to learn," and then let go of the
old belief or feeling that does not serve you before it takes hold.
If you learn from these experiences, you will become a better you.

You will find in time you will learn to recognize when it is an
Egoic thought versus an authentic, true thought. The Ego is part
of your journey to your true self. You are not in conflict with the
Ego; you are to learn from it and then release what doesn't benefit
you moving forward.

I have included a sheet on the next page to help you evaluate
where you exist in regard to your Ego. When you complete the
Ego Evaluation, you can start to change your life.

Ego Evaluation

When people go through the Ego Evaluation that follows, their
first reaction to some of the questions is "well, everyone feels that."
I used to believe that too. Yet, I have learned that isn't true. I used
to do most of the things on the list and now rarely do any of them
because I am aware that they are Ego and not the real me, and I
have learned to catch and stop myself if I start thinking this way.

Find a quiet place where you can concentrate and feel whether
you hold any of the emotions, belief systems, or patterns that are

listed on the next page. Find a pen or highlighter or two so you
can mark the items as you read. Ask yourself, do I ever feel that
way? If it is yes, even a little yes, then checkmark it or highlight
it. You can highlight the really strong tendencies in a different
color, so they become your priorities, or put stars next to the ones
that are most prevalent in your life.

Most of my clients say yes to 80 to 100% of the emotions, patterns, and belief systems that are on this list. That is OK. You do
not want to say, "Oh, I never do that" if you do it. It is better to be
honest and face them straight on. If you don't own it, it is tough
to change. When you become aware that these ways of *BEING*
or thinking are not the real you, you can start identifying these
thoughts and feelings as separate from the real you and begin to
eliminate them one step at a time. When you are able to recognize them, and release them, you will find your life transforming
right in front of you.

EGO EVALUATION		
Emotions		
Worry	Bored	Fear
Anxiety	Dissatisfied	Defensive
Stress	Resentment	Unhappy
Anger	Annoyed	Defeated

Patterns		
Guilt	Unexpressed Feelings	Need to Play the Game
Shame	No Power, No Control	Need to be Liked
Projecting	Manipulate Situations	Critical
Blaming	Live in Past or Future	Judgmental
Complaining	Experience Same Problems Over and Over	Label Others
Afraid of Rejection	Depressed	Consistent Pain in Body
Stifle Emotions	Need to be in Control	Sabotage Yourself

Beliefs		
Powerless	Seek Approval	Bad Person
Should/Would/Could Have	Seek Acceptance	Something Wrong with You
Pleaser	Unworthy	Not Enough
Self-Doubt	Not Valued	Never Good Enough

Journaling Time

Pull out your *BEING Journal* or notebook and go through the Ego evaluation.

· Highlight or write down all the items from the Ego list that you do even a little bit of the time. It is OK to mark yes on all of them as this is what will help you identify what to begin to recognize in your habits and let go of them.

· Make notes on which ones you do the most as those are the ones you want to focus on first.

· Create a list of your tendencies so you stay aware of when they show up so you can address them when you feel them and begin to eliminate them from your life.

The Ego's Enemy

The Ego's greatest enemy is the present moment. You might wonder why. Think about it. When you are present, you are very aware of everything around you, and are more likely to respond in a measured way instead of being reactionary, which is what the Ego does. When you are calm and in the present moment, if a negative thought pops in your head, you are more likely to have the foresight to ask yourself some questions such as: Why am I having this thought? Is it true? Do I want to let this thought define me? and so on. The goal of this chapter is to help you learn to live from your heart, in the now of the present moment. When you do, you will find that old belief systems and negative thoughts begin to lose their power over you, and that alone is transformational.

When you are connected to your heart and listen to it, you will always make the right decisions for yourself and feel happier and better. When you open your heart and allow those "real you" messages to flow in, you will become one with your true self, your inner self, your intuition, your inner wisdom, or that higher being. You will find your life beginning to change when you operate from your heart instead of the voice in your head. You might start saying "no" to events that you don't want to attend instead of forcing yourself to go. You might start choosing to listen to the music you like while in the car with others instead of always letting them choose. You might decide to change your job for something more fulfilling, and so on. You will also discover circumstances and people appearing who are helpful and cooperative. I call these synchronicities, and it is when the magic begins to happen.

Client Story: Jake answered yes to every item on the Ego Evaluation. He felt terrible; he thought something was wrong with him. There is nothing wrong with him at all. He is just the victim of his life experiences. I encouraged him to take this on as a challenge to change his outcome, to change his life. He is competitive and took it on with a vengeance. By actively catching himself in Egoic thoughts and throwing them away (which you will learn about next), he is now living life fully.

As you are beginning to understand, the Ego is not the real you—it's made up of compulsive, repetitive thoughts and beliefs that aren't even all yours. You also now know that you don't have to continue to let the Ego run your life. You can learn to catch your Ego by memorizing the words you highlighted on your Ego Evaluation. Those emotions, patterns, and belief systems are all excellent representations of your Ego. Once you know your tendencies and you catch yourself thinking or saying an Ego-based statement or belief, use the Throw It Away tool described below to get rid of it.

Tool #14: Throw It Away

When you feel angry, or have an angry or negative thought, pay attention to where in your body you feel the anger or negative emotion. In your mind's eye, take your hand and reach toward that part of your body. It might be your head, your heart, or your core. Pull out the feeling (anger) like it is a physical thing that you can hold in your hand. As you hold the emotion of anger in your palm, talk to it. Say, "thank you for being there and alerting me. You have done your job. Now I am aware and can handle it." Then wad it up and throw it away.

At some level, it may sound silly to throw away your thoughts. But I have found after working with so many clients that it really works to physically throw away your negative feelings or emotions. This seemingly simple tool is potent and a favorite of my clients. Give it a try and see how it works for you. There is a recording of the Throw It Away tool at www.TheBEINGZone.com/tools.

Journaling Time

THROW IT AWAY JOURNALING EXERCISE #36:

Pull out your *BEING Journal* or notebook. Make notes on how the Throw It Away Tool worked for you.

- Describe how you feel after using this tool: relief, feel lighter, change in energy? Provide as much detail as you can.
- What areas do you want to make a commitment to continue to work on?
- Will you continue to use this tool?

Tool #15: Catch Yourself & Write it Down

Intentionally sit back as an observer in your own life and catch yourself saying things that don't benefit you. You may hear yourself say, "I'm not good enough," or "I'm not smart enough." You may say, "I'm tired," or "I'm stressed." Guess what? If you say that, it will be your reality. Writing it down helps you become aware of how often you do it. The more you can increase your awareness and notice your thoughts, feelings, and emotions, the better chance you will have to stop them. And you can use the Throw It Away Tool once you complete your analysis of how often you have these thoughts. According to a study published by the *Journal of Psychological Science*, it is best to write down your thoughts or what you are feeling so you can throw them away physically.[63]

Journaling Time

CATCH YOURSELF AND WRITE IT DOWN JOURNALING EXERCISE #37:
Take out your notebook or *BEING Journal*. Make notes on how the Catch Yourself Tool worked.

- Were you able to catch yourself thinking negative thoughts? If so, how did you do that?
- What was that process like for you?
- Do you feel it is something you can build into your life? If so, make notes on how.
- Describe how you might use this tool to create positive thought patterns.
- What are the other tools in this book that you feel might be effective in helping you *SHIFT* this negative thought pattern? List them here.

Tool #16: Turn It Off

This is a simple, intuitive process where you catch yourself in your Ego and visually imagine a switch (like a light switch) that you can turn off. Say to yourself, "that is not me. I am no longer allowing those old beliefs or feelings in my life," and then turn the switch to off in your mind's eye.

Journaling Time

TURN IT OFF JOURNALING EXERCISE #38:

In your notebook or *BEING Journal*, make notes on how the Turn It Off Tool worked for you.

- Could you Turn It Off just like that? Describe what happened.
- Describe how you feel after using this tool.
- How easy do you think it will be to use this tool in the future?

Tool #17: Angel Versus Devil

This is a useful tool where you tune into your guardian angel while brushing away the thoughts you don't need. Much like in the cartoons, imagine that your devil lives on your right shoulder and feels heavy and dark. Your angel lives on your left shoulder, above your heart, and will feel light and warm. When negative thoughts, feelings, or emotions show up, talk to the devil and tell it "thank you for showing up," let it know you understand, and then flick it off your shoulder. Turn to your guardian angel on your left shoulder (over your heart). Ask your angel what you are meant to learn and know. Feel the warmth or positive feelings go through your body and trust what you hear or feel.

Journaling Time

ANGEL VERSUS DEVIL JOURNALING EXERCISE #39:

Pull out your notebook or *BEING Journal* and start writing.

- Make notes on how the Angel Versus Devil technique worked for you.
- Describe how effective this tool was for you.
- Could you visualize the angel and the devil?
- Did you feel your heart warm thinking of the angel? Could you feel the heaviness of the devil?
- How do you think you might use this tool in the future?

Recognizing Ego & Triggers in Yourself and Others

The first step in overcoming the Ego is to catch it in yourself! What you say and what others say makes a big difference in how you feel in your daily life. Once you get good at detecting what triggers you and understanding what your Egoic responses tend to be, it is easier to let them go. This awareness allows you to move on to identifying the Ego in others with more kindness.

When you realize other people have the same kinds of issues with Ego, it allows you to recognize and accept that it's not the real them attacking you or projecting their beliefs on you but is their Ego. It is much easier to let situations and comments slide without getting defensive. It becomes easier to stop, breathe, and send them forgiveness and compassion. They can't help it if they have not learned about how their Ego (Subconscious) is controlling their lives. We aren't taught this in schools—yet.

Learning not to take things personally when the Ego is involved also helps you respond to situations in life with more ease and grace. In this chapter, you will learn to identify and remove emotional triggers and negative beliefs. When you are triggered or have a negative belief system, it is often a result of an incident in your childhood where you had similar feelings that haven't been cleared up or dealt with. You will find that this simple process will help clear the past and result in you having less conflict and more joy.

Journaling Time

IDENTIFYING TRIGGERS AND BELIEFS JOURNALING EXERCISE #40: In your *BEING Journal* or notebook, take time to respond to the following prompts, which will help you decide which Triggers and Beliefs to *SHIFT* or release.

· Identify and write down your top one to three emotional triggers.
· What causes you to be most upset and thrown off balance in relation to those triggers?
· Can you remember the first time in your life when you were triggered and felt this way emotionally? This is the memory you want to clear because it will clear all the related incidents that followed it.
· What are your underlying belief systems that cause you conflict in your life?

- What is your earliest memory of conflict from this belief system? This is what you want to clear as it affects all related future incidents.
- Go back and use the *SHIFT* tool, the EFT tool or another tool of your choosing on the earliest memory related to each trigger point and belief system. Write about your results.
- Write about how you might incorporate this tool into your life in the future.

Tool #18: Reprogram Negative Beliefs

Since you know now that your thoughts become things, you need to reprogram how you think. Start with one trigger that has the least emotional charge and begin to reprogram it. Tell yourself, "This belief is not reality." What's true is, "I am lovable, capable, and smart." Substitute the negative belief with a positive, more realistic one. Keep saying what you want. Repeat this day after day.

You identified some negative family belief systems in Exercise #34 that have an impact on your life. What were they? Take time now to reprogram your thoughts with what you do want. What is no longer going to be true for you, and what do you now choose to think about and focus on? You will need to continue to say and feel what you do want so you bring that into your life. Some people get results immediately; some it will get stronger over time.

Client Story: Judy grew up in an abusive home but kept that truth under wraps most of her life. As a result, she operated from her Ego most of the time and was struggling in life. She was triggered by others who were successful and bragged about their accomplishments. She put on a happy face and covered up the truth of her pain. It eventually caught up with her, though, and she was miserable and no longer able to feel anything except depression. After we worked together, she has made remarkable progress transforming her life by knowing how to catch herself in an Ego response, learning from it, letting it know she no longer needs it, and throwing it away. She utilizes the reprogramming negative beliefs by replacing what she has thrown away with the feeling she does want. Once Judy learned the tool to stop the triggering feelings, there was no stopping her. She told me she is feeling lighter and happier than ever before.

Journaling Time

REPROGRAM NEGATIVES BELIEFS JOURNALING EXERCISE #41:
In your *BEING Journal* or notebook, make notes on how this tool worked for you.
- Describe what you were able to reprogram.
- How has that reprogramming impacted your life?
- Describe how you plan to use this tool in the future.

Creating a Heart-Based Life You Love

To create a heart-based, authentic life, you will need to learn to reprogram your subconscious and reverse your thinking by focusing on and saying what you do want, rather than what you don't want. It is all about learning to listen to your natural intuition, which is centered in all three of your "brains" (heart, gut, and head), described below. When you tune into your three brains, you will always feel confident in your decisions, because these are the places where your intuition and universal guidance reside.

Responding to your intuitive nudges happens when you operate in *The BEING Zone*, where you are very present in the here and now. When you are in this heart-based zone, you are much more likely to "allow" instead of "push," which will bring to you what you desire.

Client Story: Claire operates in her Ego mind almost 100% of the time and is always unhappy. She complains about everything and blames everyone. I know she feels in her heart from time to time as I see the softness or the pain. I have offered to work with her, but she doesn't want that because she would have to deal with issues in her life that she doesn't want to face yet. So, she continues to live in her head and feels that everything is someone else's fault.

Listen to These Three Brains!

THE THREE BRAINS

Head   Heart   Gut

The Conscious Brain

This is the brain you think you use most of the time, but scientists say we use very little, proportionately. It comes in handy for studying or creating. Most of your creativity and logic lie here, in the left and right brain. Your conscious brain provides your reasoning. It also controls all the actions that you do intentionally when you are completely present and conscious. Historically, we believed the brain controlled the heart, we have since learned, that communication between the heart and brain actually is a dynamic, ongoing, two-way dialogue, with each organ continuously influencing the other's function.

The Heart Brain

The most powerful brain in your body is your heart brain. The HeartMath Institute has measured the heart's electrical field with an electrocardiogram (ECG). They have proven the heart brain is about 60 times greater in amplitude than the conscious brain. HeartMath studies show this powerful electromagnetic field can be detected and measured several feet away from a person's body.[64] The findings point to the human heart as playing a pivotal role in the intuitive process, and a recent study at the HeartMath Institute concludes the heart receives intuitive information faster than the brain.[65] The heart sends more information to the brain than the brain sends to the heart and also manufactures and secretes oxytocin, which acts as a neurotransmitter and commonly is referred to as the love or social bonding hormone. According to the HeartMath Institute, the concept of a heart brain is widely accepted today, and they believe that the heart has independent intelligence, so pay attention to your heart and how things feel to you. If your heart feels warm and happy, it is in coherence and you want to listen to it. If it cools down and seems off, that is a warning sign.

The Gut Brain

The gut brain gives you warnings if something isn't safe or right. It often shows up as a gut-clenching feeling. People say, "I feel it in my gut," or "my gut is telling me not to do that" or "not to trust that person." Listen to that feeling. It is real. Your body is talking to you. For example, have you ever been in a situation where you felt a fear inside your gut? You might have felt a tightening or clenching? Possibly on a dark road at night where you hear an unfamiliar sound? Or being alone in a home and hearing noises that don't feel right? Visualize that moment and pay attention to whether your gut responds again.

Jay Pasricha, MD, director of the Johns Hopkins Center for Neurogastroenterology, has researched the enteric nervous system that has garnered international attention. He says, "The enteric nervous system doesn't seem capable of thought as we know it, but it communicates back and forth with our big brain—with profound results."[66]

According to *Psychology Magazine*, there's an entire ecosystem of bacteria and a vast neural network operating in our guts.[67] This ecosystem is our second brain and comprises some 100 million neurons—more than the spinal cord. There is increasing evidence indicating that your gut's health strongly influences your emotional state and mood.[68] According to scientists, the vagus nerve runs from the brainstem into the abdomen and acts as an intercom system. This system delivers messages back and forth from the gut to the brain. Scientists say 90% of the fibers in the vagus nerve carry information from the stomach upwards to the brain, rather than the other way around.[69] In other words, this "gut-brain axis" serves as a communication system whereby your gut and brain are in constant contact. Listen to it.

Tool #19: Open-Heart Meditation

This is a great meditation that helps build your ability to live more in your heart. Utilizing this tool will help you become more aware of each of your three brains that you want to listen to.

Take a moment to close your eyes and breathe deeply to center yourself. Now visualize a feeling of unconditional love for yourself and all others. Visualize a smile generating deep inside your heart and moving outward. Feel your heart opening and expanding with love. Expand that to a feeling of complete and total gratitude for all life, the world around you. Feel a feeling of absolute love radiating from your heart out and around you. Visualize that it is expanding and that feeling of pure joy is filling up the room around you. Now just sit in that kind, loving energy for a few minutes. Go to www.TheBEINGZone.com to listen to the Open-Heart Meditation recording.

Journaling Time

OPEN-HEART MEDITATION JOURNALING EXERCISE #42:
In your notebook or *BEING Journal*, make notes on how this meditation worked for you.

· How do you feel after doing this meditation? An expansion in energy, good feelings, happier? What else?

· How will you use this tool in the future?

How to Listen to Your Three Intuitive Brains

Your body knows what is best, because it is where your intuition resides.[70] When you trust your body to tell you the truth, you will begin to have more confidence in your decision-making, and it becomes an internal compass for directing your life. Beyond listening to how your heart feels or paying attention to your gut instinct, below are three physical tools you can use for tuning into your intuition.

I encourage you to practice the three tools on things you know for sure and then gradually make it harder. In each activity, you'll tell yourself something true and something that is a lie so that you can see the ways your body reacts. Start with very basic truth statements, like "my son's name is_____," or "I love my dog _____." Once you have a positive response, then try lies. Again, start with something easy. Make up an outrageous name and say, "my son's name is _____," or say, "I don't like dogs." You can make a game out of it.

When you get reliable responses every time on something you know for a fact, you'll become more confident asking questions about things in your life where you are not sure. Pay attention to any messages or hunches you may get in the process. Also, tune into how your body feels in each situation.

Each person I work with feels one tool is more effective for them than the other two, so it's up to you to determine what works best for you. I encourage you to practice with the tool you connect with best until you know what truth is and what it isn't. Let your body naturally respond; don't force it. Don't ever try to force an answer that you want to hear, because that will not help you in any way at all. You'll be lying to yourself because you want something so much.

Tools for Listening to Your Three Intuitive Brains

 Tool #20: Sway Test

Learn to listen to the wisdom of your body with the Sway test.

- Stand with your feet about hip-distance apart. Keep your knees slightly bent and set yourself in a firm stance, where I would not be able to tip you over easily if I came and pushed you.
- Drop your hands by your sides with your palms facing forward in a relaxed manner.
- Say a true statement and pay attention to what your upper body does. Look for movement.
- Say a lie and notice what your upper body does. See if you notice movement.
- **True/Yes/Beneficial:** If you are telling the truth or asking a question that the answer is yes, your body will lean into truth. It will slightly sway or move forward, or you will feel an expansion in your chest or upper body.
- **False/No/Harmful:** If you are telling a lie or asking a question that is a no answer, your body will fall back. It will sway back, constrict or collapse.

Do not force this! Allow your body to move naturally. It will tell you whether it is a yes or no. A small percentage of people may sway the opposite direction.

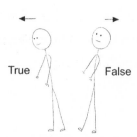

True   False

Journaling Time

SWAY TEST JOURNALING EXERCISE #43:

In your notebook or *BEING Journal*, make notes on how this tool worked for you.

- Could you feel a slight movement forward or back? Describe what it looked like and felt like to you.
- Or did you experience no movement at all? If this was the case, you might try again with a more obvious question, like "my name is..."
- Or was your experience more extreme, which made things extremely clear for you? If so, this may be the tool for you. Describe what that looked like and felt like to you.
- How do you see yourself using this tool in the future?

Tool #21: Muscle Tests

Muscle tests are your body telling you what is true or not. A variety of health practitioners (naturopaths, chiropractors, acupuncturists, etc.) use muscle testing as part of their practice. Typically, they will have the patient hold their arm out and then ask them yes/no questions. When the arm holds, it is the truth; when it drops, it is a no. When you are doing this on your own, it is easier to do Finger Muscle Testing. There are two ways to do finger muscle tests on yourself:

Finger Muscle Test #1 (On Self)

· Make an OK symbol on your left hand by touching the tip of your pointer finger to your thumb.

· Put your right thumb up through the opening and bring the right pointer finger down to touch the right thumb. In essence, you will have two OK Symbols attached. Hold them very lightly, no pressure. This is not about strength.

· Move your finger/thumb back and forth against each other very lightly without pressure.

· When you say a truth statement, your fingers will hold as you see in the diagram on the left.

· When you lie, they will slip as you see in the photo on the right.

Journaling Time

FINGER MUSCLE TEST #1 JOURNALING EXERCISE #44:
In your notebook or *BEING Journal*, make notes on how this tool worked for you. Every tool works differently for different people; you need to determine which tool is best for you.

- Did your fingers hold on truth and release on false? If so, a lot or a little? Was it clear you were getting answers and not forcing your fingers to respond one way or the other?
- What results did you get, and how do you feel about those results?
- What kind of situation do you see yourself using this tool in?

Finger Muscle Test #2 (On Self)

The same premise holds for this finger muscle test. When your fingers hold, the statement is true, and when they slip, it is false. The setup is different and works better for some people.

- Put your pointer finger pad up to your thumb pad on your left hand, making an OK symbol. This time hold it tight. For this exercise, try to keep it together.
- Put your thumb pad and pointer finger pad together on the right hand and slide them inside the circle on the left toward the top opening.
- Tell a true statement and try to force your left-hand fingers apart with your right-hand fingers. If they hold, it is a yes or truth. If they open, it is no or false. See illustration below for the visual of this exercise.

Journaling Time

FINGER MUSCLE TEST #2 JOURNALING EXERCISE #45:

In your notebook or *BEING Journal*, make notes on how this second finger muscle test tool worked for you.

- Was it easier for you to use and be confident in your results with this different type of muscle testing?
- Did your fingers hold on truth and release on false? If yes, did you feel it happened naturally and you weren't forcing the results in any way at all?
- Describe the difference you felt between your true and false questions. Did you feel confident in the results?
- Will you use this tool again? In what type of situations do you feel it will work best for you?

Tool #22: Warm Heart

This is a favorite of many who are in tune with how they are feeling.

- Think of someone or something that brings you unconditional feelings of love, like a pet or baby, or someone, something, or some place that has no conflict or stress attached. The reason is you want to feel the love in your heart with no reservations or judgement.
- Visualize that person, place, or thing and how it makes you feel. Focus on feeling that unconditional or open-hearted love you feel when you are with them or at that place. Take a moment to

bask in the feeling of that pure love for a moment. What does that feel like to you? Heightened energy, an expansion feeling, a warming feeling, a tingly feeling?

· If you are not sure if you are feeling anything, try thinking of something that makes you upset and notice how your body feels differently than when you are feeling love. There is typically a visceral difference in the way your body feels and responds to positive and negative stimuli. You just want to start feeling that difference and be in a loving place when you start the activity.

· Ask Yes/No questions.

· If your heart warms, it is yes.

· If it cools, it is no.

Go to www.TheBEINGZone.com/tools for the Warm Heart recording.

WARM HEART JOURNALING EXERCISE #46:

In your notebook or *BEING Journal*, make notes on how this warm heart tool worked for you.

- Did you feel your heart warm on truth and cool when not true? If you could clearly feel the warmth and felt you got clarity, this may be the tool for you.
- What was the difference you felt between true and false? Like warming and cooling, or expanding and contracting, or what else?
- Describe the situations where it might be useful for you to use this tool again.

Client Story: Amber, a 37-year-old stressed and driven mom, is an analyst in the health care industry. When she learned how to move from a head-based existence into a calmer, intuitive, heart-based place, she was promoted into a leadership position at work. She also became a heart-centered role model for her children, increasing the joy and fun in her household.

Your Greatest Pain Is Your Greatest Gain

Once you are good at listening to your three brains, you will be in a better place to support yourself by learning from your challenges. By taking time to find the silver lining in life situations you will begin to move into heart-based living.

I always say your most significant pain will bring your greatest gain. My best lessons, most extreme growth, and transformation came from major upsets or disruptions in my life. All my illnesses were an amazing wake-up-call that taught me about self-love, self-care, and self-healing. Getting laid off moved me towards getting trained as a Life Coach, which has resulted in creating a life I love. Losing my mom to cancer hurt deeply but gave me a better understanding of how much control each of us has in our health and vitality which makes me a better coach. I now see those traumatic events and times as the greatest gifts I could have received as they got me out of my head and into my heart. They were the impetus to changing my life. It would have been hard to let go of where I was unless it was ripped away from me through stressful events or situations.

Gratitude Brings More Of What You Want

Gratitude has all kinds of benefits and puts you deeper into your heart-space. It creates a state of happiness and optimism within your heart and body.[71] When I am grateful, more and better things happen to and around me. Scientists and psychologists have conducted studies that show some of the fantastic benefits of just being thankful for the good things that happen in your life.

· **Better Physical Health:** A 2012 study in *Personality and Individual Differences* indicated grateful people have fewer aches and pains and are healthier.[72]
· **Improved Psychological Health:** Robert A. Emmons, PhD, a leading gratitude researcher, has conducted multiple studies on the link between gratitude and well-being. His research confirms that gratitude effectively increases happiness and reduces depression.[73]
· **Sleep Better:** A study published in *Applied Psychology: Health and Well-Being* showed that participants slept better and longer.[74] Ever since I read that, I've encouraged my clients to write their five gratitude statements before going to sleep, and I suggest you do too.

Once you see how much you have lived in your head, you will see the value of living in your heart and being grateful. When you listen to your heart, your authentic life will unfold in front of you.

Key Messages

· Your thoughts, feelings, words, and emotions become your reality and most of us are programmed for the negative because we live in our subconscious (Ego) mind.
· You now know how to recognize your ego and turn it off so you can begin to reprogram your subconscious belief system.
· You want to listen to all three brains (conscious, heart, and gut) as that where your truth and intuition resides.
· Learning to operate from a heart-based place and listening to your body's messages (sway, muscle test, and warm heart) will lead you to your truth and a life you love.
· Embrace your challenges and obstacles as gifts. They are there to tell you that it is time to step back and re-evaluate your path.
· Gratitude brings more of what you appreciate and attracts more of what you desire.
· Create a life you love by moving from a head-based life into a heart-based life.

> **This Chapter's Gifts:** You will learn how to "turn off that voice," the head-based, negative thoughts and emotions that dominate your daily life. You will learn to tune into your body, listen to, and follow your intuition to move into grateful, heart-based living.

CHAPTER 5

Moving To The BEING Zone

"There are moments when all anxiety and stated toil are
becalmed in the infinite leisure and repose of nature."
— Henry David Thoreau

I N CHAPTER 4, you learned about living a heart-based
life and how your Ego or subconscious brain impacts
your reaction and response to various stimuli in the world. You
may not see a light at the end of the tunnel yet, but you will soon.
What you learn in this chapter will help you flow through life
with more ease and grace.

At this time in history, our society and culture encourage us to
live in a survival or stress state, always on the go and doing things.
Most people don't understand the value of *BEING* present in the

moment; we rarely stop just to *BE*. Instead, we surround ourselves with things to do or are preoccupied with background noise (television, cell phones, radio).

When we live in this *DOING Zone*, we are in the fast-moving Beta or Alpha brainwave state. We have non-stop thoughts, trying to figure things out and juggling responsibilities. It is an analytical state where many perfectionists or stressed-out people exist. It is often so intense that it is difficult to put your attention on one thing or absorb new information.

There are many different reasons you may end up in the *DOING Zone*. Maybe you want to keep up with the Joneses. Or maybe you are trying to earn love or approval, or maybe you are trying to survive and get the bills paid. You may not listen to your heart or your body because you are too focused on success, proving yourself, not failing, or making ends meet. When you live in the *DOING Zone*, these things seem like bigger priorities, at least until your health starts failing.

If this describes you, you may find that your attention exists primarily in the future, where you are thinking about what you must do and by when. You might go into an overwhelmed or stressed state because that voice in your head has taken you there. You might overpromise or overcommit. You might be addicted to stress because you like being busy and it makes you feel important and needed. I was like this and didn't know how to turn off or quiet my mind.

The good news is that you can learn to calm your system, quiet that external noise, and learn to operate in *The BEING Zone*, which is your natural state of happiness, health, harmony, abundance, friends, and laughter. It's a calm state of mind and body where you are present with yourself, have a clear head, and are in tune with your surroundings. It's an optimal place to start your day from, end your day with, and return to all day long.

Most people in the world today do not operate in this natural state because it requires an investment of time, and when you are living in the *DOING Zone*, even a few minutes can be too much. A large number of people in our crazy, busy world feel stuck, as I used to be, living in their heads in their own *DOING Zone*, and they often don't realize what it is doing to them. I didn't. They get up every morning, go to work, and come home at the end of a long day to more work: shopping, cooking, laundry, cleaning, parenting, and supporting. They fall into bed exhausted and drained, only to repeat the same thing the next day. When someone asks, "How are you today?" they might respond "good" or even "great," but in truth they're dissatisfied. Deep inside they know there must be more to life than the *DOING Zone's* motto of success as described by Malcolm Forbes: "He who dies with the most toys wins."[75]

Continually striving for that kind of success leaves us feeling empty. Studies have shown that we buy things to try to alleviate our inner discontent. Materialism provides short-term happiness but doesn't last.[76] Even when you are allegedly "winning" because, by outward appearances, you have attained success—the high-paying job, the big house, the big car—you may be miserable on the inside.

I know because the more I tried to find happiness and satisfaction in my life of achievement and outward success, the more miserable, exhausted, and unhappy I was on the inside. I wasn't listening to my body. Through illness, weakness, and lethargy, my body was always speaking to me, telling me to slow down, but I kept pushing through until I couldn't anymore.

Every time I speak to groups about how to move out of the *DOING Zone*, I display this slogan inspired by Kurt Vonnegut: "You are a human being, not a human doing." That message described me perfectly: I was a human doing, not a human being.

Understanding that I was more than the sum total of my outward achievements was crucial to having a genuinely happy and authentic life. I would never have learned who I truly was inside, and I would have missed out on some of the most beautiful and meaningful parts of my life, if I had stayed busy only focusing on success, or just trying to survive the day until the weekend.

I used to be "Exhibit A" for the perils of living in the *DOING Zone*. I didn't know how to turn off. I was going and doing all the time because I found value in feeling needed. Our world, our society, and many of you operate in the *DOING Zone* because you are focused on success, achievement, acceptance, or survival depending on what was role-modeled and preached to you during your formative years. As a result, you may live more in your head than your heart. Learning how to move out of your *DOING Zone* into your personal *BEING Zone* is the foundation for overall health and happiness that enables you to choose the life you want, not the life you were told would make you happy. Yes, your life is a choice!

Do You Listen to Your Body?

I have found that most people do not listen to the messages that their bodies are sending them. If you pay attention and listen, you will continually get little whispers or signs. For example, you may have tension or indigestion show up if you're working yourself to exhaustion, or your body may react negatively when a certain person calls you. You may get an unexplained rash or inflammation that results from too much stress, not turning off, or slowing down when your body needs you to. You may have a sore throat or chest congestion, and instead of resting and allowing your body to heal naturally, you pop pills. You never think to ask why, because you are too busy operating in the *DOING Zone* to notice, or you might think you don't have the time to deal with being tired or ill.

Eventually, your body will hit a point where it cannot keep going at that pace. Instead of giving you small messages, it will eventually give you one that stops you in your tracks. I know, because I did precisely that. I ignored the tension in my neck and shoulders and kept pushing through. Then I would tell myself "I don't feel good," which made me feel even worse. My words became my reality. Then I would try to cover up the pain. Instead of tuning into why I had a headache, I would take Tylenol to try to make it go away. And if I felt a sinus infection starting, I would take medicines instead of figuring out why it was developing and naturally healing it.

This type of response caught up with me. By continually taking over-the-counter medicines and never taking a minute to ask what was going on with me, I ended up messing up my body's natural ability to heal itself.

Client Story: Fran, a 32-year-old mom of two, poured herself into her responsibilities. She tried to balance her high-pressure job with being a mom with young children and found herself existing in a state of worry and stress. She got to the point where she didn't know how to turn off. It showed up in her body as migraines, inflammation, indigestion, etc. She was existing in the *DOING Zone* and wasn't comfortable just *BEING*. When she started working with me, she was exhausted, over-whelmed, and unhappy with all the seemingly benign health issues that were affecting her life. She struggled with leaving her job, as the money was too good. She felt a responsibility to stay even though her body was telling her to leave. She was too worn out to figure this out on her own, so after getting to a breaking point, she turned to me. Fran began to recognize that she had to change something. She moved into a part-time role working from home. She is beginning to understand how to create a healthier lifestyle one step at a time.

Journaling Time

DO YOU EXIST IN THE *DOING ZONE* JOURNALING EXERCISE #47: In your notebook or *BEING Journal*, make notes on how much time you live in the *DOING Zone*.

· How much time daily do you spend going or *DOING?* This would include things like working, shopping, cleaning, getting projects or chores done, volunteering, driving, etc.

· List anything you are doing where your mind, body, and spirit are not at rest. Make notes on where your time is spent and how much time on each activity.

· Look at total hours in each area so you have a good understanding of what you might want to work on. Highlight the areas where you could make the most progress.

· How much of the time do you find your thoughts or words are putting you into worry, stress, or the *DOING Zone?* What type of things are you thinking or saying?

Your Body Is Not Designed for the *DOING Zone*

When you live in the *DOING Zone*, you often feel excited, fearful, nervous, or stressed as a result of the thoughts in your head and your ingrained belief system, which results from past trauma or abuse, or issues happening in your life right now that are increasing your feelings of helplessness or overwhelm. When you operate in this place regularly, you increase the adrenaline in your body, causing your body to tense up and feel more stressed. Some people even go on overload and can even end up with a panic attack or heart issues.

Your body is not designed to run in the *DOING Zone* full-time. A stressful situation can trigger physiological changes like a pounding heart, muscle tension, and quickening breath. This is known as the "fight or flight" response. It evolved as a survival mechanism, enabling people and other mammals to react quickly to life-threatening situations, but it's not meant to be a permanent state of existence.

We have the potential to become unbalanced if we live in "emergency mode" by trying to do too much. In this high stress-state, our bodies can overreact to stressors that are not life-threatening, such as traffic jams, work pressure, and family difficulties. If you live this way, it may feel like your emotions are on a roller coaster, out of balance, and small irritants turn into major problems. Your defense mechanism will go into overdrive, begin to break down, and not work as it is intended. Ongoing stress will result in illness. Over the years, researchers have learned that long-term chronic stress takes a toll on a person's physical and psychological health.

Dangers of the *DOING Zone*

One of the main culprits of doing too much is work related. Researchers say that addiction to work is a compulsive disorder that can kill people.[77] In Japan, they have a name for it: karoshi, which means death from overwork.[78]

True workaholics get a high from the adrenaline, and I would say that's true for many of my clients. Over-working and over-committing places significant stress on their system. Many of my clients with autoimmune and stress-related diseases had to learn how to "turn off" after work and build in more selfcare practices, resulting in better health.

When you feel overwhelmed or exhausted, you are not only less effective, but you may turn to comfort food or exercise less, which can result in weight gain, which will make you feel worse. Working too much also leads to health issues and can cause relationship issues.[79]

Client Story: Tina is a full-time mom and top-level executive in a company that is growing rapidly. She has told me that her exhaustive work schedule often causes her to miss her workouts, so she has less energy. In addition, she is so stressed she often loses patience with her family, and they get riled up, too. She has made phenomenal progress since we started working together in decreasing her stress by committing to her exercise program, diffusing essential oils to calm, taking breaks and walking outside at work, and getting regular massages. She has better managed her relationship with her family by going on family walks and playing at the park. It is a journey, but she is making progress building more balance in her life.

Research at Harvard Health suggests that chronic stress contributes to high blood pressure, promotes the formation of artery-clogging deposits, and causes brain changes that may contribute to anxiety, depression, and addiction.[80] The preliminary research from Harvard also suggests that chronic stress may also contribute to obesity, both through direct mechanisms (causing people to eat more) or indirectly (decreasing sleep and exercise).

The *DOING Zone* May Compromise Your Health

Researchers have proven that working long hours is linked to many health issues. According to the *Journal of Occupational and Environmental Medicine*, health care expenditures are nearly 50% greater for workers who report high levels of stress.[81] Stress-related illnesses may start with things like exhaustion, headaches, neck and shoulder tension, high blood pressure, inadequate nutrition, and insomnia. Then it can move into something like panic and anxiety attacks or chronic health problems such as autoimmune diseases, cardiovascular diseases, musculoskeletal issues, and psychological issues that are all triggered by long-term job stress.

Journaling Time

HEALTH QUESTIONNAIRE JOURNALING EXERCISE #48:

Let's take a few minutes to see how your health is impacted by your levels of stress or your tendency to live in the *DOING Zone*. Make notes in your *BEING Journal* or notebook on which impacts you the most.

- Is your health compromised? What are your symptoms?
- Do you have high blood pressure? High cholesterol? Heart issues?
- Write about how much health issues impact your life.
- Do you lose sleep? Do you have trouble concentrating? How does this affect your life?
- Is your memory failing? Do you walk in a room and can't remember why you went there? How often does this happen, and are others noticing? How does this feel to you?
- Do you have tension in your neck and shoulders? Do you frequently have headaches? How often does this happen, and what are you doing to decrease these things?
- Describe any digestion, stomach issues, or anxiety issues or panic attacks you might experience.
- Do you have inflammation in your body? Do you have low-grade fevers? Do you have any autoimmune diseases? Describe what you feel and how it impacts you.
- Do you get colds easily or have consistent problems with congestion in your head, throat, or lungs? How does it impact your daily living?
- Do you have any aches, pains, or issues in your back, legs, or arms? How do these impact your life?
- Do you get depressed? Or withdrawn? Describe what happens. What else?

The health effects of working long hours depend on the type of worker you are, according to Lieke ten Brummelhuis, PhD, assistant professor of management at Simon Fraser University in Vancouver, British Columbia. She led a study tracking 763 Dutch workers to see if there is a relationship between long work hours and things that can cause metabolic syndrome (a cluster of symptoms including high blood pressure, elevated cholesterol, and other problems). Metabolic syndrome makes heart disease and diabetes more likely.

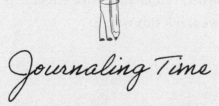

Journaling Time

IMPROVING YOUR HEALTH JOURNALING EXERCISE #49:
Pick up your notebook or *BEING Journal* and start making notes about the top issues that have emerged so far.

- Identify the top one or two health issues from the survey above that you want to address and heal.
- For each issue, ask yourself what is the underlying root cause of the symptoms?
- Search online for "what are the metaphysical reasons I have [this ailment]" and see what you find.
- Once you have identified the metaphysical reason for the ailment, journal ideas on what you can do to overcome these.

Dr. Brummelhuis also found it was not a simple matter of hours worked. The people she terms "engaged," who liked their jobs and might work long hours without worrying about it, didn't have the symptoms she tracked. "It was not the behavior; it was the work mentality, the constant rumination about work" that had an adverse effect on health, she says.[82] An engaged workaholic may put in twelve hours, close their laptop, and do something else. A compulsive workaholic will put in the same twelve hours but remain anxious about some of the tasks or decisions after work hours are over.

I believe many of us are addicted to our work or addicted to feeling needed and valued at work, so we keep trying to prove our worth to others and ourselves. Many of us look at our long hours as proof of our dedication and work ethic. It is hard to create balance when we think this way.

Journaling Time

Are You Engaged or Compulsive? Journaling Exercise #50: Pick up your notebook or *BEING Journal* and start making notes.

· Are you being filled up by your work or depleted? Describe your situation and how you feel about it.

· Do you feel more engaged or exhausted when you think about your day at work? Write about how that feels.

· Do you tend to be driven and compulsive about what you are doing, lazy and doing as little as possible, or do you just flow through the day with ease? Describe your tendencies.

· What might you be able to do to change it for the better?

Client Story: Christina is a part-owner of her company, which has grown substantially over the past five years. She easily does the work of two people and lives a full, intense but balanced life because she has the right mentality. Christina is very disciplined and has passion in all that she does. She practices yoga,

meditation, and is an avid hiker who can take on the most challenging of trails with a full backpack on the weekends. Christina
has worked with me for so long that she knows the signs of what
to watch for if she starts to get overwhelmed. For the most part,
she builds the 5 Daily B.E.I.N.G. Steps and things she loves to do
into her days, which keeps her in the flow state or *The BEING Zone.*

Your Body Tells the Truth

Once you learn to listen to your body, it's good to take time to
identify what led to any illnesses or physical symptoms you've
had. If you focus on the root cause of the problem, you will be
able to heal. Contemporary medicine has value in many ways, but
when it comes to stress-related diseases, it tends to deal with the
symptoms, not the root. I know after coaching many others with
life-altering or life-threatening illnesses that we have to focus
first on why our bodies got sick and heal that. You don't want to
wait until you have a severe diagnosis, an accident, or some big
wake-up call to slow down and listen to your body.

Client Story: Brandon's wake-up call was stage IV
cancer. He knew that he needed to change his way of operating in the world if he was going to heal. He had pushed
himself too hard to support his family and help his extended family.
He'd worked too many hours, wasn't listening to his body, and
ignored all the signs until his diagnosis. He came to me then to
help him change his lifestyle issues. The doctors could work with
him on his diet and treatment, but he needed help clearing out
his *DOING Zone* tendencies, which he knew was what put him

in this situation. Brandon had a powerful motivation to change, as he wanted to watch his grandchildren grow up. I taught him the tools to use to *SHIFT* old beliefs and focused on the importance of daily habits and operating in *The BEING Zone*. It only took two sessions and he was off and running. A year later, I met him in person, and he dropped on one knee and thanked me "for helping to save my life." He is still doing well today!

Were You Pre-Programmed to Live in the *DOING Zone*?

As you learned in Chapters 1 and 2, how you think and respond to the world is based in part on what you heard and experienced as a young child. According to Joe Dispenza in his book *Breaking the Habit of Being Yourself,* up to 95% of who you are by the time you are an adult is a set of memorized behaviors, emotional reactions, unconscious habits, hardwired attitudes, beliefs, and perceptions that function like a computer program.[83] How you think and how you feel creates your state of *BEING.* If all you saw and knew as a young child was how to work hard and live in the *DOING Zone*, then that will be how you think and act as an adult. You will keep creating the same life you have always had as it is your comfort zone, whether you like it or not. When you make a conscious decision to change your thoughts and your behavior, you can change your life!

Client Story: Elizabeth, age 36, only wanted to please others. She grew up learning to take care others before herself; she wouldn't get in trouble or ruffle any feathers that way. Her focus was to ensure everyone else was happy and taken care of, while her needs were put on the back burner. Elizabeth married a man who took advantage of her giving ways. She did everything she could to please him and create what she thought was an ideal home life. She bought their home and took responsibility for shopping, cooking, and cleaning while working two jobs to make ends meet. Her husband would hang out with friends, gaming and drinking, while she worked around them to ensure the house was clean and they had what they needed. She didn't think about herself at all. As a result of her unhappy life, Elizabeth gained sixty pounds and started to have fainting spells. It was her wake-up call. She recognized everything she was doing wasn't working, and it was time to stop. She looked around and asked herself, what do healthy people do? Many of her healthy coworkers did yoga, so she tried it, and it was a game-changer for her. She started listening to her body and her own needs and began to regain her health.

Journaling Time

WHAT ARE YOUR TENDENCIES JOURNALING EXERCISE #51: Make notes in your *BEING Journal* or notebook on the areas you need address from this survey.

- Are you a high achiever who always seems to do more than what seems possible in an eight-hour day? If so, why do you think this is true?
- Are you always trying to prove yourself, buy love, or exceed expectations? If so, why and when did this start?

- Do you mask any signs of illness with over-the-counter medications? If so, how do you feel about doing that? Is there anything you could change?
- Do you lose sleep consistently, so you never feel refreshed? Describe your situation.
- Do you keep smiling and pushing even when you are miserable? Write about any memories when you tended to smile and push through instead of being true to yourself.
- Do you tune out how you feel or what happens when you feel really emotional?
- Do you ever feel depressed, empty, disconnected, or numb? If so, describe when this happens.

Your Beliefs May Lead to Doing Too Much

- **A desire to provide well for your family.** Possibly trying to give them things you never had. Bear in mind that some studies suggest that both adults and children who attach a lot of importance to money and material possessions tend to be less happy.[84]
- **A belief that more is better.** That is what the advertisers want you to think as they try to convince you that you are depriving yourself if you don't buy.
- **An attempt to satisfy the expectations of others.** You may be trying to please your boss or your spouse, or even still be trying to impress your parents.
- **An effort to prove yourself.** The busier you are, the more important you seem. Is it about social status or being needed?

Life Demands Lead to *DOING Zone* Thinking

In a 2015 survey of full-time workers in eight countries, many respondents said that they found it hard to meet the demands of both their work and their home life. The causes they cited included increased responsibilities at work or home, rising expenses, and longer working hours. In the United States, for example, full-time employees report working an average of forty-seven hours a week.[85] Nearly one in five claimed to work sixty hours or more. I can verify that many of my high-level clients still work fifty hours or more each week, but by learning to operate in *The BEING Zone*, they learn to do it with ease. In another survey, this one involving thirty-six countries, over one-quarter of the respondents said that they often felt rushed even in their leisure time.[86] When we continuously try to do more than time may allow, we can become stressed—victims of "time pressure."

Client Story: Allie worked for a company that was known for expecting long hours and burning out their employees. She was so stressed that she couldn't even have a full conversation with me without distractions. She always had work to do, whether we talked in the afternoon, evening, or on the weekend. She would often schedule appointments with me and then cancel at the last minute, too busy or stressed to do the call. I finally had to release her as a client because we were making zero progress. I asked her to call me back when she was ready.

Where Do You Exist?

**Take the *DOING Zone* survey below to find out. Mark all
true statements.**

____ 1. I am always feeling rushed and racing against deadlines.

____ 2. I stay busy and always have multiple projects going at any
one time.

____ 3. I am a multitasker and am always doing more than one
thing at a time, such as eating lunch, answering emails, and
talking on the phone.

____ 4. I overcommit myself and try to do more than is humanly
possible.

____ 5. I feel guilty when I'm not accomplishing something

____ 6. I work late even after my coworkers have gone home.

____ 7. I take work home almost every night or I keep working
into the evening hours.

____ 8. It's hard to relax and unplug when I'm not working—even
on vacation.

____ 9. I spend more time working than I do socializing with loved
ones and friends or enjoying hobbies or leisure activities.

Interpreting Your Score:

0 to 2 Items: You're a hard worker but live more in *The BEING
Zone* and are more likely to have a good work-life balance.

3 to 4 Items: You tend to become busy and work to the exclusion
of what's important to you. You tend to operate in between the
BEING and *DOING Zone,* but with modifications, you can find
balance and prevent job burnout.

5+ Items: You are addicted to the *DOING Zone* and at risk for burnout and illness.

Journaling Time

DOING ZONE SURVEY WRAP UP JOURNALING EXERCISE #52:
Pull out your notebook or *BEING Journal* and write about your *DOING Zone* Survey score.

- What is your score on the survey? Why is it at that level?
- What can you change in your life to create more work-life balance?
- Make a commitment to change at least one thing in your life that will lead you towards the life you desire. Write it down and put in a place to remind you.

Existing in *The BEING Zone*

You now understand how operating in the *DOING Zone* can be detrimental to your health and happiness, but you may not realize how easily accessible living in *The BEING Zone* state is. I didn't!

The BEING Zone is literally a state of mind and body. It is getting into a zone, a presence and a way of *BEING* or existing. When you live in *The BEING Zone*, everything in life is more manageable. It is where the craziness is quieted, where you can turn off all the noises and distractions and just *BE* present in the moment. It is the place where you calm your mind, body, and soul, and feel connected both to yourself and something more significant. In *The BEING Zone*, you can experience self-love and a deep joy inside yourself, and it becomes easier to implement self-nurturing and self-care.

When you are in *The BEING Zone* you are completely relaxed and able to see, know, and hear things more clearly. You are able to focus your attention and reflect on your life instead of reacting to it. You get a chance to take a true breath of fresh air and just *BE*.

How often have you been able to just *BE* recently? Where there is no phone, no tv, no demands, just yourself in the present moment. We'll talk more about utilizing the energy and connection with Source tools in Chapter 7 and 8, but for now, know that when I am in The *BEING* state, my body is in a vibrational state that feels as though it is expanding out and around me like energy waves. It is almost dreamlike. When I am in this flow state, my mind, body, and spirit physically buzz (like when my foot falls asleep) and I feel completely tuned into my sixth sense.

Getting into *The BEING Zone* and tuning into my body, sensing my body's messages, is very healing for me, gives me amazing clarity and it can for you, too. The more you do the exercises in this chapter, the more you will increase your state of serenity, well-being and resilience. Once you live in *The BEING Zone*, you will flow through the day with ease and grace because you are stable and calm within. Synchronicities will start to happen because you are living in accordance with your true self. You will feel happy and joyful inside and work with others more easily.

You can choose to enter this calm energy state regularly through mindfulness, meditation, or relaxation techniques. This will help your body and mind shift out of the repetitive, negative bias loop where your subconscious mind exists. That voice in your head will become distant. Instead, you will be learning to exist in a low Alpha brainwave state, where creativity rises, or in the Theta brainwave state where you are completely tuned into to the nuances within your body.

Client Story: Anne, a forty-year-old self-employed leader in the Multi-Level Marketing world, was so used to working 10-12-hour days, including weekends, that she'd had a hard time cutting back to enjoy time with her daughter who was entering high school. Still, Anne wanted more quality family time before her daughter went to college. With a clear vision of what she wanted; it was easier for her to transition than many of my clients. First, she slowed down and committed to her 5 Daily B.E.I.N.G. Steps. Once Anne was calmer and centered, we reviewed her schedule, her habits, and her self-imposed commitments. We identified and eliminated unnecessary activities and came up with a plan that increased her sales while cutting her work time in half. Anne is now operating in *The BEING Zone* and loves spending quality family time that had been lacking. Most importantly, she is able to maintain her balanced lifestyle.

Creating Balance

I know from experience that when you have a busy life, there are many things you must do. You can't just stop everything— that's not realistic. But you can create more of a balance between *DOING* and *BEING.* The key is building simple activities into your everyday life that will calm your system.

It all starts with 5 Daily B.E.I.N.G. Steps that you will learn about in Chapter 10. Then add calming activities to that like regular massages, or a weekly yoga or Qigong class. If that's too much, just stopping to breathe deeply helps a lot.

Balance comes from getting into *The BEING Zone* even if it is just for short periods. On weekends, look at your responsibilities and commitments and see what is essential. You may be able to say no to something that you are in the habit of doing. For example, my husband and I struggled to keep up with house cleaning because we both work full-time and have busy personal lives. We decided to hire a housekeeper, which lessens our stress tremendously. I also do most of my shopping online, as it keeps me from having to run all over the place. It saves me time and gas money. These two decisions alone freed up time so I can still work long hours and also do more self-care and what I love— spending *BEING* time on the beach or hiking.

Permit yourself to take back your life! It is OK to say no. It's OK to only commit to the things you love to do and enjoy. I have a client who overcommits all the time, saying yes when he gets caught up in the excitement of the moment. Then he gets upset at himself on the way home. He has learned to stop, breathe, and center before agreeing to any more volunteer programs. He stops to ask himself, "will this fill me up?" If not, then he doesn't offer.

If you find yourself dragging your feet and delaying going somewhere or doing something, ask yourself why. You feel that way for a reason. Eliminate doing things you don't want to do whenever possible. Yes, you do have to do or arrange for the normal things that keep up your home, like laundry and dishes, but you have control over how you run your errands or what events you attend. If dealing with family or negative people is difficult for you but you feel obligated, step back and evaluate. What would happen if you decreased the number of times you said yes? Everyone would live. They might not always be happy, but most likely, you will be happier. Make a conscious decision to spend less time with people who drain you and more time with people who make you happy.

Journaling Time

LIST YOUR COMMITMENTS JOURNALING EXERCISE #53: Grab your *BEING Journal* or notebook and start writing about your commitments.

- Make a list of all your current commitments, whether it be work, home, friends, family, community, organizations, etc.
- Highlight all the ones you love doing, that fill you with joy when doing them.
- Circle all the items that are not fulfilling or valuable to you.
- Make notes about where you can eliminate, set limits, or decrease the things that that don't make you happy.
- Make notes about how balanced your life is and how happy you are.
- How much time do you exist in *The BEING Zone* or in the state of joy and synchronicities?
- Describe this part of your life. Identify all the amazing things that happen as a result of living in *The BEING Zone*.

Practical Steps to Balance for Wellness

You have the solution deep within you—you just need to learn to access it by listening to the whispers of your body and soul when it's not happy. When you can exist in *The BEING Zone* and quiet your mind, change your mindset, and believe in your body's own ability to heal itself, you will heal. When you change your thoughts and begin to create the health you desire, you will feel power and joy inside.

If you are ready to operate utilizing your internal power and natural solutions to self-heal, here are some practical steps to take you forward in that direction.

- **Refocus Your Energy to Your Inner World:** When you learn to quiet your mind, do inner work, and meditate, you can change your outer world. To get started, spend time each day breathing, getting grounded and centered, and sitting in a meditative state to be able to tune into your heart and body. You can find many useful recordings at www.TheBEINGZone.com/tools.
- **Where Your Mind Goes, Your Energy Flows:** Your energy is connected to your awareness. Wherever you place your attention— where your mind goes every day—your energy will follow. If you are focused on what you don't want, you will get more of it. Your life will stay the same. To create a new reality, you must think about what you do want and put your time, energy, and thoughts on that. Where do you want your mind to go?
- **Lower the Volume of What You Don't Want:** Lower the volume of what you don't want. When the Ego tendencies show up, use the Throw It Away Tool from Chapter 4. You do not need to listen to or be driven by your subconscious.
- **Decrease the Attention You Give to Stress or Pain:** The less attention you put on the stress, pain, or old beliefs that cause your negative thoughts, the less you will experience them. Use the tools in Chapter 3 to release old feelings. When your mind starts wandering to these areas, catch yourself and breathe,

ground, and refocus your mind on *BEING* and things that make you happy.

· **Key into the Emotions (Energy in Motion) of What You Do Want:** When you focus on joy, happiness, connection, and other feelings or emotions you wish to have, you will weaken the old bonds and addictions and begin creating new energy circuits so you can reprogram your life.

· **Focus on Health and Take Preventative Measures:** Don't think self-defeating thoughts like "I'm getting sick." Instead, choose a positive thought like "I am well and plan to stay well." Focus on believing you are healing, and those thoughts will help dictate the outcome. At the very first signs of a cold, focus on the positive message while increasing your Vitamin C intake and using immune boosting essential oils or herbs. If you have congestion, inhale dōTERRA Breathe essential oil blend or Eucalyptus oil to clear your sinus or lungs. Maybe take a bath with Epsom salt and essential oils. Slow down, nurture yourself, and get more rest at night. You can prevent almost any flu or cold by taking proactive steps at the very onset of any signs. The key is paying attention to the signs and focusing on what you want.

· **Get Grounded:** Grounding is also called Earthing. These two terms are interchangeable, and I will use both words in this book. Earthing is the easiest source of good energy, and there is a fast-growing movement emerging based upon the discovery that connecting to the Earth's natural energy is essential for vibrant health. Earthing/Grounding will be explained in more detail in Chapter 7.

· **You Are What You Eat:** Real food is the key to good health, Making conscientious decisions on what you consume is vital. You can no longer afford to ignore the facts that processed, carb-heavy, high-calorie foods are not supporting your body and happiness. Highly processed foods are a significant contributor to obesity and illness around the world. There have been thousands of studies done by major universities that talk about the negative impact of junk food and highly processed foods, which have been chemically manufactured and made from refined ingredients and artificial substances. Every time a population adopts a Western diet high in processed foods, they get sick within a few years.[87] When we replace natural foods like fish, meat, fruit, and vegetables with over-processed junk foods, we increase our risk of illness. The movie *The Magic Pill* is a great example of what happens when kids with diets full of processed, high carbs, and sugars move to a natural foods diet.[88] The transformation in happiness and health is phenomenal. There is a real need to nourish the body with healthy foods and lots of water.

Client Story: Trudie runs a company that helps people find health through diet and fitness, and she's an expert in self-care. That said, she recently orchestrated a global summit that pushed her past her ability to function. She was exercising and eating healthy but was also doing too much. She quit listening to her body. As a result, Trudie started feeling disconnected from everything. She told me she tried crying, but no tears came. She tried to read her Bible but wasn't connecting with the words. She tried to work out but felt as though her muscles were not connected with her body. She tried to journal her feelings and couldn't write. She tried Earthing and couldn't feel a thing. We did some clearing to get her reconnected to herself. She has since learned to toss away the thoughts she does not want and is watching her life turning around in front of her. Trudie has now implemented a daily practice which focuses on breathing, Grounding, and what she does want. She just texted and said, "I am glowing again!"

It's important to stay ahead of the stress and overwhelm by doing daily practices to stay in balance— once you are in the midst of the situation it is more challenging to move out of it.

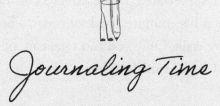

Journaling Time

YOU OWN YOUR HEALTH JOURNALING EXERCISE #54:

Get out your notebook or *BEING Journal* and make notes on what you can do to improve your health and wellness.

- List a few of the things where you place your energy every day. What are you focused on?
- Make notes on the areas of your life that are not changing where you have pain or stress. These are your areas where you need to learn to disconnect.
- How often do you get sick, and what steps do you take to fend it off?
- What does your diet look like? Is it nourishing you or depleting you?
- How much time do you spend feeling good and grounded in life?
- What do you want your life to look like? That's what you should meditate on, think about, and build into your daily thoughts and words.

Are You Listening?

Don't get to the point where you do not have the time, energy, or wherewithal to listen to your body. That can be as simple as saying no if you don't want to go somewhere. You, and only you, can make the right decisions about what will increase your joy and energy. You may choose to change your routine and allow yourself a day of rest. You might say no to doing more, especially when you aren't appreciated. If you are tired or frazzled at work, you might take a five-minute break outside to breathe fresh air and take a short walk. Only you can take care of you. Stand up for yourself and your health and happiness!

Client Story: Nina would get a headache on her drive to work most mornings, and would just pop an aspirin to get rid of the pain. After she started her *BEING Zone* practices, she stopped popping pills and decided to pay attention to when the headaches showed up. She asked herself why she was getting them. She noticed it was always on her way to work and was able to see that she was encountering stress on the way to work because she was unhappy with her environment. She sat next to a coworker who would gossip all day, and she hated it. She talked to her boss and was able to move to a new location in the office, and her headaches stopped. By paying attention to her body's signals Nina was able to change both her emotional balance at work and the physical pain in her body.

Journaling Time

ARE YOU LISTENING JOURNALING EXERCISE #55:
It's time to make notes in your *BEING Journal* or notebook on listening to your body.

· Think about any tendencies you may have toward overdoing and not listening to your body's needs. Are there things there you can change?

· Write about a time when you pushed yourself beyond what you should have committed to. How did you feel? What were the results?

· Think about times when you quit listening to your body and forced yourself to do things you didn't want to do or have time to do. What could you do differently next time?

· Journal about things you can do to reboot your mind, body, and soul. You can change your thoughts and words to revamping how you act in life.

Client Story: My clients who have had alcohol or drug addictions seem to have the toughest time with this, but once they clear old issues away, they are better able to quiet their minds and begin to enjoy getting present. Dan was addicted to heroin. He was open to coaching with me, and I am eternally grateful for that. I helped him identify and clear life issues that were making him vulnerable to the drug and holding him back. He loved music, so I encouraged him to spend his time writing music and playing his guitar, which would put him in the present moment. While doing this, he lost track of his internal desire for drugs. Dan's weekly assignment was to share with me the songs he wrote. He was always excited to do so and spent hours writing music. He wrote about his pain and problems, which was freeing for him. His songs deeply touched my heart. In time, he became heroin free. He moved to Nashville and is working full-time while building his music career.

You Can Do It!

You, too, can learn to operate in *The BEING Zone*, where calm is built into your life. The solution is to learn to identify and build thoughts, feelings, activities, and disciplines into your life that will keep you feeling in the flow. *The BEING Zone* is a place where you learn to be comfortable in the empty spaces—quieting that voice in your head and learning to *BE* present in the NOW. It took many years for me to get comfortable in this quiet space, and now I am passionate about staying in that zone and committed to sharing it with others. I have found with those who are ready, it can be a game changer.

I have helped many clients learn to quiet their minds and operate in this new silent space. They say, "I don't know what to do." I tell them to do nothing. The clients often report at first they go nuts in less than a minute. They say they are bored, and that's OK. Turn off the distractions and noise and just sit and *BE*. By the end of this book, you'll know how to reach *The BEING Zone* state, as well, through breathing, meditation, mindfulness, or Grounding and quieting the voice in your head. The easiest way to turn off is to sit on the beach, letting the waves distract you as the minutes tick by. Or lie in the grass, soaking in the sun and watching the cloud shapes float by. You might also listen to a meditation or relaxation video. The more you do this, the easier it gets. When the mind ceases to have constant thoughts, you can glimpse and tune into your true self or your soul. The secret is to stay in this zone after you come out of your meditation is to start your day with a daily practice.

Daily Practice

A daily practice of the 5 Daily B.E.I.N.G. Steps will move you into *The BEING Zone* and is life changing. The five steps are detailed in Chapter 10. When you begin to practice these steps daily and start to exist in *The BEING Zone*, everything in life is better. You start the day in a centered and grounded state, which then allows you to flow through the day with ease and grace. You automatically decrease your worry and stress. You begin to care about self-nurturing and self-love, which will change the outcome of your life. You feel happy and joyful inside and find that you blend well with others more easily.

Client Story: Jana is a fast-paced, high-level executive leading a successful company. She has embraced the value of the 5 Daily B.E.I.N.G. Steps and builds it into her daily schedule as a requirement. If she doesn't take the time, she has told me she pays for it. She starts to get overwhelmed and stressed and then realizes by not doing her daily practice, she falls out of her *BEING Zone*. She says that committing to the 5 Daily B.E.I.N.G. Steps starts her days with ease and grace and keeps her in good energy.

Ways to Build *BEING Zone* Activities into Your Life

- **Breathe:** Even if you can only spare a few seconds, take time to breathe and center yourself. There are a variety of breathing exercises in the book—discover your favorite and use it daily and repeat as needed.

- **Calming Activities:** Commit to yoga, Qigong, meditation, or spa time at least once a month. Utilizing essential oils during the day will help you calm your mind and soothe your soul.

- **Ground and Immerse Yourself in Your Surroundings:** Find time to relax and ground with the earth. Tune in to and enjoy your surroundings, whether it is on a beach or in a park. Notice the clouds, the birds, etc. Be mindful of nature's magic as you relax and fill yourself with earth energy. You will learn more about Grounding in Chapter 7.

- **Intention:** Slow down and consciously do things with a purpose. Eat slowly. Move slowly. Think slowly. Be intentional.

- **Daydream and Play:** Invoke calming imagery in your mind. You might feel like you are floating on a cloud or riding on the back of a giant eagle as it soars through the sky. Play like a child.

- **Observe Your Surroundings:** Without judging, just notice what's around you. Detach any thoughts. Be present.

- **Listen to or Play the Type of Music that Calms You:** Find music that relaxes you and listen to it often. Sign up for a Sound Healing Class or session, which can be very healing. It lowers stress, decreases mood swings, lowers blood pressure, and improves sleep. We incorporate sound into our training and workshops for those reasons.

- **Do Art or Crafts:** Make something that doesn't matter how it turns out so you can get lost in the moment with the artwork. It can be any type of arts and crafts that you can enjoy just for the fun of it. My sons laugh at me for this, but I paint heart-shaped rocks. It's very calming. I even created a Facebook group called Create Love Rocks, where members paint rocks with messages of love to share with others. The purpose is to get people to stop and paint, creating calm in their lives with the extra benefit of spreading love across the world.

· **Mindfulness:** Take a hike or a walk that isn't about exercise but about noticing your surroundings and becoming one with the earth and nature. Just let your eyes enjoy the feast of our natural world while quieting any thoughts.

· **Do What You Love to Do:** Get lost in time, doing **whatever feels right to you.**

Journaling Time

BEING Zone **COMMITMENT JOURNALING EXERCISE #56:**

Get out your notebook or *BEING Journal* and begin to make notes.

· What commitments can you make to increase the amount of time you are spending in *The BEING Zone*?

· Be specific about when you will build these new activities into your schedule, so they happen.

The BEING Zone System

You have just learned how the mental state of *BEING* surpasses the mental state of doing every single time, and how operating in *The BEING Zone* can transform your health and happiness. Now let's continue on to *The BEING Zone System*, which has all the tools and practices you will need to change how you are operating in the world.

After my healing journey, as discussed in the introduction of this book, then coaching hundreds and hundreds of clients, I designed *The BEING Zone System* that will help you rediscover and reconnect with yourself while improving your happiness and health.

You may be living a life that does not reflect who you really are. *The BEING Zone System* empowers you to release those difficult and stuck areas of your life. You are learning how to free yourself from guilt, shame, regret, and habitual negative habits by learning to operate from a place of love within yourself. *The BEING Zone System* will help you reconnect with your true self and learn to trust your intuition while building in daily practices and happiness boosting activities that will take your life to a higher level. You will experience the magic of inner growth and transformation when you apply *The BEING Zone System* tools and practices into your life.

Client Story: Linda is a 57-year-old woman who used to overdo in all areas of her life and had a hard time shutting off. She is in the nursing field and would give all day at work and then would go home and give more by volunteering in the community. She was unhappy, started getting sick, and turned to me. At first, Linda quit volunteering so much but felt guilty about dropping it completely. She committed to *The BEING Zone System*, released ingrained blocks and beliefs, and today practices tools and techniques daily that have transformed her life. She has a very full yet balanced life, spending more time doing things she loves while still keeping a balanced life. This is the life I want for all of you.

Key Messages

- The *DOING Zone* is a stress state where we overthink and over analyze everything.
- You might exist in and be addicted to the *DOING Zone* and not even know it.
- You exist in this state when you are driven by your subconscious mind and don't listen to your body that is talking to you all the time.
- If you exist in this state, you tune your bodies messages out, mask your symptoms, and move into a "fight or flight" state, which compromises your health.
- Your body tells the truth. Ongoing headaches, digestion issues, exhaustion, etc. are not normal states of *BEING.*
- You might live in this place because of life's demands and your belief systems around success, achievement, acceptance or survival.
- You can turn off the noise and distractions and learn to enjoy the silence of *The BEING Zone*, a place of calm connectedness where you want to exist.
- *The BEING Zone* is accessible to anyone; you just need to make a conscious decision to find balance and learn to exist there.
- You can be driven and still exist in *The BEING Zone* if you are in tune with your body and engaged, not anxious or worried.
- *The BEING Zone System* will help you rediscover and reconnect with yourself while improving your happiness and health.

This Chapter's Gifts: You learn to understand and let go of any *DOING Zone* tendencies while learning to embrace the qualities and stillness of *The BEING Zone* existence so you can create your own personal flow state.

CHAPTER 6

Discovering Your True North

> "I find the great thing in this world is, not so much where we stand, as in what direction we are moving."
> —Goethe

YOU WERE BORN with natural intuition, but most of us stop listening in favor of chasing outward success in the *DOING Zone*. In Chapter 5, you began to understand how important it is to operate in *The BEING Zone* instead of the *DOING Zone*.

Sometimes it feels impossible to figure out who you are and what you are meant to do in this world. Using your intuition and staying in *The BEING Zone* will help you work through the exercises in this chapter with a greater sense of knowing. When you unearth your intrinsic gifts, you will discover your True North (aka your life's purpose).

You will be more effective working through this material if you get into *The BEING Zone* first as it makes it easier to access your intuition (using the tools introduced in Chapter 4) while completing the activities in this chapter. With your internal knowing, you will be able to better identify your True North, also known as your life's purpose, which will serve as the compass for your daily life and future goals.

A critical thing to understand about discovering your life's purpose, or your True North, is that it is not just one thing or a final destination—it is a process or a journey. Part of this process is listening to the messages or issues that show up in your life. When you have challenges or setbacks, it is your soul speaking to you and a gift. You want to pay attention as they are meant to be part of your journey to your True North.

I started my journey in the perfect position in Corporate America, and I have moved on to be a Life Coach. Life keeps unfolding right in front of me, while I am being guided to do bigger things from writing this book to getting my message and teachings out to a broader audience. My journey continues to grow and expand and yours will too. My new path is more fulfilling than I ever could have imagined. I just had to learn to listen to what felt right.

The exercises I will take you through in this chapter will give you tremendous clarity on who you are at the core and what is important to you. It may or may not describe a specific job or career. What it will define is what your natural gifts are, which will give you a general idea of what you should be doing, and your job is to figure out how to capitalize on that information. For instance, I know my gifts are empathy and intuition, and I know I am meant to be helping people heal and find happiness within. That is pretty general, but, in my case, it is also the core of what I do as a Life Coach and now as an author.

Client Story: Erin had a very successful career in a large accounting firm but was limited to dealing with tax clients, which was not challenging to her. She went through the exercises in this book and gained phenomenal clarity on what made her happy and what she wanted to do in life. Through the work we did together, she confirmed that strategizing and envisioning new things were essential parts of her core gifts, and we were able to redirect her career. We updated her resume and she applied for a new job that was more exciting to her. She has moved into a new position with the same firm, where she is now focused on developing talent and performance strategies. She is challenged and fulfilled at a deeper level.

Stuck in Life

I have identified some commonalities across most of my clients that might apply to you as well. You may feel stuck in your life or in a job you don't love because your beliefs, messages, and stories got you to where you are today and are keeping you stuck. You possibly didn't realize how much was programmed into you at a young age, or how that led you to your current career. You may feel the realities of your life will not allow you to make a life transition at this point because of other issues. Your level of income and financial commitments may be keeping you trapped.

When you start unraveling your past, exploring the nooks and crannies of your life, many nuggets will be uncovered. You may have to go through some pain to get to your gain, or you may breeze through the exercises and have extreme clarity by the end without a struggle. Some of my clients do not remember their childhood because it was abusive or traumatic, and they have blocked that out. If this also describes your situation, these blocks will impact your ability to truly get to the core of who you are and what you are meant to do in this world. Be assured I have been able to help many clients reconnect with what they have blocked, and they have come out stronger on the other side. I have so many stories about clients who healed and found themselves and redirected their lives to one they love as a result of this work. The more honest you are through this entire process, the better your results will be.

Your Purpose

You were born with a purpose. There is a reason you are on Earth at this point and time. My goal in this chapter is to help you excavate your life and discover what it is that you are meant to be or do in this world. You will use some of the tools you learned in the first part of this book, such as breathing, Grounding, and intuition, to complete your homework from a heart-based place that will speak directly to you.

Some of you know what makes you happy already, and some of you may struggle with this question a lot. Are you holding yourself back or are your circumstances impacting your decisions? The key is when you can truly discover who you are, what you should be doing, and start doing it, you will come alive! You will re-engage in life and have a deep fulfillment inside your heart and soul.

Listen to Your Heart's Desires

One of the most essential things in this discovery process is to feel worthy that you deserve this full life you can create for yourself. You possibly don't see how you can get from where you are to the dream life you will identify in this chapter. I am always amazed at how many of my clients do not think they can transition to a job they love even if they are miserable where they are. They might feel too much responsibility to provide for others, and so stay chained to the job or life they have fallen into. Or they may not feel confident or worthy enough to transform their life into one they love entirely.

Learning to listen to your heart's desire deep within you will stir things up. It is often a place of discomfort at first, as you face your deeply ingrained perceptions of who you think you are, because that is how you have always been. When you begin to connect with your heart, you will start to know and feel you are worthy of happiness, peace, joy, love, and compassion. You might find your heart's desires are very different than the actual life you are leading today. This can be a little scary at first, but trust what you are feeling and continue learning to listen to, respect, and trust that these yearnings are your first steps toward accessing a higher consciousness, which leads to authentic fulfillment.

Client Story: Adrianne, a 60-year-old healthcare professional who had been working remotely for years, had a boss who was hard to work for. He was disrespectful and critical. She was often in tears but felt tied to her job because it was lucrative and flexible, so she stayed stuck. Adrianne went through the healing process to eliminate the self-confidence issues that had arisen as a result of the disrespect she felt from her boss. She then started training as a Life Coach and healthcare trainer, as she knew from firsthand experience how emotionally draining nursing can be, and how it affects not only the caregivers but the patients too. Adrianne knew deep inside that she wanted to make a difference in the lives of the dedicated souls within the health-care industry. She successfully launched her own company, and she is now helping nurses, nurse leaders, and healthcare professionals reduce burnout and stress while rekindling their passion—which is precisely what she did for herself.

Homework Tips for Extracting the True You!

This next section will be full of homework to help you get to the core of who you are. Before we get to the homework, I have a few tips for you to bear in mind.

- **Heart-Based Approach.** Stop, breathe, center, and ground before you get started each time. The more you are in a centered, connected state, the more quickly the answers will come to you.
- **Journaling** will help you fine-tune and evolve your thoughts during the homework and discovery process, but also afterwards when you have more clarity on your life purpose.
- **Your Dreams** are your subconscious talking to you. Listen to them and learn what you are meant to. Keep a blank notebook near your bed with a pen. In the early morning hours, when you become aware that you are dreaming, grab your notepad and pen and make notes that will assist you in remembering the nuances of your dream. There are many amazing books out there that will help you decipher what the dream means, or you can search the internet and ask, "what does this dream mean?"

Homework

After you have completed all seven homework exercises listed below, you'll come to a section called "How to Process the Homework Information Gathered." This is critical to gain insight and information about extracting the true you, your true passions, and talents. Please do not move forward to the next section until you complete all your homework, as this is what will give you clarity on who you are and where you are going.

Journaling Time

EXCAVATING YOUR LIFE JOURNALING EXERCISE #57:
Get out your notebook or *BEING Journal* and answer the questions below.

1. **Who Do You Admire?** List three to five people you admire the most in the world. They can be friends, family, or famous. They may have passed or are alive and well. You do not have to like every single thing about them, but you must genuinely admire something about what they say or do. Make a list of the three to five people you feel are truly amazing. Write about the qualities that you like in each of them. Why do you like them? What is unique about them? What makes them special to you?

2. **List Your Peculiarities, Idiosyncrasies and Flaws (PIFS).** This is one of your most essential exercises. Honesty is the key, so detail all that you can think of. When you have run out of ideas, ask your spouse or family to help you add to your list. What do you do that

drives your family or friends nuts? It might be something as simple as you always interrupt, or you always second guess yourself. Maybe you have to have a clean kitchen before starting to cook. These PIFS are so innate in you that you don't even realize you do it.

3. **What Drives You Nuts About Other People?** As above, list as much here as you can think of. You could start your sentences "I dislike it when…"

4. **What Causes Do You Care Most About?** What are the top one or two causes in the world that hurt you or affect you at a deep level? These are the issues where you might feel real pain in your heart when you hear about them. They are the things you want someone to do something about or wish you could do more to resolve.

5. **What Did You Love to Do as a Child?** Think about your childhood ages two to seven. How did you spend your time where you would be lost in the moment and so happy that the day would fly by? If you don't remember your earliest years, ask a family member who might.

6. **Reconnect with the Joys of Your Early Years.** Looking back on your entire life, what were your favorite times, activities, and memories? What filled you up the most or made you the happiest?

7. **What is Your Legacy?** What would you want people to say about you? What do you want to be remembered for?

8. **"Ask Open-Ended Questions."** What energizes you today? What drains you? What industries or jobs excite you when you think about them? What type of work or jobs would you hate doing? What buzzwords energize you? What words depress you? What do you feel your greatest strengths are? What are your weaknesses? What are your top three work-related favorite memories, where you felt excited or energized?

Going Deeper

Tool #23: The Heart Chamber

The Heart Chamber Experience is a life-altering exercise I learned from David Morelli, where you will travel deep within your heart to get answers to your calling. It is a very deep, meditative visualization experience. Start by finding a quiet place, turning off your phone, and settling into a comfortable position. Put on headphones if you have them and start listening to the Heart Chamber interactive recording at www.TheBEINGZone. com/tools.

Journaling Time

THE HEART CHAMBER JOURNALING EXERCISE #58:
Have your notebook or *BEING Journal* ready to take notes in.
 - Once you listen to the recording and are ready, write about what you heard, experienced, felt, and learned during the Heart Chamber visualization. This exercise may provide some real ah-ha's for you.

Tool #24: The Movie Director

The Movie Director Experience is another audio experience. You are the writer, producer, director, and actor in your own life. When you own that, you can begin to transform yourself.

This is a great tool to go through your life to pick up what you want and let go of the rest. Once again, find a quiet place, turn off your phone, and settle into a comfortable position, either sitting or reclined, to go through this interactive visualization exercise. You will find the Movie Director recording at www.TheBEING-Zone.com/tools.

Journaling Time

Movie Director Experience Journaling Exercise #59:
Grab your notebook or *BEING Journal* to make notes in. Once you listen to the recording and are ready, start writing.

- Write about what you heard, experienced, felt, and learned during the Movie Director visualization. This exercise will help you iden-tify issues to release and ideas on where you might be headed.

Tool #25: The Mirror

The Mirror Exercise is a hypnotic-type tool that allows you to reflect on your life and begin to create visually what you want it to be. You will be looking at where you currently exist and transforming it into what you desire. Find a quiet area where you will not be disturbed and visit www.TheBEINGZone.com/tools to get started.

Journaling Time

Pull out your *BEING Journal* or notebook to capture your memories. Once you listen to the recording and are ready, begin to document.

· What did you feel, experience, and learn during the Mirror Exercise visualization? Make notes on what you can change in your life to incorporate your key ah-ha's from this session.

· This exercise will help you identify issues to release as well as provide visuals of what you do want.

How to Process the Homework

Wait until you have completed all your homework to read this section, so it doesn't impact how you answer your questions. It is imperative that you answer them honestly in the moment and not based on the answer you want to get.

Exercise #1 Processing: Who Do You Admire?

You are the sum of all the people you admire most in this world. The reason they resonate with you is that their values align deeply with yours. Take time to highlight the words you wrote about each individual. These words relate to your inner dreams and desires or that are at the essence of who you are. Take these highlighted words and combine them into a paragraph that speaks to your heart. This paragraph will become part of your 5 Step Daily B.E.I.N.G. practice, which is described in the final section of this book. It will help you move toward your true self when you review these daily.

Exercise #2 Processing: Your Peculiarities, Idiosyncrasies, and Flaws (PIFs)

Your PIFS are your greatest natural gifts. By listing the PIFS and finding the benefits, you will find your personal strengths, the part of you that is so inherent in you it couldn't be removed if you tried. Look at the lists you made and group like statements or things together. You can arrange them in bubbles, or you can use a spreadsheet to make a list in columns. When that's done, you will want to create a title for each group that identifies the benefit of those particular PIFS. You will understand the significance of these titles as you continue through this section. If you can't identify the benefits, search the internet: what are the benefits of being messy? You will find it means you are creative at the core.

As an example, a client turned in these PIFs:

- The kitchen has to be clean before I start cooking
- I clean the kitchen while I cook
- I can be opinionated and stubborn
- I love reading and can go on book binges
- I replaced all the plastic straws in the house with paper
- I am health-oriented and eat only natural foods when possible
- I always stock up on items so I have what I need
- I am a dreamer and do not live a conventional life

· I love to exercise and go over the top
· I hate clutter
· When I share an emotional story, my voice cracks—I feel it
· I don't watch TV
· I love to organize and rearrange things
· I get excited about something and am sad if it doesn't happen
· I am honest, loving, and caring

I took all these items submitted and grouped them into like categories. I chose to make several big circles on the page, listing all like things into each of the bubbles. Here are two bubbles with like items from the above list. Once they were all grouped, I titled each bubble with the advantages of all those PIFS.

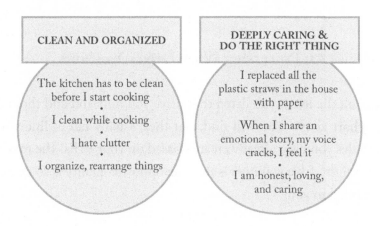

CLEAN AND ORGANIZED	DEEPLY CARING & DO THE RIGHT THING
The kitchen has to be clean before I start cooking · I clean while cooking · I hate clutter · I organize, rearrange things	I replaced all the plastic straws in the house with paper · When I share an emotional story, my voice cracks, I feel it · I am honest, loving, and caring

Another way to process this homework is to create a spreadsheet and put like items into the same column. Then put the proposed Title (the advantages of those PIFS) at the top.

CLEAN & ORGANIZED	DEEPLY CARING & DO THE RIGHT THING	LOVE SELF, OTHERS & EARTH	PASSIONATE DREAMER & DOER
I like to start with a clean kitchen, then I clean while I cook.	I replaced plastic straws in the house with paper.	I am health-oriented and eat only natural foods.	I love reading and will go on book binges.
I always stock up on items, so I have what I need.	When I share a story, my voice cracks.	I love to exercise.	I am a dreamer, and don't have a conventional life.
I hate clutter. I love to organize, rearrange.	I am honest, loving, and caring.	I don't watch TV.	I get over-excited and am sad if doesn't occur.

Exercise #3: Processing What Drives You Nuts

Take all the items you listed that drive you nuts and add them to the chart above. You will find that they usually fall in line with the titles you have already created based on your PIFs. The reason they might drive you nuts is that the opposite quality is so deeply ingrained in you.

Here are the actual items submitted by the same client about what drove her nuts:

· I don't like it when people load the dishwasher with knives up
· Arrogance and condensation
· Inauthentic, lack of integrity
· I despise it when people want to spread their limited beliefs onto me

- People who are not respectful or negative nelly, backstabbing (gossipy) and judgmental
- Passive-aggressive behavior
- When people use dirty sponges over and over again
- People creating drama with mean spirited purposes or control issues
- Anyone who doesn't treat animals or others nicely
- When people don't take care of their bodies
- Dirty & cluttered houses
- When people complain yet don't do anything do change their circumstances—hypocritical

Summary Spreadsheet of What Drives You Nuts

Once again, I grouped like items these into bubbles and into a spreadsheet and labeled them with the right titles.

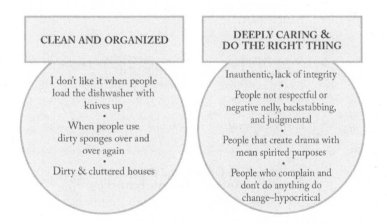

Exercise #4: Processing Your Causes and Passions

Look at the list of issues in the world you identified as really affecting you along with your passions and what energizes you. Look at the titles in the charts above and see if they fit. Most likely they do. In the case of our example, they both clearly fall under loving self, others, and the earth.

CLEAN & ORGANIZED	DEEPLY CARING & DO THE RIGHT THING	LOVE SELF, OTHERS & EARTH	PASSIONATE DREAMER & DOER
I don't like it when people load the dishwasher with knives up.	Inauthentic, lack of integrity.	Arrogance and condescension.	I despise it when people want to spread their limited beliefs onto me.
When people use dirty sponges over and over again.	People who are not respectful or negative nelly, backstabbing (gossipy), and judgmental.	Passive-aggressive behavior.	
Dirty & cluttered houses.	People that create drama with mean spirited purposes or control issues.	Anyone who doesn't treat animals or others nicely.	
	When people complain yet don't do anything do change their circumstances. They are hypocritical.	When people don't take care of their bodies.	

Love Self, Others, and the Earth
Cruelty to Animals, Human Trafficking

In summary, the titles you come up with are the benefits of your PIFS. They may get refined as you add what drives you nuts about others and what causes break your heart, but in general the titles you decide upon by the end of this exercise are your greatest natural strengths, the parts of you that are so inherent they can't be taken away. They are your gifts and the things you are meant to be utilizing and capitalizing on as you work toward your purpose. Now that you know your inherent gifts, take the time to evaluate how you are capitalizing on those today and look for little ways you can build them into your current life as you work toward your purpose.

Journaling Time

YOUR ANSWERS AND FEELINGS FOR PROCESSING
JOURNALING EXERCISE #61:

Get out your *BEING Journal* or notebook to write in.

· When you read back through all your journaling, notice when your words or descriptions cause an emotional or physical reaction in your body or heart. There will be some things that, when you re-read them, make your heart sing, or you may feel a deep sadness, or you may feel irritated or angry. Highlight these and note your reaction.

· Think about how they might tie into the chart you created above. Color code your reactions by what fills you up or makes you happy (yellow highlight) and what drags you down (blue highlight). These are important to know as you move forward in life.

· Use the tools learned in Chapter 3 to continue clearing or *SHIFT-ING* what drags you down. Group like things together from your highlighted list and decide what tools might work best to clear these issues. Make notes on what tools you used and how effective it was for you.

· Write down all the items that fill you up will need to be considered as we identify your True North.

More Than Halfway There

Hopefully, the work you have done so far has taken you to a place where you have more clarity on who you are and what your deepest values are and how you might be able to make a difference in this world. The goal is for you to do this work by listening to your heart.

When you take on roles that you don't feel connected to, your internal flame is dampened and often extinguished. When you do not have passion for what you are doing in life, and you don't have that excitement for what life is about, you will start to move into a place of feeling despair, disconnection or depression. But when you are passionate about what you are doing, you will feel more connected to life itself and regain a sense of hope that fuels your creative potential and your heart.

You've gone deep within to increase your clarity and your passion utilizing the Heart Chamber, Movie Director, and Mirror exercises. They helped you tap into your subconscious in a more profound way. The next few exercises will take what you learned and journaled about during your deeper meditations and apply it to your current vision of who you are and where you are going. You will begin to see how what you heard in those deep meditations applies to the big picture. By reviewing your notes along with your current homework, you will begin to see correlations. The Heart Chamber, Movie Director, and Mirror Exercises you listened to at www.TheBEINGZone.com/tools are powerful exercises to get you into a deeper place with your true self.

Journaling Time

PROCESSING THE GOING DEEP JOURNALING EXERCISES #62:

Grab your *BEING Journal* or notebook to review your notes from Journaling Exercise #58-60. These deep explorations from the recordings you listened to and journaled about will shed more light on what you need to clear or where you need to go. You listened to and journaled for the following three recordings: Heart Chamber Exercise, Movie Director Exercise, and the Mirror Exercise.

· As you listened and journaled, you may have received messages from dreams if you can remember them or received downloads when in meditation.

· Take time to go back through all your notes that you wrote and see how it applies to the bigger picture.

· Highlight or note the most important ah-ha's.

· Make a few notes on things you want to address in your life.

Time to Dream

We can think, walk, and talk, but we also have a responsibility to dream. As you went through the deep exercises, hopefully you allowed yourself to dream of the life you want to live and the world you want to see, where we can all live in peace and harmony. The intent was to awaken yourself to the pieces of yourself that have led you to where you are, and tune into what you want to change.

Don't close the doors when overwhelming issues of life hit you; instead, wake up, learn from them and move toward the bigger picture. Tune into your heart to access the great wisdom within you that will lead you on the right path. It is the time to reconnect to your truth and live by your authentic values.

When you are in a meditative state or during your daily practice, you are going to continue to get messages and ideas. Keep a log of them as they are clear messages and ideas that are meant to guide you in life. I get a handful of these daily when I go out on my deck in the early hours of the morning and connect with the Universe. I feel connected and ask questions and get answers. The answers I get lead me through my daily activities and have been extremely useful in helping me write this book in a way that will connect with you.

Things happen all day long, and when I am operating in my *BEING Zone*, I am more likely to notice because I am present and mindful. When I tune in and listen to those stirrings deep inside me, I can be consciously aware of things that are meant to jump out at me and guide me. The same thing can be true for you. If you listen to your heart, follow your intuition, and pay attention to the synchronicities and the things that show up unexpectedly, you will find that they are there for a reason. Being intuitive is about noticing things, listening, and following hunches. It is a deep knowing that can't be ignored. These messages always lead me to something greater and amazing opportunities, and they can for you too.

Client Story: Stay-at-home mom Jeanette loved cooking healthy meals and ensuring her family valued exercise and self-care. Her children were getting self-sufficient because of this, and she was ready to step out and do more in life.

Her passions centered around health—from what we eat to how we exercise. Her friends and acquaintances were always asking her for advice for their workouts or getting recipes from her. She decided to launch her 85-15 Lifestyle Coaching company, which has skyrocketed in growth from day one. She started by putting on workshops about creating healthy eating habits. She quickly expanded into coaching others in life, exercise, and diet to help them become happier, healthier, and fit. She is flourishing in life because she is doing exactly what she is meant to be doing. It fills her up and makes a difference in the lives of others.

Be a Light

Some of you might know how it feels to be in the presence of a person who lights up the room with love, who makes you feel accepted and embraced for just being who you are. I have found that many of my clients want to be that kind of light in this world and feel like they are making a real difference for the greater good. Are you one of them? Do you have an inner desire to be just like the enlightened spiritual guides, leaders, or everyday people who make you feel good inside just by *BEING* who they are?

I believe everyone is capable of learning how to exist in the place where they can radiate their own light and make others feel amazing. When you complete the excavation of your life, unearth your gold nuggets, and begin to integrate your passions and unique gifts into your life, you too will begin to shine from the inside out. You will know when you get to this state as you will wake up happy every day and put out good vibes based on how amazing you feel. It is a place where you feel uplifted and inspired, and people will feel your positive energy. You will then begin to see the world around you reflecting your own inner state of consciousness.

You already have this gift of inner light within you; you just need to learn to access it. Once you figure out who you are at your core, what you are meant to do and build it into your life while simultaneously existing in *The BEING Zone*, you will shine from the inside out! Instead of staying focused on *DOING*, you will *BE* present and able to hear your heart's desires and do what "feels" right moving forward. When you operate in this enlightened state, you will find that things around you change through your presence. You will naturally become a positive force and part of the change that is meant to happen in our world. Shine your light as you step into life you dreamed of.

Key Messages

- Trusting your instincts and intuition enables you to create the life you dream of.
- Whether you realize it or not, you are always being guided; you just need to learn to listen to your body and, most importantly, your heart.
- You can capitalize on the gifts and challenges that are there to guide you.
- Your natural traits are your greatest strengths!
- You are fascinated or attracted to certain things for a reason.
- When you identify your purpose in life, it will serve as the compass for your life.
- You can shine your light!

This Chapter's Gifts: Using the tools in this chapter, you can identify your natural attributes and passions so you can clarify your True North, also known as life's purpose, and begin to shine your light.

PART III

Connecting
With Source

CHAPTER 7

We Are Energetic Beings

"The energy of the mind is the essence of life".
—Aristotle

I N CHAPTER 6, you became an excavator and arche-
ologist of your own life. In this chapter you will begin
to learn about energy tools that will help you confirm what you
already know, allowing you to move forward with purpose. You
will learn to awaken to your energy and expand your potential.

The idea that the world, including your body, is made up of
matter is an illusion. As mystics and practitioners of Eastern and
Indigenous medicine have always known, and quantum physicists discovered in the 20th century, everything is energy! You
are an energetic being connected to the quantum "Field," aka the
energy of the Universe. When you learn to tune into the Univer-

sal and Earth energy, you can bring good energy to yourself and feel immediately better. And when you understand energy, you can learn to recognize and remove stuck energy, which, invisible as it is, blocks you as surely as a reinforced wall.

What Is Energy?

Energy exists in many different forms. Examples are light energy, heat energy, electrical energy, earth energy, and so on. Even humans have energy. You might hear a family member or friend say, "I have amazing energy." This might mean they have slept well, are well-nourished, and are energized to take on the day. When you hear someone say, "I have no energy," it may mean their body is fatigued and they have an overall feeling of tiredness as a result of doing too much or too little and not taking care of themselves.

When we are young and full of energy, we can keep on going. When we get older, we start to slow down. We have less energy as we get more oxidized or possibly more out of balance, and we begin to feel more depleted. I am a firm believer that we all have energy within our body, and we can increase that energy by our lifestyle choices and practices.

There are many ancient practices are based on this concept of energy within us including yoga, acupuncture, Tai Chi, and Qigong among other—all of which I utilize. These practices have been around for thousands of years. As you read earlier in the book, the first time I ever did yoga, I felt energy in my body. Since that time, I have been very aware when the energy in my body is good and when it's not.

Leonard A. Wisneski and Lucy Anderson wrote the book, *The Scientific Basis of Integrative Medicine*, which bridges the gap between scientific Western medicine and energy-based Eastern medicine.[89] They provide the science behind the mind-body connection and energy healing. The book explains that you have energy within your body systems, and there are many other leaders in energy medicine that speak to this phenomenon in a variety of ways, as you will see below.

What the Experts Say

What we are talking about here is energy and energy waves. Bruce Lipton, a best-selling author, scientist, and biologist, explains in his book, *The Biology of Belief*, that we are energy beings and communicate with energy.[90] He goes on to say that each person has approximately 50 trillion cells in our body, and these cells are living entities. Every cell has a negative voltage on the inside and positive voltage on the outside, making them each a tiny battery that has about .07 volts, according to scientific sources. When you multiply 50 trillion cells x .07V = you have between 3.5 trillion volts of electricity in your body. Others can feel your energy, and that impacts how they respond to you.

In simple terms, you have a field of energy in you and all around you, with moving electrons which make up energy waves. Lipton goes on to explain that the energy waves between humans, animals, and plants communicate with vibration. Vibration is measured in Hz, which is a frequency.

Everything has a frequency. Bruce Tainio, of Taino Technology and Professor at Eastern Washington University, built a frequency monitor and discovered that the body resonates frequency between 62 to 72 MHz when happy and healthy. If your body vibration drops to 57-60 MHz, you are more susceptible to colds and flu and severe diseases like cancer.[91]

What I know from my own personal experiences and the experiences of my clients is the more we are aware of this vibrational energy and follow or create good energy, the more productive, happier, and healthier we are.

In his book, *Breaking the Habit of Being Yourself*, best-selling author Joe Dispenza also teaches that all energy has a frequency.[92] He agrees with Taino that disease shows up when you are vibrating at a lower frequency, which is also a sign that you have negative thoughts or feelings. The way to think about it, according to Dispenza, is that your thoughts, feelings, and emotions all have different weights to them. When you have positive thoughts, feelings, or emotions, you will feel lighter. When you have negative thoughts or experiences, you will feel heavier. Your energy changes as a result of how you feel. Joe is using the knowledge he has gained about frequency to help people evolve their consciousness and heal themselves of illnesses including even terminal diseases.

In his book *Vibrational Medicine*, Dr. Richard Gerber includes references to clinical research showing that our thinking patterns have a profound effect on our body's vibratory field.[93] Quite literally, "energy flows where thought goes."

You can become aware of how the energy in your body changes based on how you are thinking. When you learn to tune into your thoughts and your energy, and move it from negative to positive, you experience better health.

Feeling Energy

The first step is to realize you and everything around you is energy; the second step is to tune into your body so you can actively feel your own personal energy and then see if you can notice or feel the energy around you. When I teach workshops, I use dowsing rods to demonstrate the power of personal energy. Dowsing rods react to the energy in a person just like they respond to water or metal in an area, which is how they have been used for centuries, dating back to 400 BC. Before we start the demonstration, some of the people in the group believe in dowsing rods and some don't. By the time we're done, everyone is amazed. Some of them still think I cause the rods to react to good and bad energy, so I allow participants to try it, and they get the same results.

Dowsing rods literally read the energy of a person in the room, picking up on what we cannot see with our eyes. A person displaying anger will cause a different response in the rods than a person full of joy. The impact the different types of energy can have on an entire room is shocking, especially when people get up and try it themselves.

You will successfully connect with good energy when you are living in *The BEING Zone*. You will also learn ways to bring in good energy to reboot yourself. Surrounding yourself with people, things, and circumstances that fill you up will increase your energy and keep you vibrating at a healthy level. Below you will find several simple techniques to make feeling energy easier if you have never consciously felt it before.

Tool #26: Rub Hands Together

This is a simple one that all of us can feel easily. When you rub the palms of your hands together rapidly, you feel the friction and warmth increasing. You may not realize it, but that is energy.

Journaling Time

RUBBING HANDS TOGETHER JOURNALING EXERCISE #63:

Pull out your notebook or *BEING Journal* to make notes in.

· What did you feel on this exercise? Describe the sensations.

Tool #27: Tai Chi Ball

Hold your hands up like you are holding a small invisible basketball. Very slowly bring your hands toward each other and back again (without touching). Repeat until you feel a warmth or tingling between the two hands. This energy can be very subtle.

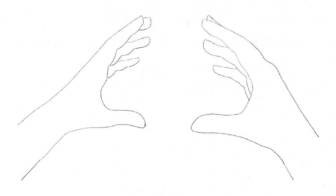

Journaling Time

TAI CHI BALL JOURNALING EXERCISE #64:

Take out your notebook or *BEING Journal* to make notes in.

· What did you feel between your hands? Describe the sensations.

· Was is stronger or weaker than what it felt like when you rubbed
  your hands together?

Tool #28: Stand On the Earth

Close your eyes and visualize for a moment the power of
the earth. Stand on grass, soil, or sand in your bare feet. Feel the
earth's energy pushing up into the bottom of your bare feet. Feel
your feet begin to tingle and/or warm from that energy flowing
into them. You can allow that energy to move beyond your feet
into your calves, up into your thighs. Allow it to move past your
hips into your core and all the way up to your neck and head.

Most people are able to feel this right away, others take longer—be patient. Just take a few minutes to try and feel this powerful energy flowing through your body. If you can't feel it, imagine it flowing through your body, and eventually you will feel it. You will learn more about Earthing/Grounding later in this chapter.

Stand on Earth Journaling Exercise #65:

Bring out your notebook or *BEING Journal* to make notes in.

· Could you feel anything? Describe your experience.

· If you felt something, describe the sensations you felt through the bottom of your feet.

Tool #29: Lean Against a Tree

Most of my clients are amazed when they do this exercise. A tree is a living, vital thing. When you sit under a tree, you breathe in the fresh oxygen it releases. When you lean against the tree and tune in, you can feel a vibration running up your back.

As the energy inside the tree vibrates, the tree's healing energy helps you feel more calm, secure, stable, and at peace.

Journaling Time

LEAN AGAINST A TREE JOURNALING EXERCISE #66:
Pull out your *BEING Journal* or notebook to write in.

· Could you feel anything?
· If so, what did you feel? How would you describe it?

In this chapter, you will learn more about negative energy, including how to eliminate, remove, or block lousy energy so it doesn't drain you or drag you down. Understanding what to avoid—whether it's a cluttered room, a negative person, a bad situation, or how someone is treating you or talking to you—is critical.

Feeling Negative Energy

Let's start with understanding negative or draining energy. Have you ever walked into a room and intuitively known that something didn't feel right? Or have you interacted with someone who makes you feel small or tense without them even saying a word? It might be a look or their stance that causes your physical or emotional reaction. When there is negative energy in people around you, you might feel a sense of being judged, demeaned, constricted, or attacked. You intuitively feel unsafe or on guard. It feels heavy or draining in your body and you can feel the off-putting vibes.

An example of this might be a person whose negative or aggressive comments make everyone else feel defensive or protective. They complain, or blame, or accuse. These people give off negative energy as a quality of their being. This can poison everyone's energy around them. Think about a time when someone yelled at you and how it felt to you. You may have felt the blood drain from your face, or your heart sink, or felt your body tense up with fear. You might have even begun to feel physically ill. You might start to feel that again, just thinking about the past event.

This is also a time in history where we are seeing the convergence of science and spirituality, especially when it comes to energy. As you will learn in this chapter, just spending time connecting with the earth's surface can calm your system and heal your body. When you don't have the ability to connect with the earth's natural healing energy, you can feel depleted. We are energetically drained by working too much and living in cement and steel buildings. Dealing with the dysfunction and craziness that seems to fill the world today can drain your energy. Watching negative news, witnessing violence on TV shows, movies, video streaming, and other programming brings your energy down and impacts your psychological well-being.

According to the author of the *Anxiety Epidemic* and a professor of psychology at the University of Sussex, Graham C. L.

Davey, PhD, we have known for a long time that the emotional content of films and television programs can affect psychological health.[94] It can do this by directly affecting your mood, and your mood can then affect many aspects of your thinking and behavior. Dr. Davey indicates that people who had watched negative news spent more time thinking and talking about their worry and tended to catastrophize their fears. Catastrophizing is when you think about a worry so persistently that you begin to make it seem much worse than it is in reality—basically making a mountain out of a molehill.

In her book, *Mind Over Medicine*, Dr. Lissa Rankin shows how thoughts, feelings, and beliefs can alter the body's physiology.[95] She lays out the scientific data proving that loneliness, pessimism, depression, fear, and anxiety damage the body, while intimate relationships, gratitude, meditation, sex, and authentic self-expression flip on the body's self-healing processes. These activities will increase your energy. You will soon learn about the Vase tool that can be used to make you more aware of good and bad energy.

Journaling Time

**DESCRIBE TIMES YOU FELT NEGATIVE
ENERGY JOURNALING EXERCISE #67:**

Pull out your *BEING Journal* or notebook to write in.

- List all the situations you can think of where you felt bad energy.
- What did bad energy feel like to you? How would you describe it?

- Explain some of the situations you were in where you felt bad energy.
- How did each of those situations make you feel? Physically? Mentally? Emotionally?

Is Your Life What You Thought It Would Be?

Are there things in your life you would like to change, but don't feel you have that much control? Do you feel stuck or unhappy? Do you feel like people don't understand you or connect with you? Do you tend to rub people wrong or cause conflict? Most likely, it is because you are living a life based on what you "think" you should be or do and not based on your intuitive "feelings" or "knowing." You might be giving off bad vibes and people are reacting to that. You can change that! When your energy is tuned into your feelings and inner knowing, you'll be working with your own energy, and that is the first step toward creating good energy within you.

Your Body is Like a Vase

I learned in the Enwaken Coaches training that when you do things you love, like surrounding yourself with people you like or putting yourself into a place you love, your vase (your body) fills to brim and overflows with love. You will feel the vibration in your body as a result of visualizing yourself full of this energy and love. Know that when you are disorganized or around people or things that drain you, it is like putting holes in your vase and all your good energy will drain right out. When you witness violence or watch negative news or spend time with negative people, it drains your energy. Your goal is to identify what fills your vase and do more of that.

Tool #30: Fill Your Vase

Close your eyes and visualize yourself as a vase. Notice how full your vase is and visualize the things in your life that are filling up your vase. Now look at the bottom of your vase and notice if there are any holes, cracks or drains. Now visualize who or what is causing those cracks or holes to appear. Make a conscious choice to avoid those people who drain you. Now visualize patching up all those holes and see yourself hanging out with people who fill up your vase and see your vase filling and even overflowing with love.

Journaling Time

FILL YOUR VASE JOURNALING EXERCISE #68:

Take out your notebook or *BEING Journal* to make notes in.

· Identify anything or anyone that you want to begin to close out of your life or build boundaries with. Make conscious decisions to start the process.

· Identify everything that fills you up and make plans to bring more of that into your life.

· Make notes on the difference you feel in your life as a result of beginning to make these changes.

Client Story: Using the tools in this chapter and Chapter 3, Alexa, a 36-year-old professional in the banking industry, did a lot of energy-based work, releasing a painful and abusive history. She began to build energy-enhancing tools into her life and has just taken the leap of faith to move toward becoming a full-time energy healer. She is now the epitome of what we all strive for, radiating good energy ("vibes") every day as she does energy work on others to help them transform their lives.

What Can You Change?

· **Turn It Off:** We've talked already about how the evening news is typically negative and energetically draining. "If it bleeds, it leads," but watching violence, hearing about war, killing, and conflict is stressful on our psyches. For the same reason, watching intense movies or playing violent video games also decreases your energy. Even negative politics can leave you zapped or binge-watching shows can drain you.

· **Clean It Up:** A house that is extremely messy and cluttered, or one that doesn't feel safe, can also be draining. Feng Shui explains that an untidy home blocks the energy in the home from flowing so it can weigh you down. It might be time to organize it and keep it up.

· **Stand up for Yourself:** If you are treated poorly by your spouse, your family, or your boss, you will feel defensive or depleted every time you are around them. When you live in this type of energy for long periods, it restricts your flow, and it will begin to manifest in your body as inflammation. Stand up for yourself, change your circumstances or avoid these people when you can.

Journaling Time

WHAT CAN YOU CHANGE JOURNALING EXERCISE #69:
Take out your notebook or *BEING Journal* to make notes in. Take a few minutes to list things in your life that drain you of your good energy, so you are ready to respond to them when they show up. Awareness is a big part of the healing process.

· Write about people or situations that make you feel bad. Make commitments to change what you can.
· Write about people who fill you up and you like to be around. Make decisions to spend more time with them.

· Make notes on places in your life where you feel stuck or unhappy. What can you clean up or change?

· List areas in your life where you can start standing up for yourself.

· Take a look at each item on the list and think about how you can turn it around. Make notes on what you feel you can commit to.

Removing or Deflecting Bad Energy

There are many ways to keep bad energy from impacting you. The most important part is recognizing negative or harmful energy by tuning into how your body feels and reacts, so you can do something about it. For example, when I start my day in good energy and am happy and flowing, and all of a sudden, I feel heavy or weighed down, I look around me to determine what is causing that feeling. It might be someone near me who has very heavy or negative energy, and I can feel it strongly. I must take the time to clear it and block them.

There are a few different ways to clear away and block bad energy. Some are methods that you most likely already use. Have you ever heard someone say, "I have to take a walk to clear my head"? If you've ever felt that way, you might recognize your head was filled with thoughts or stress that you needed to release or work through. Later in this chapter, you will learn the power of movement in ridding yourself of negative energy. Walking refocuses your attention on something other than what was causing heaviness in your body.

Other techniques discussed throughout the book include breathing techniques and use of essential oils that will also help clear negative energy. Below you will find a few new energy tools to try that will also clear or block negative energy. energy. I thank David Morelli for teaching me powerful energy tools including the Vase, the Magnet in the Bubble, the Waterfall, the Golden Vacuum, Cutting Energetic Cords, and Root, Release and Receive. The value of these tools shows why it is so important to find good teachers and sources for personal growth.

Tool #31: Smudging

Smudging is an Indigenous tradition. In ceremonies, sacred plants were burned as a powerful spiritual cleansing technique where they called upon the spirits of the sacred plants to drive away negative energy and to restore balance to an individual, a group, a space, or all three. Typically, dried sage or palo santo is used. Both can be purchased online loose or in bundles used for smudging.

In 2006, a scientific paper called *Medicinal Smokes* was published. The research reviewed information from 50 countries over 5 continents and found that, dating back to ancient times, smoke administered medicinally is typically used to aid lung, brain, and skin functions.[96] Research shows the smoke from a variety of herbs is highly effective in reducing airborne bacteria for up to 24 hours. Many of the pathogenic bacteria had not returned to the same room even after 30 days. It was the combination of the smoke from the medicinal sacred plants and the mantras or sounds made in this process that helped clear negative energy from participants and the place.

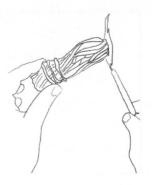

Journaling Time

Smudging Journaling Exercise #70:

Pull out your *BEING Journal* or notebook and start writing.

- Have you done smudging before? Or did you try smudging for the first time after reading this section?
- Did you like the smell? Did you like the experience? Did you feel any different?
- Describe any observations or feelings you had during or after smudging.

Tool #32: Magnet in the Bubble

If you are experiencing tightness or tension in your head, jaw, neck, or shoulders, try this tool to pull that heavy energy out. Visualize a bubble (like the type a child would blow) floating above your head. This bubble has a magnet in it, the most powerful magnet in the world. Visualize the magnet pulling out of you all the stress, worry, anxiety, tension, tightness, and pain. The bubble will get bigger and bigger and darker and darker but will keep floating above your head. Keep visualizing all the dark, heavy energy getting pulled out of you until you feel lighter. Then reach up, visualizing touching that bubble, and watch it float up into the Universe and dissipate. Then take a deep breath and relax. You can find a recording of Magnet in the Bubble tool at www.The-BEINGZone.com/tools.

Journaling Time

MAGNET IN THE BUBBLE JOURNALING EXERCISE #71:
Grab out your notebook or *BEING Journal* to make notes in.

- How did this Magnet in the Bubble tool work for you? Most people feel instant relief. If that was not the case, try again.
- If you did feel lighter, describe how you felt.
- Write about your plan to utilize this tool in your life.

Tool #33: Waterfall

When you stand in the shower with the water running over your head and down your body, close your eyes and visualize that a waterfall is cleansing and cleaning and rinsing away all the toxins and negative energy from your body. If you live in area with warm waterfalls, use the real thing—that is even better.

Journaling Time

WATERFALL JOURNALING EXERCISE #72:

Pull out your notebook or *BEING Journal* to make notes in.

- Did you like this Waterfall tool? Did you feel lighter?
- If you did feel lighter, describe how you felt.
- Write about your plan to utilize this tool in your life.

Tool #34: Golden Vacuum

If your whole body feels exhausted, or you are sick or have pain in your body, visualize a Golden Vacuum sitting next to you. It is the most powerful vacuum in the world. At the end of the hose is a life-sized suction cup that you can put over your head and around your entire body. The other end of the hose leads to the center of the earth where all of the heavy energy burns up in the core. Turn on the vacuum and feel it begin to pull out anything and everything that doesn't serve you. Feel the heaviness, tiredness, and illness getting suctioned right out of you. It just keeps getting pulled out and pulled out until you feel light. When you turn off the vacuum, you should feel lighter. You can find a recording of Golden Vacuum tool at www.TheBEINGZone.com/tools.

Journaling Time

GOLDEN VACUUM JOURNALING EXERCISE #73:

Get out your notebook or *BEING Journal* to make notes in.

· Did you feel lighter from this exercise? If that was not the case, try again.

· If you did feel lighter, describe how you felt.

· Write about your plan to utilize this tool in your life.

Tool #35: Cutting Energetic Cords

Many of us do not realize that people who are around us or interact with us each day can become connected to us energetically. It is called cords of attachment and is an invisible, energetic connection that exchanges emotional energy between the bodies of two or more beings. When the cords attach to us, the other person has the power to decrease our energy. You can undo this by going through a cord release process every day. Say the words, "I release the emotional attachment to all those who connected to my energy today" until you feel the attachments release. You can also visualize using a sword or light saber to cut all the cords. Visualize them dropping to the ground. You can find a recording of Cutting Energetic Cords Tool at www.TheBEINGZone.com/tools.

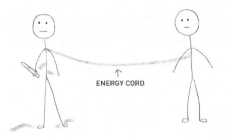

ENERGY CORD

Journaling Time

CUTTING ENERGETIC CORDS JOURNALING EXERCISE #74:

Pull out your notebook or *BEING Journal* to make notes in.

· Could you visualize and see the cords dropping? If not, try again.

· If you did, describe how you felt.

· Write about your plan to utilize this tool in your life

You Can Feel Negative Energy from Afar

When you feel negative energy, it might not be something or someone in the room with you. You need to be aware that this energy can impact you from a distance. For example, when I jump on a coaching call with a client who is stressed or overwhelmed, my head, neck, or shoulders will start to hurt. I will stop and do the Magnet in the Bubble exercise with them, releasing their pain and what I am feeling. They are always amazed that I can feel it, that I am picking up their energy. I explain to them that we can all feel energy, even if we are not entirely aware of it. Our bodies feel it intuitively and react accordingly. The more practice you have getting in touch with yourself and feeling good, the more you'll notice when someone's energy is affecting you or when your own energy is off.

Tools for Protection

Tool #36: White Light of Protection

The White Light of Protection is like a force field that cannot be penetrated—like the Force in *Star Wars*. The White Light boundary will protect your energy from negativity around you. Close your eyes and visualize a bright white light above you and see the rays coming down around you from the Universe and providing a protective barrier. The White Light can be called upon by anyone for assistance, healing, and protection from negative energies or wonky vibrations. You can find a recording of the White Light of Protection tool at www.TheBEINGZone.com/tools.

Journaling Time

WHITE LIGHT OF PROTECTION JOURNALING EXERCISE #75:
Find your *BEING Journal* or notebook to write in.

- Could you visualize this light? Did you feel a difference?
- Describe how you felt.
- Write about your plan to utilize this tool in your life.

Tool #37: Mirror Shielding

For this Mirror Shielding Technique, close your eyes and visualize your body surrounded by mirrors facing outwards. It is like a wall of mirrors around you, above and below you, encasing your body like a cocoon. The mirrors work as a way to deflect any negativity that is directed at you by reflecting it away from you and back at the initiator. Visualize others energy being deflected off the mirrors and moving back at them. There is a recording of the Mirror Shielding at www.TheBEINGZone.com/tools.

Journaling Time

MIRROR SHIELDING JOURNALING EXERCISE #76:
Take out your notebook or *BEING Journal* and make notes.

- Could you visualize the mirrors? Did it work for you?
- Describe how you felt.
- Write about your plan to utilize this tool in your life.

Tool #38: Fortress or Wall Protection

The key is visualizing protection around you that cannot be penetrated. Close your eyes and visually create in your mind's eye a large wall surrounding you (it can be brick, cement, metal, or whatever comes to mind). It can also surround your room, your house, your car, etc. In your visualization, see the wall as strong and sealed and have inner confidence that it cannot be breached. Visualize this wall protecting you from all bad energy that is around you. There is a recording of the Fortress or Wall Protection at www.TheBEINGZone.com/tools.

Journaling Time

FORTRESS OR WALL PROTECTION JOURNALING EXERCISE #77:
Pull out your *BEING Journal* or notebook to write in.
- Could you visualize the barrier? Did you feel protected?
- Describe how you felt.
- Write about your plan to utilize this tool in your life.

The easiest method is to stay away from draining places and people, so you don't have to spend as much time clearing or blocking. Sometimes it is unavoidable. I was speaking at a Mind-Body-Spirit event, and someone walked in the room with horrible energy. It felt like a weight on my neck and shoulders, crushing me, and my head started pounding. I immediately left the room, used the Magnet in the Bubble to clear that energy, rebooted my energy, then I protected myself with the White Light of Protection and came back in, and that individual with the heavy energy no longer impacted me.

Energy Building Tools

Now that you know how to eliminate and block bad energy, it is time to learn how to recognize and increase good energy.

Tool #39: Root, Release, & Receive

This multipurpose tool is powerful. First, stop and do your Three-Part Breathing to center. Then visualize you have a cord, a rope, or a flexible hose that is tied around your hips, so it is secure. Visualize the other end of that cord flowing down into the earth and rooting or anchoring into the crystallization in the Earth's core, connecting you to the earth to ground you.[97] When you are grounded and secure, visualize anything and everything that doesn't serve you flowing or draining down that cord, into the earth where it will dissipate. You can use this tool all day long to release heaviness, negativity, and bad energy.

Now visualize golden light flowing into you from the Universe, filling you up with positive energy to replace everything you have just released. It will also cleanse and strengthen your cord, rope, or hose, keeping it open and clear. It is a vibrational energy that makes you feel good inside. Feel this happy golden energy filling your heart and soul.

Journaling Time

Root, Release, & Receive Journaling Exercise #78:

Grab your *BEING Journal* or notebook and start writing.

- Write about how it feels to be rooted or connected to the earth.
- Note how it feels to be able to release or drain all the negative, heavy energy.
- Write about how it feels to fill up with golden, vibrating Universal energy.
- Write about how you will build this process into your life.

Tool #40: Earthing/Grounding

Let's learn more about Earthing, also called Grounding. The Earth's surface is negatively charged, full of free electrons willing and waiting for us. The Earth is meant to be a docking station for us, a port we can plug into to receive a head-to-toe, inside and outside neutralization of inflammation. There is a great documentary called The Earthing Movie that explains the science behind this concept.[98] Within the documentary you will see that experts from both the science and medical world tell us how powerful it is to spend time connecting with the energy of Earth. The Earth is full of natural energy, which is why all the trees, plants, oceans, etc. thrive. That energy can lower our blood pressure and heal our minds, bodies, and souls.

Take a minimum of one minute up to hours to sit on our Earth, and it will reboot your energy and your health. It is your own personal healing resource or battery if you learn how to use it.

Options for Earthing

· **Earthing simply means putting your bare skin on the earth and allowing the energy to flow up into your body.** You might stand, sit, or lay on the beach or in your yard, watching the clouds drift by. The important part is to have some part of your body touch the earth so you can soak in the powerful energy. The energy will flow through light clothing. I recommend being barefoot when possible.

· **You might lean against a live tree.** You will be able to feel the energy flow up your back. Most people laugh when I tell them this, then they go try it and are amazed that they can actually feel it. Go try it today.

- **Put your hands in the soil while gardening.** Your hands in the dirt without plastic gloves is powerful also. Plants are a source of good energy.

Earthing has the potential of awakening you to the beauty and magnificence of your true nature, as well as the beauty of our planet itself. If you visualize for a moment your current life, how often do you notice the beauty of the earth surrounding you? I know when I was working full-time in corporate America, I rarely took time to notice my surroundings. How about you? Are you like most busy people, where you might drive through your day just thinking about what needs to get done? You might live in a cement world where you move from building to car and back home without ever connecting with nature. If this is the case, you most likely don't have time or the wherewithal to stop and smells the roses. You probably rarely touch the Earth's surface or connect with it at all. When you choose to become aware of your surroundings and begin appreciating the natural beauty, it can change your mood and energy almost immediately. Why do you think so many people plan vacations where they can rest and relax or connect with nature? It might be on a tropical beach or hiking in the mountains. They do this because it rejuvenates their spirit, re-energizes their body, and heals their soul.

Instead of existing in the past (reminiscing about what you should have done or said) or living in the future (thinking about what you have to remember to do tomorrow), take the time to be completely present where you are right now. If you decide to enjoy your drive home and forgive all the other crazy drivers on the road with you, you can have a whole different experience.

There are some excellent studies and information on how helpful Earthing is to your health, including lowering your blood pressure or decreasing your hypertension. Integrative cardiologist Howard Elkin, MD, who practices in Whittier and Santa Monica, California, conducted a small study of 10 patients with hypertension.[99] The objective was to test the validity of such reports by measuring blood pressure among grounded hypertensive patients over time. Multiple measurements over several months while they were grounded resulted in significant improvement of blood pressure. Subjectively, they reported better sleep, more calmness, and fewer aches and pains. Some Japanese companies have a requirement that their employees go forest bathing, which simply means spending time on a wooded trail that they have built into their cement city. Young workers were dropping dead because of stress, and they found forest bathing helped them calm and lowered their stress. I earth daily. Sometimes it is for a few minutes and sometimes hours. Don't wait for a vacation. Make this a daily habit; you will begin to feel alive and vibrant! Your energy will increase, and your health will improve. There are excellent resources regarding Grounding from Dr. Josh Axe[100] and Dr. Laura Koniver.[101]

Journaling Time

EARTHING/GROUNDING JOURNALING EXERCISE #79:

Get out your *BEING Journal* or notebook and write your responses to the following questions:

- Have you ever felt the life force of the ground vibrating through your body, making you feel part of the greater whole?
- Where in nature do you feel alive? Which of the following are you more drawn to: oceans, rivers, desert, forest, mountains, or where

else? Each of these natural terrains brings something to the individual seeking connection, seeking calm, seeking health.

· Think about all of the natural places you love to be at and write about which one is your favorite and why.

· Go outside and sit in the grass or on the beach and take time to tune in with your senses. What does it feel like? What does it look like? What does it smell like? What do you hear? What do you see? How do you feel?

· Write about how you will build Grounding into your daily life.

Client Story: Susie was so stressed out that she felt disconnected and couldn't feel sadness or happiness inside of her. No matter what she tried, she couldn't connect. I tried to help her visualize bringing in energy, and she just felt empty. Finally, I asked her to take off her shoes and walk outside and stand in her grass. She gasped when she got there, indicating she could feel the Earth's energy in her feet.

Tool #41: Connect with Universal Energy

Connecting with Universal Energy is a powerful way to bring positive energy. Some people visualize golden energy coming in from Source. As I've said before, I go outside every morning from spring through the fall to watch the moon set and the stars melt away as the sun begins to rise. I sit on my deck (all bundled up in the colder months), and I can feel myself filling up with this universal energy. Sometimes I am out there for 10-15 minutes, and sometimes hours fly by as I get downloads from Source that I told you about, and those fill me up inside. The fantastic thing that I now realize is I have always had this ability, and you have it also. When you quiet yourself, connect with the moon and stars, and ask for guidance, you will be amazed at what might show up for you.

Journaling Time

CONNECT WITH UNIVERSAL ENERGY JOURNALING EXERCISE #80:
Pull out your notebook or *BEING Journal* to make notes in.

· Take the time to go outside and connect with the moon, stars, and constellations.

· Journal on how it feels and what you experienced. Keep practicing until you know without a doubt that you are experiencing the energy from this activity.

· Write about your experience and how you will utilize this tool moving forward.

Tool #42: Spending Time Doing What You Love

When you spend time doing things that you love and make you happy, which you will explore more in Chapter 9, it decreases your stress and increases your positive energy.

Pay attention to how it feels in your body when you are doing different activities. If time flies by and you aren't even aware of it, that is a good sign that what you're doing is an energy-boosting activity for you. If you have to force yourself to finish something and it feels almost painful, then not so much. For instance, my husband loves to play music or go fishing. His stress lowers, and he is in his happy place. Whatever you choose to do, take time to notice and be mesmerized by the calm you feel when you are in your happy place.

Tool #43: Spend Time with People You Like

When someone has good energy, their good vibrations will attract us, similar to the way that we enjoy upbeat music because of how we feel when we listen to it. The good energy picks us up and increases the good vibrations within our bodies. When we were babies, we naturally read the energy or vibrations of others. If it felt good, we would willingly go into a stranger's arms. If their energy was heavy or the person was uncomfortable with babies, we might start crying as we "felt" their fear or angst. It was an intuitive knowing of good and bad energy.

Have you ever been drawn to someone because they make you feel fabulous, so you want to be around them? They are fun, or they make you laugh, or you feel good when you are with them. You can feel their goodness. You want to spend time with them. Pay attention to their life and activities and events. If they are filling you up, schedule them into your day. Just being in their presence will increase your serotine, also known as your good endorphins. Make your life one full of good energy and happiness. You own your life and well-being! Make it what you want!

Journaling Time

CREATE A LIST OF THINGS AND PEOPLE YOU LOVE JOURNALING EXERCISE #81:

Find your notebook or *BEING Journal* to make notes in.

· Make a list of things and activities that you love to do.

· Make a list of all the people from home, family, friends, work, and the community who make you happy. Who do you enjoy being around and feel better after spending time with them?

· Create an intention and plan to spend more time with them and put specific commitments into your calendar.

Tool #44: Tree Grounding Visualization

Visualize yourself as a tree, standing tall and proud out in your field. Feel the sun's rays coming down and warming your branches and leaves (your head, shoulders, arms and hands). Feel the warmth and energy from the sun flowing down through your trunk (or core). Feel it flow all the way through your legs and down to your feet, where the roots of your tree flow out the bottom of your feet. Feel those roots flow into the soft soils of the earth that are full of life force, rooting and grounding you to the earth.

Allow the power of the earth's energy to flow back up into your roots and into the bottom of your feet. Feel your feet begin to tingle and warm. Feel that warmth and tingle flow from your feet up into your calves and up to your thighs, where your entire legs are warming and tingling. Feel that flow across your hips and up into your core. Feel that flow all the way up to your neck and head, warming and tingling, and then across your shoulders down your arms to your fingertips and turn up the volume like you would turn up the volume on a stereo. Just resonate in that powerful energy. And then take a deep breath. Listen to a recording at www.TheBEINGZone.com/tools.

TREE GROUNDING VISUALIZATION JOURNALING EXERCISE #82:
Find your *BEING Journal* or notebook to write in.
- How did the Tree Grounding Visualization feel to you?
- Could you feel the energy flow through your entire body? If not, how far could you feel it for? Each time you do this practice, you

will get stronger and able to take it further up through your body's energy system.

· Write about your experience and plan to continue to use this tool.

Tool #45: Breathe and Tighten Energy Centers

This is a very powerful way to increase the energy flow in your body as it addresses the energy centers that run up your spine. Take a deep breath in through your nose and tighten your pelvic floor (like doing a Kegel), then release through your mouth. Take another deep breath in through your nose and tighten your stomach and core muscles below your belly button, and then release your breath through your mouth. Take another deep breath in through your nose and tighten your abdomen and then release. Then deeply breathe in as you tighten your chest, or pectoral muscles, and then release through your mouth. Take a deep breath in and tighten your throat muscles and jaw, and release through your mouth. Take one more deep breath in through your nose and tighten your forehead and scrunch your eyes before you release through your mouth. When you take your last breath, you will feel lighter inside as the energy flow has been increased in your energy center all the way up through the top of your head. Go to listen to a recording at www.TheBEINGZone.com/tools for breathing and tightening your energy centers.

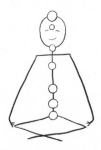

Journaling Time

BREATHE AND TIGHTEN ENERGY CENTERS

JOURNALING EXERCISE #83:

Pull out your notebook or *BEING Journal* to make notes in.

- When you tightened each energy center, did you feel anything in that specific area? Describe what you experienced.
- Could you feel the difference of energy or flow through your body as you tightened each area? Talk about how it made you feel.
- When might you use this tool moving forward?

Tool #46: Breath of Fire

This is a very powerful way to increase the energy flow in your body and is often used in yoga practices. It takes time to build up to the full practice of the Breath of Fire. Beginners should start with a 30 second practice.

- Sit up tall, visualizing and intending to lengthen the space between your navel and your heart.
- Breathe in and out through the nose and start to pull your abdomen in during the exhale and press it out during the inhale.
- Imagine your belly filling up with air during the inhale and use your abdominal muscles to push the air out during the exhale.
- Start to shorten each breath and pick up the pace. The breathing should be loud and quick. Focus on making the inhale and the exhale in both strength and length.

Listen to the Breath of Fire recording at www.TheBEINGZone. com/tools.

Journaling Time

BREATH OF FIRE JOURNALING EXERCISE #84:

Take out your *BEING Journal* or notebook to document your thoughts and feelings.

- What was different for you with the Breath of Fire compared to what you experienced with other breathing exercises?
- How did it make your body feel?

Tool #47: Energy Movements

Practices such as yoga (especially Kundalini Yoga), Tai Chi, and Qigong are all good options for increasing the energy in your body daily. Each one offers different movements that will act on the body in different ways. You can watch videos online or sign up for a class.

Journaling Time

ENERGY MOVEMENTS JOURNALING EXERCISE #85:

Get your *BEING Journal* or notebook ready to write in.

· What are the energy movements that you can commit to or try?
  Yoga? Tai Chi? Qigong? Other?

· Find the one that works best for you and build it into your schedule.

Tool #48: Tune into Energy

When you learn to reconnect with your energy or your feelings, it will start to feel right to make decisions that flow for you. You will instinctively begin to know how to avoid situations, people, and things that decrease your energy and follow things that fill you up or increase your vibrations.

· Stop and breathe deeply to get centered and present so you can bring in good energy using one of the techniques you learned above.

· When you are trying to decide something, ask yourself how it feels in your body. Your body knows best. If it warms or feels good inside, follow it. If you feel cooling or tension, it's a no.

· Listen to your body. If it is tired, let it rest. It will always tell you when to stop if you listen.

· Only fill your body with food or things that will make you feel good. If you are continually eating things that don't agree with you or are unhealthy, that will decrease your energy flow.

· Move your body through exercise, stretching, walking, yoga, Tai Chi, and Qigong to keep your energy flowing.

· Follow your instincts because your feelings are always right. You will feel and know what is right for you.

Journaling Time

TUNE INTO ENERGY JOURNALING EXERCISE #86:

Pull out your notebook or *BEING Journal* to make notes in.

- When you have good energy flow in your body and are asking questions, your body will respond. It will feel more flow if the idea resonates with you and you will feel a tightness or a decrease in flow if the idea is not good.
- Take some time fill your body with energy and ask questions and journal about what you hear or feel.

Managing Your Energy

You have learned many ways to feel energy, when to bring in good and when to release bad. Now the goal is to balance this in your daily life. Managing your energy will unlock many happy doors for you, as you will find yourself more and more energetic, alive and ready to take on daily challenges. You also know when to avoid people and situations that bring your energy down and how to remove stuck energy when it happens.

When you are tuned into your energy and manage it daily, you will exist in a flow of positive energy and you'll be able to watch as the magic unfolds in your life. As best-selling author, life and business strategist Tony Robbins says, "Where your attention goes, your energy flows."[102] Therefore, you must set intentions so your energy flows where you want it to, not where you don't want it to. Run in good energy and good energy will run to you.

We all have the natural ability to tune into energy or vibrations like this, but it was often turned down or off when we were young. As we grew up, we heard things like "big boys don't cry," or "you are too sensitive," or "Be tough or don't be so touchy/feely." Adults encouraged us to go after material success instead of following our feelings, and so we turned off the part of us that knew how to read the energy waves. We were told to stop listening to how life felt when, in truth, we are meant to listen to how everything feels. To help you better understand this concept, imagine that you had a great day at work. You just got home and are feeling great and are full of good energy. A few minutes later, a family member walks in the room and yells at you for something. Almost immediately, you will most likely feel different. You may feel upset or defensive, and you will feel that good energy you just had drain out of you. Now you know how to react in a situation like this, remove the negative energy, bring in positive and protect yourself.

Energy Limits

Most of the time, your goal should not be to run in super high, intense energy. If you are a really hyperactive person, or super focused, your energy, though not negative, might be overwhelming to people. When you vibrate at too high of a level like that, it can feel intense and be off-putting to those around you. You want your energy to be grounded and balanced.

You can be almost too electric if not. People resonating in intense energy often don't even know it. I didn't. When I received my energy training, David Morelli said someone's energy was invading the stage, and he instructed us to pull it back. I had no idea what he was talking about until he had us do an exercise that made it clear. I was so excited to feel energy, I was floating in powerful vibes and had no idea about how to control it. To demonstrate how to control our energy, David had everyone walk in a big circle around the room. He told us to walk in whatever direction felt best to us so there were people walking clockwise and others walking counterclockwise. When he walked past me, he had such strong energy I could feel it as we passed which made understand what he was trying to say. I was astounded that someone could have such strong energy that others could feel when passing. It was an authentic lesson in how powerful energy is and how important it is to keep it close to you and at the right level. Since then, I've learned to keep my energy within one foot of my body, in a calm state. If I just visualize my energy within a foot of my body, it will stay there.

Key Messages

- The Universe, the Earth, your body, and everything around you is energy.
- You can tune into your body to move stuck energy within you followed by bringing in good energy.
- You have learned to recognize how energy (people and situations) impact you which allows you to protect yourself and change your circumstances.
- Your mind is the creator of your life. Where your attention goes, your energy flows.

- Your thoughts, feelings, emotions, and words affect your energy and become your daily reality. Change your thoughts in order to change your life.
- Tuning into your body, increasing its energy flow and releasing tightness and pain improves your health and happiness.
- Your body's openness and movements have a significant impact on keeping invisible energy flowing. Energy-based healing modalities are amazing for effecting fast, enduring change.

> **This Chapter's Gifts:** You learn how to feel, move, read, and improve your energy and know who or what energy-zapping people and situations to avoid.

CHAPTER 8

Connecting With Source

"All Creation Is One so people should try to
live a simple life in harmony with nature and
with others. I am part or particle of God."
—Ralph Waldo Emerson

IN CHAPTER 7, you learned about energy and how to
tune in to it, feel it, and manage it. Feeling and listening
to your energy will help you in all parts of your life, just as it has
helped me in my own life. Before moving on, I would be remiss
if I didn't include the other thing that was the biggest game-
changer in my own life: having an understanding and belief in
a higher power and trusting it. It can seem impossible to feel a
connection with Source. So, in this chapter you'll be shown how
and given examples, as it is life changing. Connecting with your
higher power will transcend your life.

As, I've mentioned already, I believe we are one with Source. Source resides within us and is greater than us and is always there when we are ready to listen. This chapter is all about showing you how to understand this connection and bring hope, faith, and love into your life. When you learn how to tune into it and trust it, you will most likely find it is a game-changer for you too.

Defining Source

What do I mean by Source? There are a wide variety of definitions of Source in the various dictionaries: a place, person, or thing from which something initiates; one that supplies information; or the place something comes from or starts at, or the cause of something. A few synonyms for Source include the words origin, inception, and root, which means the point at which something begins its course or existence. What does Source or God mean to you? Does connecting to a higher power play a part in your life today?

I have total belief and faith that there is something bigger or higher than all of us, yet I am not attached to a set religion. Many of my clients have strong religious affiliations or beliefs, and that is perfect for them. Most find they can follow their religion and still learn about energy and connection with Source. Every religion has its own opinions and traditions and may call Source different things. Many words can describe this higher power, including but not limited to God, Creator, Divine Source, Universe, Universal Source, The Divine, Buddha, Abba, Allah—the list goes on. Use the term that feels right to you, and what fits in your world and reality. I describe myself as spiritual and aligned with what I call Source, God, Creator, or the Universe, and I may use those terms interchangeably throughout this chapter. It doesn't matter what you call it; what matters is you believe in a higher power that you can feel and build a relationship with and turn to for guidance. When you learn to do this, you are never alone.

You don't have to belong to any specific religion or follow any set rules to connect with something higher than you. The key to connecting with Source energy is to *BE* completely present, which is why it is essential to learn to exist in *The BEING Zone*. You must turn off that little voice in your head and tune out anything and everything that is going on around you.

You Can Connect

Many clients ask me if it is really possible to connect with Source. I tell them it is not only likely, but often immediate. When you learn the tools and practice described below, you will be able to make a connection with the Divine inside of you, and you will know it. It's like riding a bike. Once you learn how and experience it, you will be able to do it time and time again.

I have read books, watched videos, taken classes, and learned from many spiritual masters about a hidden channel, and through all of my research I've come to understand that the connection to Source comes from a physical channel that connects the pituitary and pineal glands. The pineal gland is in the center of your head behind the third eye, so it's no wonder I feel my connection and buzzing firmly there. This connection has been called activation by spiritual leaders. There is some history behind these beliefs. Philosophers and spiritual seekers have long contemplated the exact function of the mysterious pineal gland. Ancient Greeks believed that the pineal gland was our connection to the realm of thought and consciousness. French philosopher Renee Descartes referred to it as the seat of the human soul, believing it to be a powerful Source of spiritual energy. Centuries-old Eastern philosophy theorized that the pineal gland was associated with the sixth energy center.

In the book *Scientific Basis of Integrative Medicine*, authors Leonard A. Wisneski and Lucy Anderson say that hope, faith, and love aid in healing and that the dimension of spirituality transcends all the five senses to help get us there.[103] Some may call it the sixth sense, or Extrasensory perception (ESP), or intuition. It simply means you are receiving information not gained through the recognized five physical senses but sensed within the mind. I refer to it as intuition which is an inner knowing and connection to the sixth sense.

The streaming service Gaia is an international member-supported media network for truth seekers and believers focused on empowering an evolution of consciousness. An article on Gaia's site, called *"The Pineal Gland and The Third Eye Chakra"* written by Andye Murphy, indicates the third eye is our greatest gift to connect us to Source, reminding us that the Universe is much more mystical than what we perceive with our physical senses.[104] The article goes on to say when we awaken the third eye and its corresponding pineal gland, we can attain supernatural feats like telepathy, psychic vision, or an intimate connection with God or Source. Andye says "rare is a conversation on consciousness well-being without a mention of the pineal gland." Its prevalence is more than a fad; many believe that awaking the third eye is a necessary step in attaining our full human potential.

Deborah King is a best-selling author, speaker, and attorney. In her article, *"The Secret to Connecting with God,"* she talks about the pineal gland or third eye as a channel.[105] Deborah says, "Our ancestors were not only aware of this channel but were adept at using it to connect directly to Source regularly. It was almost like picking up a phone for the ancients—tapping into the God force within themselves and expressing the light of Source through their human bodies was a regular activity."

Journaling Time

YOU CAN CONNECT JOURNALING EXERCISE #87:

In your notebook or *BEING Journal* make notes on what works for you.

· Write about when you feel more connected to yourself or a greater Source.

· Pay attention to your surroundings, the situation, the time of day, the sounds, and how you feel when you are feeling a connection with Source. The more you are aware of what works for you, the more you can build on this skill.

· Write about your experiences in connecting with Source.

Preparation for Connecting with Source

Everyone has the ability, deep inside, to connect with Source. It's up to you to learn the tools to open up that power within you and expose yourself to the richer experiences that this connection provides. This entire book has been written to help you prepare for this process of connection, and as we move forward, I will refer you back to chapters that will assist you. You must learn how to turn off your thoughts—your Ego mind—and connect with your heart and soul as you learned in Chapter 4. When you learn how to operate in *The BEING Zone* as discussed in Chapter 5, you will have an easier time learning to visualize and connect with energy as covered in Chapter 7. All of these steps are imperative to your success in creating a connection.

If you have read the book, journaled, and learned the tools, you are ready. If you've only skimmed the book and didn't take the time to practice the tools, I recommend you spend a little more time getting the foundational skills in place. The following preparation steps will identify what will help you the most.

Preparation #1: Change Your Thoughts, Change Your Energy

Your thoughts are the highest frequency vibration of energy that you possess. When your thinking is negative or you're acting like a naysayer, your energy will be low. When you nurture positive thinking, belief, and trust in a higher Source, the energy you're emitting out into the Universe and inside you is much higher. The Law of Attraction says, "like attracts like." It explains that you magnetically attract things vibrating on the same frequency. If you stay positive and are full of love and compassion, you will more likely draw this type of energy back to you. When you think thoughts that vibrate at this higher level, it is easier to connect with Source, which will result in you automatically vibrating at even a higher level. Chapter 4 has the tools and information that can help you change your thoughts.

Preparation #2: Quiet the Ego, Listen to Your Heart or Intuition

The Ego is that voice in your head that isn't the real you. We've talked about tools and techniques that will help you turn off that voice, as well as guidelines for how to listen to your body, heart, and intuition. If you don't have this concept down, go back to review Chapter 4 and work on strengthening your ability to do this. My clients who master this step have great success in turning their lives around.

Preparation #3: Learn to Exist in *The BEING Zone*

A high percentage of the world today exists in the *DOING Zone*. When you can slow down and begin to live in the present moment and enjoy just *BEING* here, now, your life will change. Take the time to review the tips and techniques in Chapter 5 if you don't feel like you've mastered this. When you learn to exist in *The BEING Zone*, you have a much higher chance of connecting with Source.

Preparation #4: Improve Your Visualization Skills

Being able to visualize is essential when it comes to connection. Many of my clients tell me that they can't visualize things. I have them practice visualization skills by studying something in front of them and then closing their eyes to see if they can recreate it in their mind's eye. With enough practice, they can learn visualization skills, and I believe anyone can. If you're struggling, start by looking at an apple or another piece of fruit. Study it for a few minutes. Now close your eyes and visualize that apple or other fruit in your mind's eye.

Here are a few more techniques that can help you increase your ability to visualize.

- **Image Generation:** The first step is to generate an image. Close your eyes and picture a past experience. Imagine the details. Take a few minutes to think through the scene of what happened. When you are ready, describe as much of the event or scene in words as you can. Write it all down. Draw pictures of it if that helps. Keep writing and drawing until you have created your memory in enough detail on paper. This will build your visualization skills.

- **Reflection:** Close your eyes again and take yourself back to a specific day, event, or scene. Imagine you are in the middle of that situation once again. See yourself there. Visualize where you are sitting or standing. How does that seat, or the ground beneath your feet, feel? Are you comfortable? How does your body feel? Are you warm or cold? What are you feeling? Are you happy or sad, or what? What are you thinking? Are you enjoying it and want more? This process assists you in getting more familiar with visualizing so keep trying it. Over time visualization will become easier and easier.

Journaling Time

Visualization Practice Journaling Exercise #88:
Make notes in your *BEING Journal* or notebook.

- Follow the steps for visualization practices above and document what you felt, thought, and experienced.

· Were you able to visualize and experience what you expected based on the descriptions? Write about it.

Preparation #5: Learn to Feel Energy

As explained in Chapter 7, we are energy beings. Energy is the starting point for connecting with Source. You need to know how to feel energy because that is what you will feel when you get connected. You may feel the energy in your body, your hands, a tingling of your skin, your third eye, or the top of your head, etc. Everyone is different. The entire Universe and world are made up of energy. Some of it is energy converted into matter, and that's all the material, objects, and people and nature that we see. Some of it is energy that we don't see. For instance, we can't see the energy going through our smartphones to satellites to phone lines, but we know it's there. Energy is in us and all around us whether we see it or not.

Hopefully, through the exercises in Chapter 7, you began to become aware of yourself as a body of energy. You are made up of trillions of atoms that contain energy, and those atoms are vibrating. Scientists estimate that there are about 100 trillion atoms in each cell in your body, and if you have 50 trillion cells in your body, that is a lot of atoms.[106] The atoms are creating high-pitch frequencies and sounds, and they're emitting light. That means you are a body of light; you are directly connected to the energy body of the Universe. You and everything around you are emitting light in different shades, which means everything, and everyone are interconnected. The only separation is what is in your mind. Understanding this will enable you to connect with Universal

Source Energy. Practice what you learned in Chapter 7 until you are confident in your skills to feel and read energy.

Journaling Time

WHAT ENERGY FEELS LIKE TO YOU JOURNALING EXERCISE #89:
In your notebook or *BEING Journal*, make notes.

· Describe what it feels like to you when you are in good energy or bring energy into your body. This is a feeling you want to learn to expand.

Preparation #6: Operate in the Light

In Chapter 6, you learned about finding your purpose, and you will learn about building in Happiness-Boosting activities in Chapter 9. When you are doing what you are meant to and are always filling up your free time with things that make you happy, you will operate more in the light.

I support the concept that there are two realms in life because I have existed in both at different times in my life. You have the power to choose where you exist: either in the light (oneness or love) where I exist now or the darkness (separateness or judgment) where I used to exist. It is a choice. When you are in the light, the circumstances of life have no power over you. You are full of love, and life works incredibly well. Synchronicity and serendipity are part of your everyday existence. When you are in the darkness, the circumstances of life have total power. It's easy to lose who you are at the core, and life becomes a struggle. When you are in the darkness, the experience of love is irrelevant, and it seems like everything is happening to you and most likely is not going your way. You push, force, fight, resist, hang on, and with-draw in this place. It is the realm of fear, resentment, upset, and suffering. Struggle, frustration, anger, or illness are prevalent in a life of darkness. Once you understand that you have control over these two realms, you can choose to never go back to the dark side, and you have the tools that can keep you in the light no matter what unfolds in front of you.

When you live in the light (connected to Source), the opposite happens. The circumstances of life are irrelevant. The only thing that matters is love. When you are in this state, the focus is on love, compassion, forgiveness, letting go, healing, and connecting with God. This is the realm of love, joy, peace, happiness, and miracles.

When you begin to let go of the negative, let go of fighting against the world, and let go of what doesn't serve you, it will free you up to find what's right with you and others. It will free you up to forgive all who have ever wronged you and begin to spread love and compassion in the world. Use the Throw It Away Tool you learned about in Chapter 4 to help you move from dark to light as things come up. When you start utilizing the tools daily to change your life, you will be able to start to connect with Source energy easily.

Journaling Time

LIGHT VERSUS DARK JOURNALING EXERCISE #90:
Pull out your notebook or *BEING Journal* to make notes in.

- Do you tend to operate more in what I call the light (good or positive energy)? Describe what you feel.
- Or are you more in the dark (bad or negative energy)? Describe what you feel.
- Just observe yourself and write about your tendencies to increase your awareness.

Client Story: Mandy is a perfect example of someone who lives in the light today but hasn't always been there. She was stuck in the dark for years and wondered why. When she forgave everyone in the past who wronged her, she was able to let go of her anger and pain. This allowed her to start existing in the light. Now everyone who meets her is uplifted by her presence, her smile, her authentic, genuine warmth, and unconditional love. She radiates light from the inside out. She, too, had a difficult life at times but was willing to do the work, heal and establish a connection with Source.

Preparation #7: Learn to Love Yourself First

Throughout the book, you have learned tools and techniques that will move you toward loving yourself and loving your life. When you are ready to explore this and figure out how to grow a spiritual and energetic connection or relationship with Source, it is best to start by learning to connect with yourself and to love yourself unconditionally.

When you don't love yourself, it is hard to feel connected because you feel empty inside. When you learn to love yourself, you feel happy inside and are more connected to your heart and how things feel to you. Start today by standing in front of the mirror, looking yourself in the eye, and telling yourself, "I love you!" It may be challenging at first—at least, it was for many of my clients and me. Do this daily, though, and you will find it gets easier and more comfortable. Over time, you will start to believe it. The benefit of this exercise is that it will raise the energy in your body as you radiate with this self-love, which is your light.

How do you know if you are there? You will feel better overall in your mind, body, and spirit. You will feel love and joy when you look in the mirror. Things will just seem to go the right way for you. You will start to experience all kinds of synchronicities or magic, in your life and these experiences will become daily occurrences over time. You will feel a lightness in your being, and you sparkle more, which is your light shining. You might even feel the buzzing, warming, or tingling that I experience when I do this exercise.

Journaling Time

DO YOU LOVE YOURSELF JOURNALING EXERCISE #91:

In your notebook or *BEING Journal*, make notes on the following questions.

· Do you love yourself? What does that look like?
· How does self-love feel to you?

Preparation #8: Forgiving and Loving Others

To learn to forgive and love others, you must start with loving yourself as described in preparation #7. You will find your love for yourself expands when you send this unconditional love, compassion, and forgiveness out to others. The pond exercise recording referred to in Chapter 3 can help you get to this point. The Pond exercise takes you through forgiving all those who may have wronged you in your life and gets you to the point that you can send them compassion and love. You may need to do this exercise several times.

When you get to this place of forgiveness and unconditional love for others, people are drawn to you because of how good it feels to be around you. You have probably seen this light and energy in others. Your experience will be more profound when you choose to practice unconditional love, compassion, and forgiveness. Whenever a friend or neighbor is snarky, or a child is angry, or your spouse is short or irritable, return it with unconditional love and forgiveness, and you will immediately see them soften.

The best way I have found to send unconditional love and forgiveness is stopping first to breathe and ground. I remind myself that the other person is this way because of something in their life. It's not about me. That makes it easier to forgive and send love, because I know they aren't attacking me because of me. I realize it is their stuff, and they need love and compassion, too. I send a thought or feeling from my heart of forgiveness. Sometimes I might pray for their happiness. When you live in this kind of compassionate energy, and you surrender to what is, you will find the magic increasing in your life.

Journaling Time

FORGIVE AND LOVE JOURNALING EXERCISE #92:

Pull out your notebook or *BEING Journal* and start writing.

· Who do you need to forgive in your life? Make some notes and
  think about all the people in your life who you feel wronged by
  so you can work through the forgiveness process on each person
  that hurt you.

· What do you need to forgive yourself for?

· Write about how it felt to forgive yourself and all others.

Connecting: How Do You Get There?

I will share the specific steps my *BEING Zone System* partner,
Amanda, and I use to get connected so you have real life examples on what works for us. First, I position myself in a location
that is extremely conducive to connecting for me. My favorite
place is under the stars. I breathe deeply and ground myself and
then get very present in the moment. I go through the process of
calling in the Grandmothers and Grandfathers, Spirit Guides, and
Ascended Masters which I learned from Indigenous and Eastern
traditions. My mind and body become still, and I become aware
of the quietness and emptiness of that moment in time. I begin
to experience a feeling like I am free-floating among the stars in
the Universe, and it feels as though I am in a dream. It is from
this connected place, I ask for guidance and get answers.

Amanda, on the other hand, finds a location she loves and where she is less likely to be distracted. She says, "I start with breathing, grounding, and bringing in good energy from the earth and heaven which settles me in. I then imagine I can see straight up into the sky, and I visualize that I am going into a bright light. It's like light from the sun. I go into several more bright lights, until I come up to a multi-colored light that I again go into, and through. Then I see one more beautiful, all-encompassing light and go through it. I can almost feel a string go from the heavens down to the crown of my head. I sit for just a moment to feel the connection, which to me feels like a super relaxing honey-like substance that starts at my crown and goes down and around my body. It's so grounding and relaxing I just melt into my seat. I then say a prayer or request or give gratitude or ask for guidance, and I wait for answers. I can stay in this trance-like state for a long time if not interrupted."

Making a connection is a learned activity that didn't happen overnight for either Amanda or me, but when it did happen, we knew exactly what it was. There are detailed steps in this chapter to help you learn how to get to the place where you can connect. Just remember, it takes time and practice to learn to get to that tranquil, open place in time and space. For years, I understood energy and knew there was something more, but did not really understand how to connect or what that meant or how to do it. Now I know it is in this quiet, connected, open feeling place where I can seek guidance and ask questions.

Steps for Connecting with Source

The following steps will help you cultivate a connection with Source. In the beginning, I recommend you do these steps in the order listed, knowing that each step will still be unique to you based on your preferences. Do not judge yourself if your experience doesn't feel like my experience or Amanda's. If you believe in Source and believe you can connect, you will find it is possible.

Once you begin to connect with Source regularly, you'll want to make the process your own and do it in whatever way you like best. Everyone is unique, and we each experience this magic feeling differently.

Step #1: Location, Location, Location

It is imperative that you find a quiet location where you will have no interruptions that is also a space that feels great to you. My favorite place, as I mentioned, is outside under the moon and stars in the early morning hours. My other favorites are in the woods or on the beach. In the early years, I quieted my mind on a dock or beach. I could tune into the beauty around me, watching the birds flutter about and seeing other wildlife here and there. If you live in below-freezing temperatures, getting outside may only be an option in the warmer months of the year. Take some time to brainstorm what space may work best for you. It might be on a window seat where you can look outside and see the stars and semi-connect with nature. It can be any room in your home where the energy is good, and you feel happy being there.

If you are in your home and don't have the opportunity to connect with the stars or nature, then put on some headphones, close your eyes, and listen to meditative sounds. I love the sounds of nature, like waves flowing or the soft pitter-patter of rain, to calm my mind. Choose what sounds work for you, or no sounds at all if you find them distracting.

Journaling Time

LOCATION JOURNALING EXERCISE #93:

Take out your notebook or *BEING Journal* to make notes in.

- Write down several locations where you can be comfortable connecting with Source energy. Look around your home and community and decide on the places where you feel most grounded and feel you would have the ability to connect, whether it be with the Universe or the Earth.
- List several options depending on weather or time of year to ensure you stay comfortable.
- Write about what time of day is best for you. I like early morning but figure out what time of day works for you.
- Make a commitment to days and times you will connect and write it down.

Step #2: Breathing

You must *BE* completely present in the moment to connect with Source. I get to this present state by breathing and grounding. There are a variety of breathing exercises included in Chapter 3 and we will cover more in Chapter 10. Start by focusing on your breath. Just breathe in through your nose, watching your chest or belly expand as it comes in, and then breathe out through your mouth, seeing your chest or stomach sink. Breathe in another deep, full breath, where you can see your belly filling with air, and then release it through your mouth as your belly flattens. Breathe in again, breathing in love, and release through your mouth, letting go of all thoughts.

Step #3: Grounding

Grounding yourself allows you to get out of your head and to bring energy in from the earth. The most effortless Grounding practice is the Tree Visualization process in Chapter 7, where you can feel the sun warming you from your head down, and then feel the energy of the earth coming back up through your roots into your feet and body. In this centered, grounded space, you can begin to just *BE*. You can also go outside and sit on the earth and get to that same place.

Step #4: Call in Your Guides

Once you feel present, call in your guides, whatever that means to you. They can be your guardian angels, your angels in general (sometimes I call in my mom and grandpa who have passed on), the Archangels, or the Grandmothers, Grandfathers, Spirit Guides, Star People, and Ascended Masters. You can even call in your Higher Self. I use the words, "Calling in Grandmothers and Grandfathers from all four directions, Spirit Guides, Star People and Creator, please help guide me today." Amanda says, "I request the presence of my Higher Self, Guardians and Guides, Loved Ones and the Creator of all that is to assist me for the highest good of myself and the world." Do and say what feels right to you.

Step #5: Feel Energy for Answers

You will feel energy when you are getting answers from Source. There are a few of my clients who have what they call a knowing, and that works, but for the majority of people I work with, answers come with a physical, visceral response of buzzing or vibration in their bodies or third eye. If you haven't felt this yet, go back to Chapter 7 and practice feeling energy or do some Earthing, sitting in the grass or on the beach, and feel the energy radiating out of the earth into you. When you can feel energy and know it, move onto Step 6. If you are having difficulty, you may want to work with a certified trained energy practitioner to see what is keeping you from feeling energy. Everyone has the ability to feel energy; you just need to figure out how it resonates in you.

Step #6: Mastering the Quiet Mind

Connecting with Source is all about surrendering in the present moment, which goes back to Preparation #3: Getting into *The BEING Zone*. This is probably the hardest step of all; at least it was for me at first. I lived in the *DOING Zone*, so quieting the mind was almost impossible. I always had so many things to do and places to be. Quieting your mind is about learning to exist in a meditative type state where you are entirely present. You basically want your mind to stop. This is just about sitting and *BEING*. Every time a thought or worry comes up, pull it out, leave it behind, and go back to the present moment with no thoughts. In the beginning, slowly say the words, "here, now" over and over to pull you back into the present moment.

One way to do this is to get in a comfortable position and close your eyes. Warm your heart by thinking of a pet or child that loves you unconditionally or visualize a place you love to be. You will naturally create feelings of love and joy. With each breath, inhale more joy and allow these feelings to radiate throughout your body gently. Expand that feeling throughout your body, to the space around your body. While you are experiencing this love, imagine *BEING* in the presence of Source. Bask in the warmth of this love and peace.

Step #7: Connecting with Source

When you are in this connected, quiet place, ask Source to be there with you and guide you for the greater good of all. Then just sit and wait. If thoughts come, let them glide by. You may get answers or guidance, or you may get nothing at first. Be patient and know that in time, you will get more information. With practice, sitting in this peaceful place takes your awareness away from any pain in your physical body and your chaotic, always-thinking mind. It might be an odd thing to experience at first, but you will find that time can slow down...or at least that's what it can feel like. Regular practice of getting to this state will help you to feel like part of something much bigger than you. It can also bring you a tremendous sense of peace and calm, as well as a feeling of being detached from the pressures, complexities, and interactions of being human in our crazy busy world.

Step #8: Keep Practicing

Practice until you feel it and know you are connected. If you do this work daily, pretty soon it will become so natural that you can connect and get answers amid your everyday life. I now connect with Source as part of my daily practice, which you will learn about in the final chapter.

Waiting for Answers

I believe when you seek help, you have a much higher chance of connecting and getting messages and guidance if your purpose is to make our world better, rather than seeking self-gain. When I connect with Source, I ask to be helpful and contribute what is needed in this world. Many people are interested only in their own benefit and may do fine, but it doesn't resonate with me. You need to follow what feels right to you.

You want to make sure you don't approach Source with pre-conceived ideas of exactly what you want, how you want it and when you want it. Be open to the bigger picture, stay detached, and watch as your answers unfold. You'll find ideas, messages, and things come to you that are beyond what you could have imagined. Best-selling author and spiritual leader, Marianne Williamson, describes a supreme power in the Universe that is bigger and more powerful than our small mortal selves.

> "Spiritual growth involves giving up the stories of
> your past so the universe can write a new one."
> —Marianne Williamson

I believe in the concept; we are not Source, but Source is in us, which is another way of thinking about it. I believe this as truth because once I became aware of and learned to feel the energy in my body and how to quiet my mind, I began to feel that connection with Source.

How Source Shows Up

As explained earlier, this connection will show up differently for everyone. It might be a physical feeling, an emotional response, a deep knowing, and so on. Personally, my connection shows up in several ways. Once in a while, my entire body will give me messages in the form of pain or illness that I believe is Universal Source getting me to slow down and stop. Other times I feel warm in my heart or from head to toe when something is right, and when something isn't right for me, my heart and body cool. I receive a powerful vibration or buzzing sensation in my third eye in my forehead when I am connected; this might show up for you as well. I get clear energetic messages—the downloads I told you about.

Be open to how Source shows up in your life. Trust what you feel, hear, or know as it will be unique for everyone. For instance, you may feel expansion or positive energy when something is right or contraction in your body when something is wrong, which is different than what I feel.

Synchronicities

When you do the steps explained in this chapter daily, you will find synchronicities start to show up in your life. I believe synchronicities, what some people call "moments of meaningful coincidence" or "the stuff you just can't make up," are Source's way of getting us moving in the right direction, and so they happen for a reason. For instance, have you ever thought about someone, and the next thing you know, they call you or you bump into them? That's synchronicity. Nothing is by accident. I believe those encounters are the higher organizing power making these serendipities a reality. I love the magical power of synchronicities, especially when I need help with something and voila, the answers pop into my inbox. A recent example for me is the same week an executive at a publishing company told me I should write a book, I received an email reminding me I had signed up for an online writer's workshop four years ago, and it still was there waiting for me. How cool is that?

Now that you have a handle on how to connect with Source, here is a tool you can use to make it stronger. It's a powerful and helpful tool that that my clients and I both utilize often.

 Tool #49: Connecting with Source Energy and Replacing Feelings

This one requires you to believe and trust in a higher Source. (Again, use whatever name you'd like for your higher Source.)

Process for Replacing Feelings

· Take a deep, cleansing breath and close your eyes.
· Start by visualizing a white light flowing down from the heavens into the top of your head. Begin to feel a tingling or buzzing on the top of your head or in your third eye, which is located between your eyebrows in the center of your forehead. These are your top two energy centers.
· When you feel the tingling, ask Source to replace an unwanted belief or feeling with something you do want. For instance, you may say, "Source, please replace the fear inside me with a feeling of confidence that everything will be alright. Thank you, Source. I now feel complete!"

· You can also ask Source for guidance while you are feeling that connection. Ask yes/no questions and see what you get. In the long run, you can put bigger, open-ended questions out there and get what I call downloads, but this takes time and practice.

When to Use This Tool

Whenever you feel stuck or frustrated and are tired of feeling that way, this tool is the right choice. Just go ask Source to help you replace the feeling. The thought, belief, and words make it possible to transform how you feel about something.

I use this tool daily for direction in my own life. I ask yes/no and open-ended questions. This process helped me take this book to a higher level, so people can better connect with the words and stories. For instance, using this tool, I received the feedback not just to explain the tools in the book but to tell people when to use the tool and to share a client story.

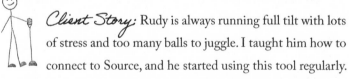

Client Story: Rudy is always running full tilt with lots of stress and too many balls to juggle. I taught him how to connect to Source, and he started using this tool regularly. It has changed how he thinks and acts. Rudy now asks Source frequently to replace his stress and overwhelm with a calm, clear focus. He spends more time operating from a more peaceful, clearer place. I can feel the difference when we talk. He used to try and fit a million things into our calls. Now when he calls, we have a more calm, focused conversation.

Journaling Time

CONNECTING WITH SOURCE ENERGY AND REPLACING

FEELINGS JOURNALING EXERCISE #94:

Grab your *BEING Journal* or notebook to start writing.

- Make notes on how well the Connecting with Source Energy and Replace Feelings exercise worked for you. Did you have any ah-ha's or messages that came to you?
- Did you feel a connection? What did that feel like for you?
- Did you feel like you were able to change how you felt physically, mentally, or emotionally? Write about that. Is this an exercise you will use moving forward?
- What was the time of day or location where you felt most connected?
- What steps worked best for you? How did you get to that place of connection?
- What did you feel? What did you hear or learn?

When you welcome Source guidance into your life, you open up the doors to unprecedented coincidences and opportunities.

Key Messages

- When you focus on creating the highest good for all, you will be a happier, kinder, more positive soul.

· It takes time. Learning to connect with Source doesn't happen overnight.

· When you incorporate your learnings from the early chapters in this book and follow the preparation steps, it makes connection with Source much easier.

· Visualization is powerful and helpful when you are ready to connect with Source.

· Begin to operate in the light. Our world of competition and success focus keeps most of us in darkness. Start to operate from a place of love, and you will find the light!

· Find the right location, breathe, ground, and call in your guides. You will be thrilled and surprised at what happens when you ask for help.

This Chapter's Gifts: Learning to connect with Source is the game-changer. If you are seeking a significant transformation and want to love your life without exception, this is the step to embrace fully.

PART IV

Creating a Life You Love!

CHAPTER 9

Happiness-Boosting Activities

"One of the first conditions of happiness is that the
link between man and nature shall not be broken."
—Leo Tolstoy

I N C H A P T E R 8 you learned about Source and how to
cultivate your personal connection to Source. That bond
brings hope, strengthens faith, and increases the opportunity for
fulfillment and balance. Now it is time to identify what to add into
your life to make it better. It can feel overwhelming to think about
building more things into your life. But do not worry, you will find
when they are Happiness-Boosting activities, they will fill you up
instead of depleting you. Increase your Happiness-Boosting activities to balance your life.

What Drains You?

What you might not realize is that you could be spending a lot of time each day doing things that drain you instead of making you feel good. You may not recognize the impact these repetitive activities have on your energy. I learned in my Energy Based Life Coach training that watching or listening to the news is draining. News programming prioritizes sensational information; their motto is "if it bleeds, it leads." I quit watching the news because it was depressing and increased my stress. Now when I overhear negative news, it feels draining and exhausting. I only read the news headlines online, so I have an idea of what is happening in the world, and only delve in if it has the potential to impact me directly.

Are you one of those people who spend your free time watching news or mindless shows, browsing social media, gaming, or doing things that are not filling you up? I have discovered that some of my clients spend 40+ hours a week making a living and then spend much of the rest of their time on activities that can be depleting. Scientific studies have shown that prolonged television viewing increases the risk of obesity and related diseases such as diabetes. It's also been linked to mental health problems. A recent Texas A&M study revealed that binge-watching is tied to feelings of loneliness and depression.[107]

Researchers have shown that people live longer and happier lives when they spend their free time doing fulfilling activities and spending time with people they enjoy. For over 75 years, Harvard's Grant and Glueck study has tracked the physical and emotional well-being of two populations: 456 poor men growing up in Boston and 268 male graduates from Harvard.[108] According to Robert Waldinger, director of the Harvard Study of Adult Development, "The clearest message we get from this 75-year study is: Good relationships keep us happier and healthier. Period."

WHAT DRAINS YOU JOURNALING EXERCISE #95:

Pull out your notebook or *BEING Journal* to make notes in.

- Write about what drains you in your life. Is it your job, your friends, your family, how you spend your time?
- Identify what is no longer working for you once you understand all the things that can drain you.
- What fills you up? Make a commitment to exchange a draining activity with something that fills you up.
- Write about what that would be.

The 5 Spheres of Life

Everyone's favorite Happiness-Boosting activities will be different. My favorites include exercise, yoga, eating healthy foods, hiking, being outdoors, beach time, doing art projects, and spending time with friends. My suggestions may or may not resonate with you. Everyone has to identify and connect with what works for them.

I believe there are five areas in your life that should be considered when you take the time to think about increasing your Happiness-Boosting activities as you want to maintain an overall balance. I call these the 5 Spheres as they represent the primary areas in your life that you can influence. When you are aware of each of these categories and make a conscious decision to keep them in balance, you will find that you will create a life that you enjoy more.

The 5 Spheres, in no particular order because they are all important, include:

1. Health and Wellness
2. Spirituality
3. Relationships
4. Happiness-Boosting Activities (Hobbies)
5. Career and Achievement

I offer suggestions under each of the 5 Spheres to help you plan these Happiness-Boosting activities so you can improve the overall quality of your life. However, I encourage you to think about what works for you and add the things that you do that you know will fill you up or make you happy. I recommend that you review the 5 Spheres and determine what falls under each sphere for you. What can you do to balance these areas of your life much more, even if you spend a high percentage of your time working during the week? Is it possible to build more happiness-boosting activities into your schedule? The more you do, the better you will feel, and the more productive you will be at work.

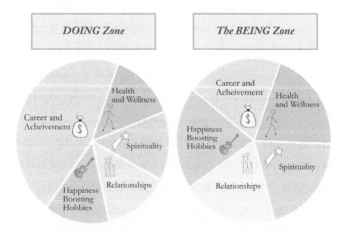

Sphere #1: Career and Achievement

> "Choose a job you love, and you will never
> have to work a day in your life."
> —Confucius

When you have a job where you feel that you are making a difference in the world and are authentic in what you are doing, you probably love to work. When you can do your job with integrity from your heart, with your core values intact, your job will feel even more meaningful to you.

If you're like most of the people I meet, you are likely to feel happiest when your job is in service to others and not just focused on yourself or your gain. When your job puts you in a position where you can be gracious, generous, show appreciation, and feel supportive and supported, you will be more engaged. When you feel challenged and excited by what you are doing, you will love your job even more. Bear in mind, even when you love your job and you feel it is challenging, exciting, and dynamic, you can still burn out.

My challenge to you is to evaluate your career, your job, and your employer. Does it fill you up? Does it make you happy? Do you feel challenged? If you answered those questions with a resounding no, do not despair. If you do not like your current job but are not in a position to change jobs or careers at this moment, there are things you can do to improve how you feel. You can boost your happiness by focusing on what you like about your job. Maybe it's the people you work with or the location of your workspace you like. When you focus on what you enjoy, it makes life easier and more fun.

Client Story: Barry was burned out and unhappy in his job. He worked long hours, going above and beyond to get things done, but was never appreciated. It frustrated him that there was never any consistency, and the directions of the projects he managed were continually changing, causing everything to spiral out of control. He finally made the decision to leave this company, and when interviewing for a new job, he asked potential employers a lot of questions about work-life balance and spent a lot of time looking at company dynamics to ensure that he would go somewhere with more clarity and firm direction. He eventually found the perfect company for his skills and knowledge.

Happiness-Boosting Activities for Career and Achievement

- **Identify what you love most** and see how you can build more of that into your job.
- **Spend your breaks** and free time doing things that fill you up.
- **Take classes** or workshops to learn new things.
- **Cross train** in another area that interests you more than what you are doing.

Journaling Time

CAREER ENRICHMENT JOURNALING EXERCISE #96:
In your notebook or *BEING Journal*, make notes on the following:

- Think about and document what you love to do at work or what you love about your job.
- Take time to identify things you can do during your work breaks that will re-fuel or energize you. It could be things as simple as taking a stretching break or walking at lunch with friends or building in work activities that you enjoy.
- What do you love about your company culture, co-workers or teammates? If you take time to think about what you like about the culture, when times are troubled, you can stay focused on what you do like.
- Make a list of all the things you like about your company and its environment. Keep this list in mind when you get frustrated at work. Examples might be you like the location of your job because it is near trails or shops or has beautiful grounds. Or you might like the décor inside because its calming.
- Write down how many hours you can commit to your career on a daily basis and still maintain happiness. You want to keep it at a reasonable level so you can spend more time doing activities that fill you up outside of work.
- Journal about how much time you spend working and brainstorm ways you may be able to be more efficient so you can spend more time doing activities that fill you up outside of work. Make a list of what some of those activities might be.
- Review your notes in your notebook or *BEING Journal* from Chapter 6 around your purpose and fulfillment to help you move forward in your career? Once you refresh your memory, begin journaling about what conscious decisions you can make to improve your work life, job or career to make it more fulfilling whether it be learning new things or cross-training in another area.

· Now that you have more clarity around your purpose or what is fulfilling to you, is that part of your current job? If not, can you build it into your current work or life by volunteering or having a new hobby?

· Or is it time to start looking for a new career? Consider working with a Career Coach to begin to plan your next step based on your answers.

Sphere #2: Health and Wellness

"The part can never be well unless the whole is well."
—Plato

Your health and wellness are a significant part of your happiness! As you learned in Chapter 5, you are responsible for quieting your mind and listening to your body so you can manage your own health and wellness. The first step is to ask questions when you have symptoms. What is happening in your life that could relate to this type of illness? What is off in your body or your mindset? Listen to what your body is telling you. If you get a heart-palpitations every single time you are driving to work, it could mean work is overwhelming or stressful or it could mean you don't like your job, your boss or your coworkers. Stop and ask yourself, what is it that isn't working for you? That is most likely the root cause of your racing heart. This will provide knowledge so you can start to heal from the inside out as your awareness starts the healing process.

The key to maintaining wellness is to do activities that help your body naturally heal. I've listed some of them below in the Happiness (and Health) Boosting activities. You will find that when you incorporate healing activities into your life, you will feel more uplifted and joyful in your healing process.

Client Story: Jessica told me, "I cannot live like this anymore!" Her life was stressful; she was working too much, zoning out in front of the TV at night, and then staring at the ceiling trying to sleep. She decided to try yoga and meditation out of frustration. She found the practice so calming and relaxing she began to sleep better. As a result, she had more energy in the morning, was able to get a head start on the day and worked this Happiness-Boosting activity into her life for good.

Happiness-Boosting Activities for Health and Wellness

I have listed 10 Happiness-Boosting activities that I enjoy but take the time to brainstorm what works for you.

- **Grounding or Spending Time in Nature:** Grounding is where you spend time sitting on or standing barefoot in the grass or on the earth. The Earth's energy is known to be very healing and can increase happiness. This is my #1 daily health and wellness activity. You learned about Earthing/Grounding in Chapters 5, 7, and 8.
- **Qigong:** The National Qigong Association describes Qigong as a mind-body-spirit practice that improves one's health by integrating posture, movement, breathing technique, self-massage, sound, and focused intent. Learn more by searching YouTube for videos with Qigong. I personally like Simon Blow, who I found on the Qigong Institute website at https://www.qigonginstitute.org/.
- **Yoga:** There are all kinds of yoga. I personally like Yin Yoga, Flow Yoga, or Kundalini Yoga, all of which I find to be healing and calming, which brings better energy into my body. Find an online course or a class near you.
- **Meditation or Relaxation:** Building these into your daily practices calms your system and decreases the likelihood of illness.

There are many examples throughout the book, or at www.TheBEINGZone.com/tools and you can find free or low-cost options online. There are also many good meditation apps.

- **Sound Healing Classes:** Sound and vibration can re-tune a body. Sound therapy is powerful for healing your mind, body, and spirit. Vibrating sound therapy has proven to have significant results on human health, both physiologically and mentally. The low vibrations increase cellular movement, thus increasing energy and cellular regeneration in the body. Consequently, both inflammation and pain reduce because of this treatment. You can create your sounds, listen to many healing sounds online, or attend Sound Healing classes.

- **Diet Decisions:** Eat what makes you feel good and gives you energy. Your body responds best to naturally grown, minimally processed food instead of highly processed food. The best foods don't have a label or ingredient list. It is hard to be perfect all of the time. I follow the 85-15 rule, where if you eat well 85% of the time, you can allow more indulgences the other 15%.

- **Supplements:** Your body has the natural ability to heal, and much of your diet can achieve what you need if you eat the right foods. For things your body lacks, you may need supplements. You can find the right combinations intuitively or work with a good naturopath.

- **Essential Oils:** Essential oils can be game-changers in health. They were instrumental in my own healing and are primarily what I use today to maintain my health. Oils are powerful solutions for all ailments as they are natural and from the earth. Herbs and essential oils have been used for literally thousands of years, starting with early healers and Shamans. Oils utilize the power of the natural earth in healing your mind, body, and soul. Learn more here: https://www.doterra.com/US/en/site/practicalsolutionszone

- **Acupressure:** This is an easy-to-learn practice that you can do at home in just minutes. You can search online for acupressure points for specific ailments or pains and find images showing you exactly where the points are for that complaint. It involves putting a small amount of pressure on and massaging specific points along the energy pathways that run through your body (which are the same points acupuncturists utilize). Just the small amount of pressure in the right location helps to correct imbalances in the body which helps to heal you. It is a daily practice for me depending on what is going on in my body.

- **Sound Sleep:** Your health, happiness, and well-being are intrinsically tied to the soundness of your sleep. If you are not a sound sleeper or cannot fall asleep quickly, there are many things you can do. Diffusing lavender into your room or putting it on your palms and rubbing together and breathing in the smell in deeply is a helpful way to get your mind quieted. You should turn off all electronic stimuli at least an hour before bed—read a book or journal, instead. If you wake up at night, repeat the process. The last thing you want to do is say "I can't sleep," as that will become your reality.

Journaling Time

HAPPINESS-BOOSTING ACTIVITIES FOR HEALTH
AND WELLNESS JOURNALING EXERCISE #97:

Grab your notebook or *BEING Journal* and make notes.

- Write about spending time in nature or outside and how it feels to you.
  Write about your Grounding experience if you got outside to try it.

- Write about your Qigong or Yoga experience if you got online and tried it out or took a class. Talk about how you might build qigong or yoga into your life.
- Describe how you can build more meditation into your life. Think about the time of day, the source of the meditation. What is your favorite part of meditation?
- Identify some relaxation exercises that resonate with you and describe how it makes you feel and how you might be able to build a meditation practice into your life.
- What experiences have you had with sound healing? How did it feel during and after? Is this something that is a good match for you? If so, make notes on how you will build sound healing into your life.
- Think about what diet changes may be the most beneficial for you and write about it. What healthy foods can you add to your diet? What do you want to delete from your diet?
- What supplements may be the most beneficial for you? Is it time to see your doctor or naturopath to help you make these decisions?
- Make notes on what physical, mental, or emotional issues are impacting your life most. Then do an online search to see which essential oils would be helpful in your healing process. You want to be sure you are using therapeutic grade oils to ensure the best results.
- Describe the aches, pain, ailments, illnesses you would like to correct in your body. Then search online as to which acupressure points would be most useful for you, or you can schedule an appointment with a reflexologist or acupressure specialist or acupuncturist for treatment. Create a daily regimen of the points you would like to focus on if you are going to do acupressure on yourself.
- Write about your sleep habits and do some research on what might help you the most. Bear in mind that essential oils and acupressure can be very effective.
- What are the health and wellness activities you already do that are not on the list?

Sphere #3: Spirituality

"The spiritual life does not remove us from
the world but leads us deeper into it."
—Henri J.M. Nouwen

Spirituality, in this context, means spending time daily connecting with someone or something greater than yourself. It isn't about religion. It is about spirituality, and that word means something different to each of us. Do what you feel is right for you. There is no right or wrong here.

When I talk about spirituality, what I am talking about is more like good old-fashioned prayer or asking Source for guidance. It is about connecting directly; I do this many times throughout the day. It's never a wrong time to get connected to Source—you can do this any time. One of the upsides of having a spiritual connection every day is that you'll never feel alone. You'll know you have guidance and support available to you at a moment's notice. The key is to look for divine guidance and hold it with reverence, by showing and giving appreciation too. I myself am incredibly grateful for all I receive. I always offer my services for the greater good of all while in prayer, and I know everything will unfold exactly like it's meant to. I trust the process because I know it's for the betterment of not just myself but the world.

Happiness-Boosting Activities for Spirituality

Here are a few ideas but take the time to brainstorm what works for you in the journaling section below.

· **Grounding**: Grounding is one of my favorites for wellness and spirituality. You will learn to feel the energy flowing into you from the earth and begin to feel deeply connected to Source while doing this. Go back to Chapters 5, 7, and 8 to refresh your memory on Grounding techniques.

· **Connect with Universal Energy:** This is a great activity for connection whenever the sky is full of stars and constellations. It is a beautiful way to go into a deep meditative state and connect with Source through vibrations in your third eye. When you are in this deeply connected state, ask questions and look for guidance.

· **Morning Prayer:** Here is an example of a morning prayer you can use, or create your own of course. "Thank you, Spirit, for directing me where you would have me go for the highest good of myself and the world today. What does the world need from me? How may I best serve? Show me the way. I am open to all messages and signs and will hold your guidance with reverence."

Journaling Time

HAPPINESS-BOOSTING ACTIVITIES FOR
SPIRITUALITY JOURNALING EXERCISE #98:

Grab your *BEING Journal* or notebook and begin to journal.

· Write down how you will build Grounding into your life to increase your connection with Source.

· Write about how you plan to build connecting with Source into your life.

· Write about your current prayer practices or the new ones you would like to adopt.

Sphere #4: Relationships

"If civilization is to survive, we must cultivate the science
of human relationships—the ability of all peoples, of all
kinds, to live together, in the same world at peace."
—Franklin D. Roosevelt

Our mental health and personal well-being are all tied up in the quality of our personal relationships and connections. The more closely we are connected to the people we love, the happier we feel, and the more personal satisfaction we have in our lives. When surveyed, people rate moments of connection and shared enjoyment with their loved ones as some of their most important life experiences.[109]

These critical relationships include not only family and personal friends, but also the groups we join. Having a sense of community contributes to our long-term well-being, whether it is a larger local social group, like the Yacht Club my husband and I belong to, or a group of neighbors who like to watch sporting events together. You may have friends who go to art or music events, or who like to cook with or visit fine restaurants. We tend to gravitate to others like ourselves, who share our interests, and that makes relationships fun. So, gather your friends who love doing art projects and sign up for classes to learn new things together, or find people to golf or bike or rock climb, or whatever activity speaks most to your heart. Having a sense of belonging with other people adds to your sense of personal meaning and fulfillment.

 Client Story: Peggy has a very demanding and stressful job and has learned to maintain balance by eating healthy and incorporating exercise and yoga (on top of her 5 Daily

B.E.I.N.G. Steps practice) into her schedule. Instead of zoning out in front of the TV, she fills herself back up by spending time with friends doing activities that make her happy. She loves to knit and has joined a knitting group where they socialize and "solve the world's problems." Peggy has another group of friends that she hikes with on the weekends. She lives a much more balanced life than she did when we first met.

Happiness-Boosting Activities for Relationship Building

Below I have listed a few ideas but take the time to brainstorm what works for you.

- **Get Active:** Whether you are biking, hiking, bowling, or golfing for enjoyment or competitively, spending time with friends doing sports or active activities you enjoy is a happiness booster. This can include both individual and group sports or physical activities.
- **Play Games with Friends or Family:** Gather around a table and enjoy each other. Card games and drawing games are great for groups. Puzzles are a favorite of many families. You can also add in a few active outdoor games like badminton, bocce, volleyball, or croquet.
- **Join a Book Club or Watch Movies with Friends or Family:** Books are often more fun to read when you can discuss them with others at a social event. Movies that you share at home, outdoors, or in the theaters can also be conversation starters to make you laugh or think.
- **Cooking Clubs, Classes, or Entertaining:** Spending time with friends planning and preparing meals, and perhaps enjoying a

nice glass of wine, will boost your joy. If you're not much of a cook, consider taking cooking classes with friends and experimenting with new ideas.

- **Attend Events with Friends and Family:** Make an event out of a sporting, musical, comedy, or arts event by planning a meal before or after the event to create space for conversation.
- **Join Groups, Clubs, or Exercise Classes:** Join an exercise class or a club. Over time, you will find you build rapport with those who attend with you.

Journaling Time

RELATIONSHIP BUILDING JOURNALING EXERCISE #99:

In your *BEING Journal* or notebook, take time to write.

- Write about which type of relationship building activities you might enjoy the most. They may not be included in the above list as everyone has different interests. Make a commitment to at least one activity that you can begin building into your life today!
- Write about what activities you love to do, inside and out.
- What are some of your favorite games and who might be interested in playing games with you?
- Identify potential friends to have book club or movie night with to bring more enrichment into your life.
- What groups or clubs can you join?
- Are there any classes or events you have an interest in that you could plan on attending?

Sphere #5: Happiness-Boosting Activities

"Happiness is when what you think, what you
say, and what you do are in harmony."
—Mahatma Gandhi

When you spend time doing things you love, it fills you up. Even when you are exhausted, you can choose calming activities that refill your reserves and do not drain you more than you already are. For instance, as we've seen, taking an art class is more rejuvenating than watching TV. Taking a walk on the beach is much more relaxing than surfing the web. There are so many things you can do that are fulfilling, Happiness-Boosting, and fun!

Happiness-Boosting Activities

Below are many different ideas for boosting your happiness. You will also want to brainstorm things that you believe would make you happy have wanted to try and put them on your list.

- **Art or Crafts:** Art therapy is making a tremendous impact in the healing world. Art increases your brains flexibility, adaptability, and ability to heal.[110] Try to do at least one art or craft project every month. You don't have to be an artist, and it doesn't even matter how the project turns out. What's important is getting lost in the moment with what you are working on, and art does that. Some fun ideas I have tried includes stone carving, fused glass, raku, pottery, jewelry making, basket weaving, painting, printmaking, etc.
- **Use Music for Healing:** Just listening to music or singing along is very healing and improves memory function.[111] Researchers have found that learning to play a musical instrument can

enhance verbal memory, spatial reasoning, and literacy skills.[112] Playing an instrument makes you use both sides of your brain, which strengthens memory power. It is also a stress reliever. You don't have to pick up a difficult-to-learn instrument. I have an Indigenous rattle and drums as well as sound bowls, which all increase my energy when I play them. Just listening to music is very healing.

· **Writing:** Picking up a pen, pencil, or even keyboard is a very healing and releasing process.[113] You can journal your feelings, thoughts, and ah-ha's; hand write a grocery list; post a note or letter to a friend; or set out to create your family history or write your first book. The art of writing is a healing and therapeutic activity.

· **Spend Time with Those You Love:** Being social and spending time with others increases your health and happiness.

  · **Family or friends help you cope with stress.** A study conducted by Carnegie Mellon University found that people use their family and friends as a stress buffer, talking about their problems instead of seeking harmful coping mechanisms like drinking alcohol, smoking, or doing drugs.[114]

  · **May lengthen your life.** An article in the *American Society of Aging* noted that older adults with more extensive social networks have better memory and better cognitive functions.[115] Having a good relationship with a spouse, children, siblings, and friends contributes to these positive health effects.

  · **Improves your psychological well-being.** One study found that people who view their friends and families as supportive, reported a greater sense of meaning in life and felt like they had a stronger sense of purpose.[116]

  · **Is good for your cardiovascular health.** Having good friends and a strong social support network can relieve stress, and lower pulse and blood pressure.

- **Practice Gratitude and Keep a Gratitude Journal:** Gratitude (also called thankfulness) is strongly and consistently associated with greater happiness as discussed in Chapter 4. When you are grateful, you are more likely to feel better, have more positive experiences, and build stronger relationships.[117] If you buy a new car, you might begin to notice that car everywhere. The same is true with thankfulness. If you are thankful for kindness, you might start noticing and receiving more kindness. A gratitude journal is simply a place to write down what you are grateful for. Just taking the time to write it is very powerful.

- **Keep Active:** This can be anything from individual sports to team sports or playing pinball machines. Finding a physical activity that you enjoy is important for physical movement and keeping your body flexible. Exercise helps you control your weight which can reduce your risk of heart disease and help your body manage blood sugar and insulin levels. It is also known to improve your mental health and mood. Just get outside for a walk and pay attention to how good you feel afterwards. In general, it's widely known that exercise is good for the body and mind.

- **Explore Nature:** Getting outdoors is extremely healing. You can sit in your yard, work in your garden, or take a hike. Or you might be happier exploring a local trail, a park near your home, or find a place where you can experience water as it is known to be a powerful healer as explained by marine biologist and author of the 2014 book *Blue Mind*, Wallace Nichols.[118] He states, "People can experience the benefits of the water whether they're near the ocean, lake, river, pond, swimming pool or even listening to the soothing sound of a fountain." The important thing is to enjoy these places from a *BEING* standpoint, where you are present in the moment.

· **Try New Things:** Some of your favorite things for building happiness may be things you haven't tried yet. Have you ever gone skydiving, ridden in a hot air balloon, or gone ziplining? What about going to a Native American pow wow? How about axe-throwing or a soapbox derby? Be creative.

Journaling Time

HAPPINESS-BOOSTING ACTIVITIES TO

INCORPORATE JOURNALING EXERCISE #100:

Grab your *BEING Journal* or notebook and make some commitments.

· Which Happiness-Boosting activities would work the best for you? Make a commitment to add one or two of these to your daily routine.

· Are you open to arts, crafts or music? If so, which?

· Do you like to write? What type of writing activities can you build into your life?

· Who do you love to spend time with? How can it help you?

· Do you have a gratitude journal? Do you use it? Can you commit to trying this? Write about what you will commit to now.

· What activities can you add to your life that will keep you active or outdoors in nature?

· What new things can you try?

Bottomline, Happiness-Boosting activities will increase your mental, physical, and spiritual well-being.

Key Messages

- The foundation of good health and happiness is based on a healthy mind, body, and spirit.
- Become aware of and avoid anything or anyone who drains or exhausts you.
- Build Happiness-Boosting activities into your life. The more you do things just because you love doing them, the more energy you'll have and the happier you will be.
- There are five spheres in your life to focus on achieving balance and they include health and wellness, spirituality, relationships, hobbies, and career.
- Working in a job you love while doing things that fill you up is the answer, whether it is engaging in meditation or yoga, listening to music, doing art, spending time outdoors, spending time with friends, being grateful, eating right, and taking care of yourself.
- Balancing all spheres of your life will lower your stress, boost your immunity, decrease depression, and increase your happiness and health.

> **This Chapter's Gifts:** The opportunity for you to identify healthy activities in all 5 Spheres of your life from your career, health, spirituality, relationships to Happiness-Boosting hobbies that you can integrate into your busy schedule to bring more balance and joy into your daily life.

CHAPTER 10

The 5 Daily B.E.I.N.G. Steps

"We carry inside us the wonders we seek outside us."
—Rumi

MOST OF MY clients whose stories I include in this book have told me that the 5 Daily B.E.I.N.G Steps have become the most critical part of their day. You may not yet see the value of building this practice into your day, and I am here to tell you, it will be well worth your time. Your consistency will be the game-changer.

These 5 Daily B.E.I.N.G. Steps are the daily practice that I encourage all my clients to implement in their lives, so they are able to stay in *The BEING Zone*. My clients say the difference between doing the daily practice and not doing the practice is the difference between having a good day and a bad day. I can attest to the same. I must do my morning practice, or I will be off kilter for the entire day. My clients tell me they do these steps and get results in less than 10 minutes per day.

To ensure that your 5 Daily B.E.I.N.G Steps practice becomes as routine as brushing your teeth, post it on your mirror, save it in your phone, set reminders on your calendar (with alerts), and do whatever works best for you, until it becomes a way of life.

What Are the 5 Daily B.E.I.N.G. Steps?

Step #1 - B: Move into Your *BEING Zone*

Step #2 - E: Change Your **Energy**

Step #3 - I: State Your **Intentions**

Step #4 - N: Affirm Your True **North**, AKA Purpose

Step #5 - G: Ask for Universal **Guidance**

This chapter will offer you many tools for building your practice, as no one way works for everyone. There are many ways you can design and enhance your practice to fit you, your lifestyle, and your uniqueness. You will find a sample or foundational practice below that is an example of how I usually get my clients started on a daily practice. Following the sample, you will see a form that will assist you in customizing your practice. This outline will help guide you in making decisions to replace the sample foundational practice with any of the tool options found throughout the book that resonate with you.

I am always amazed by how quickly my clients get clarity on what will work for them and automatically build that into their daily practice. It makes it individualized, and they become more committed to the process. Some people can do their daily practice in as little as eight to ten minutes and some like to spend up to an hour or more. Let's start with a sample plan so you understand what we are looking for before you start customizing your own plan for the long run.

Sample *BEING Zone* Plan

Below, you will find a sample of easy-to-do B.E.I.N.G. steps to get you started. You will want to follow this sample and build it into your everyday life until you feel comfortable making it more individualized. You can download a PDF or listen to a recording of this sample 5 Daily B.E.I.N.G. Steps at www.TheBEING-Zone.com/tools.

Step #1 - B: Move into Your *BEING Zone*

 Three-Part Breathing
(Tool #2 from Chapter 3)

Take a deep breath in through your nose (breathing in love) for a count of three, hold it for a count of three, and release (all that doesn't serve you) for a count of three. Repeat three times.

Tool #50: Beach Relaxation

Visualize yourself on a beautiful, secluded white sand beach in a tropical location.

· See yourself lying in a soft, comfortable hammock in the shade of two palm trees, where enough sunlight filters through to keep you warm. There is a light breeze in the air that flows through the soft strands of the hammock.

- The hammock hangs low to the ground, so when you drop your hand or foot over the side, you can feel the warmth of the sand beneath you. Visualize scooping up a small handful of sand and drizzling it through your fingers with ease.
- As you lie in this hammock, listen to the waves flowing in and out, calming your body and your soul. You can see beautiful birds in the trees around you. Sink into the depth of their songs. You can smell the exotic flowers that surround you as well as the salty smell of the ocean, relaxing your mind and soul.
- As you lie in the hammock, tuning into the sounds, smells, views, and textures all around you, you begin to feel your body physically relax. Your toes and feet begin to tingle and go numb. Feel the warmth and comfort begin to flow up into your legs and up into your core. Feel it flow into your neck and head and down your arms to your fingertips.
- Turn up the volume of this feeling as your body melts into your hammock and the experience. Stay in this space until you are ready to move. Listen to a recording of this tool at www.The-BEINGZone.com/tools.

Step #2 - E: Change Your Energy

 Magnet in the Bubble
(Tool #32 from Chapter 7)

Visualize a bubble floating above your head (like the kind a child would blow). In that bubble is the most powerful magnet in the world. Allow that magnet to pull out of you anything and everything that does not serve you. Feel any tightness in your head, jaw, neck, or shoulders get magnetized up and out. Allow all of your stress, worry, or concerns to get sucked up into that bubble. That bubble will get bigger and darker but will keep floating above your head. When you feel light and energized, put your hand up, touch that bubble and watch it float up into the universe and dissipate.

 Tree Grounding Visualization (Tool #44 from Chapter 7)

Visualize yourself as a tree. Not just any tree, but the most beautiful tree in the world. It can be any kind of tree that you like. Feel the sun's rays coming down and warming your leaves and branches (your head, shoulders, and arms). Feel that warmth flowing down through your core and legs (your trunk) and out through the bottom of your feet as your roots seep into the soft soils of Mother Earth. Feel the powerful Grounding energy from the Earth flowing back up those roots into the bottom of your feet. Feel your feet begin to tingle and warm. Allow the energy, warmth, and tingling to flow up into your calves, your thighs, across your hips up through your core, to your neck and head, and then down across your shoulders, through your arms to your fingertips. Sit and resonate in that energy.

Step #3 - I: State Your Intentions

What Is an Intention Statement?

Intention statements are words that help you create a vision and set the tone for what you want to achieve in life. They should be closely related to your values.

What Do Intentions Look Like?

Intentions are meant to be clear and specific, believable and realistic. The three simple guidelines for writing an intention statement are:

· Write it as if it is happening now or in present tense.
· Focus on how it feels.
· Build in gratitude.

Example Intention Statements (to say out loud or to yourself)

· I am grateful I am able to easily move through this day being grounded and present.
· I am thankful that I am able to be inspired, happy, and healthy today and every day.
· I am blessed to be able to live with compassion filling my heart with forgiveness for myself and all those whom I need to release.

How to Use Them

It is best to write your intentions so you can read through them, say them in your head or out loud and feel into them. Feeling into intentions means you imagine how it would feel in your body if they were a reality. For instance, to feel into the first intention statement, I would visualize myself feeling present and grounded in that moment, as well as seeing myself go through the day feeling the ease of being grounded and very present. When you have written intentions, you will have a history that you can tweak as you grow and begin to feel like they are becoming a reality and you want to take them to the next level.

Step #4 - N: Affirm Your True North, AKA Purpose

What does it mean to affirm your True North or life's purpose? It means turning your life's purpose into a daily verbalization.

What Do Affirmations of Your Purpose Look Like?

· Your affirmations are written statements demonstrating your alignment with your mission in life or higher purpose in this moment.
· You want to affirm what you want and not what you don't want.
· They are based in the now and therefore usually start with the statement, I am.
· You only want 1 or 2 affirmations so you can stay focused on what is most important.

Example Affirmations

· I am on Earth to help transform our world into a better place full of love.
· I am love and my purpose is to spread and receive love daily.
· I am the architect of my life and choose its foundations and contents.

How to Use Affirmations

Write your affirmations down and then say them out loud (or in your head if needed) and feel into them. What it would feel like if it was a reality? I often stand in front of a mirror, look myself in the eyes and repeat them as if I am speaking my truth to others. You want to focus on the meaning of each word or group of words as you say them. I recommend repeating your affirmations more than once.

Step #5 - G: Ask for Universal Guidance

What Does It Mean to Ask for Guidance?

What does it mean to ask for guidance? It means you are committed to releasing control to be led by a power greater than yourself.

What Does It Look Like to Ask for Guidance?

- When you ask for guidance, you fully surrender your Ego and open up your heart and mind to the concept that you will have faith in the messages that come to you.
- The guidance you receive can show up in many different forms. You might hear words or even just one word, like *peace*. You might get visuals, like a yellow brick road which might mean you need to follow your path to enlightenment just like in the movie, *The Wizard of Oz*. A song may pop into your head, like the Beatles song, *"All You Need Is Love"* when you need to feel more loved. Or it could be a sign, like when the numbers on your clock show 444, which is the sign the angels are sending you encouragement.

Examples of Guidance Requests (to say out loud or to yourself)

- Today, Divine Source show me the way. I am open to all messages and signs. I will listen from deep inside and hold your guidance with reverence. I will move as if there is a force of love and light waiting to aid me in every area of my life, big and small. Use me, whatever I can give, for the highest good of all. Just let me be helpful and contribute what I am meant to, to this world. Then sit in that energy and see what comes to you. When you are ready, take a deep breath and move into your day!

· Source, what does the world need from me today? What do people or others need from me? How may I best serve?

· Divine Source, how I can best resolve an issue with a family member or friend? Guide me in this process, I am all ears.

Guidance Statements

Your requests can be a longer paragraph or short sentences as shown above. The key is to be open to what you might hear when you ask for guidance and follow it. When you are in a quiet, meditative type state and leave space for listening or hearing messages after you read the statement, you are most likely to hear or feel something.

Journaling Time

SAMPLE DAILY PRACTICE JOURNALING EXERCISE #101:
Grab your notebook or *BEING Journal* and make notes.

· First practice utilizing the sample daily practice and make notes on what worked for you.

· Document what parts you liked best and what you might change when you customize it as described below.

Customizing the 5 Daily B.E.I.N.G. Steps Practice

Now that you've seen the sample and understand the steps, there are ways to make this practice your own. There are so many options to choose from, more are listed here for your customization and further exploration of each step are listed below.

Step #1 - B: Move into Your *BEING Zone*

> "If you are depressed, you are living it the past. If you are anxious, you are living in the future. If you are at peace, you are living in the present."
> —Lao Tzu

"B for *BEING*" Overview

Start your day by releasing your stress and your fears so you can be the calm, clear co-creator of your own destiny. This step is about calming your body through breathing, meditation, or relaxation exercises. You will be operating in the present or *The BEING Zone*.

Breath is essential to life. Most people tend to breathe in a very shallow way and do not oxygenate their bodies enough. As a result, they get more tension in their bodies and tend to feel more anxious and stressed. When you take the time to breathe deeply and consciously, it helps to restore balance in your mind and body while centering you. You will discover the more you practice basic breathing, meditation, and relaxation techniques, the more you will increase your state of well-being and resilience. Bottom line, you will be happier and healthier by learning to quiet your mind while tuning into, listening to, and communicating effectively with your body!

To help you get into and operate in *The BEING Zone*, there are three breathing exercises you already learned in Chapter 3, and the following pages include additional examples for Breathing and Meditation/Mindfulness & Relaxation exercises. I recommend you always include a breathing exercise to start and follow with either a meditation, mindfulness, or relaxation exercise. Use the tool appendix to find other examples throughout the book.

Tool #51: Belly Breathing

When you breathe in slowly and deeply, watching your belly and chest rise and then watching them fall, it becomes almost hypnotic and calms your system. Belly Breathing requires you to focus on filling your belly with air. You can test this by placing your hands over your rib cage right under your chest and taking in a big breath of air. Your ribs should move out in the front, sides, and back. If you feel them move this way, you are doing it right.

This breathing practice is like the Three-Part Breathing explained in Chapter 3 but focuses on the physical movement of your belly. Repeat each part three times for maximum results.

- Breathe in through your nose, filling up your belly for a count of three and holding for three. Watch your belly expand.
- Release through your mouth (for a count of three), letting everything go that does not serve you: your stress, your worry, any tension, etc. Watch your belly flatten.
- Repeat three to five breaths until you feel calm and relaxed.

Tool #52: Meditation by Walking

This exercise will help you become ultra-alert and in tune to your surroundings, especially nature. As you walk slowly, you are totally in touch with everything. It takes training, but it is fantastic once you master it.

- Choose a walk or a hike. Select a location where there is less traffic, fewer people, and not as many distractions. My favorite is a trail hike.
- Before you start, do your Three-Part Breathing to get centered.
- This walk is not about speed or endurance but is all about connection. Maintain a decent pace if you wish, but stop, smell, feel, and connect often as you go.
- With every step, be deeply aware of your surroundings. Use all your senses:
  - **Eyes:** Notice the colors of the leaves, bushes, plants, and flowers. Look at the sky and notice its color and whether or not there are any clouds.
  - **Nose:** If there is a flower, stop and smell it. Notice the differences in scents from a cedar tree to a fir tree, or the different kinds of grass.
  - **Ears:** Listen to the birds and other sounds, like the wind, and even the sounds of cars or planes or boats.
  - **Touch:** Touch the leaves or the bark on a tree. Notice the different textures. Take your shoes off at some point and feel the surfaces of the Earth on your bare feet.

The key is to entirely tune into where you are and what you're doing.

If you find yourself getting distracted by your phone or that voice in your head, pull yourself back to the present and continue. Once you get comfortable walking, invite your children or another person. You can even go blindfolded, having another person lead you. Ask them to help you touch different textures so you can guess what it might be. This exercise will help heighten your hearing, smell, and touch.

Tool #53: Mindfulness Meditation

The only thing you need is you and your breath!

· Find a comfortable seat wherever you wish. You can sit on the floor, in a chair, cross-legged, legs extended, it doesn't matter. Sit tall, with a straight spine. (If you have back pain, lay on your back but stay awake.)
· Focus on your breath. Focus on the feeling of the air entering and exiting your nostrils, or the expansion and release in your lungs and chest. It can help to breathe in and out to a count of four or six. (In…2…3…4…5…6. Pause. Out…2…3…4…5…6. Pause.) Counting will keep your mind from wandering.
· Notice when your mind begins to wander. Your mind will wander. Simply note that you are thinking (In your mind's eye, consider the word "thinking") and then go back to counting your in-and-out breaths.

The main goal of the practice lies in the "breath/mind wandering/breath" cycle. Thoughts will creep in a thousand times from your active subconscious mind. Let that happen, and then continue redirecting your focus back to your breath each time.

Start with three-minute sessions. Three minutes will feel like an eternity at first. Little by little, you can increase the amount of time you spend on this practice until you get to the ideal time for you, whether it be 5, 10, 15, or 30 minutes. Set a timer so you're not distracted by looking at the clock. There is a recording of the mindfulness meditation at www.TheBEINGZone.com/tools.

> **Note:** There is an Open-Heart Meditation Tool in Chapter 4 or you can find many meditation audio recordings online.

Tool #54: Mountain Top Relaxation

You can find a recording of this relaxation exercise at www. TheBEINGZone.com/tools.

- Start with Three-Part Breathing to calm and relax your body. Now visualize yourself at the top of beautiful mountain, leaning back against a comfortable rock that supports you beautifully. You feel so relaxed after your long hike. You are in heaven as you can see forever and ever from this place. You are looking out at other mountain tops, meadows, mountain lakes and feel as though you are on top of the world. Feast in the beauty.
- There are a few beautiful trees just above you that are filtering the sunlight, so you are entirely comfortable. You drop your hand to the ground and can feel the texture of the soft soils as they slide through your fingers. As you sit in the beautiful place, you can feel and hear the light breeze flowing through, keeping you comfortable. You see an eagle soaring and floating above you as he seeks out his next meal or resting place. You

hear a woodpecker in the woods working steadily away. Listen to the songs of the small birds as they flit about.

· As you lay back, close your eyes and begin to feel your body physically relax. Your toes and feet start to tingle and numb. Feel that warmth and comfort begin to flow up into your legs and up into your core. Feel it flow into your neck, head, and down your arms to your fingertips.

· Turn up the volume of this tingly, warm feeling as your body melts into this space and the experience. Then just stay in this space until you are ready to move again.

Tool #55: Sound and Earth Based Relaxation

You can find a recording of this relaxation exercise at www. TheBEINGZone.com/tools. Lying on the earth is very powerful while chanting Om. Om is pronounced like au-em, and you want to draw that sound from your belly, so it is deep and resonating. When chanted, Om vibrates at the frequency of 432 Hz—the same vibrational frequency of the earth.

· Go outside and lie in the grass or on a beach, looking up at the blue skies with the sun warming your body. Notice the light breeze in the air, keeping you cool and comfortable.

· As you lie on the grass or beach, close your eyes and do some deep breathing to quiet your body and mind. Listen to sounds around you. Feel yourself sinking into the depth of being present.

· As you lie there in the grass tuning into the sounds, smells and textures all around you, you can begin to feel your body physically relax.

- Then take a deep breath, filling yourself with air. As you release, quietly chant the Om sound with a long O (au) sound followed by a long M or (em) sound. Repeat 3 to 5 times.
- Notice how your body begins to vibrate with the Om sound.
- You might notice a vibrational feeling in your neck, head, and arms. You might feel that warmth and comfort is flowing throughout your core. You may feel your legs, feet, and toes begin to tingle and numb.
- Turn up the volume of this feeling as your body melts into the grass and the experience. Then just stay in this space until you are ready to move.

Tool #56: Acupressure

A very quick and simple solution for lowering anxiety and stress so you can relax is massaging an acupressure point on your ear or forehead. If you have a calming essential oil handy (such as lavender, serenity, balance, or any woods) use them to massage these acupressure points.

The ear point is called the heavenly gate point and is located in the upper shell of your ear, at the tip of the triangle-like hollow there. Stimulating this point is said to help relieve anxiety, stress, and insomnia.

To use this point:

· Locate the point in your ear. It might help to use a mirror.
· Apply firm, gentle pressure in a circular motion for two minutes.

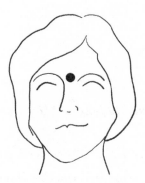

The forehead point location lies between your eyebrows where there is a small indentation. Applying pressure to this point is said to help with both anxiety and stress.

To use this point:

· Sit comfortably. It can help to close your eyes.
· Touch the spot between your eyebrows with your index finger or thumb.
· Take slow, deep breaths and apply gentle, firm pressure in a circular motion for 5 to 10 minutes.

More Helpful Practices to Get in *The BEING Zone* State

As we've seen in previous chapters, restorative practices such as Yin Yoga, Flow Yoga, and Kundalini Yoga are suitable for building both breathing and Grounding skills. Making one of these a regular practice two or three times a week will put you in a grounded, relaxed state, which will help you to exist in *The BEING Zone* even more.

Journaling Time

YOUR PLAN FOR YOUR "B" STEP FOR THE B.E.I.N.G.
PRACTICE JOURNALING EXERCISE #102:

In your *BEING Journal* or notebook, document your B Step.

- Review the above section and choose what activities resonate most with you. Write those down and create a plan to ensure it is part of your daily practice.

- Put it into your calendar or reminders. I put my steps into the Notepad section on my cell phone so whereever I am, whatever I am doing, I have access to reading and reminding myself of my current commitments.

Step #2 - E: Change Your Energy

"The more you lose yourself in something bigger
than yourself, the more energy you will have."
—Norman Vincent Peal

"E for ENERGY" Overview

The E Step is about managing your energy. In Chapter 7, you learned how to recognize bad and draining energy and how to release it, as well as how to bring in good energy which will put you in a happier state. Now it's time to apply it to your daily practice.

As demonstrated in Chapter 7, there are many negative energy-releasing exercises and tools for getting grounded and bringing in good energy, including the Cutting Energetic Cords, Magnet in a Bubble, the Vacuum, and the Waterfall Shower. Choose which tools fit you best, and what enables you to tune into your energetic body so you can release stuck energy and bring in good energy. The following tools will give you additional ideas for releasing energy. In time you will intuitively know which one is right based on how you feel that day.

A Few New Tools for Releasing or Moving Stuck or Bad Energy

Tool #57: Trap Door

Lie down, either on the floor or on a bed, and visualize opening a trap door on the back of your body to release anything and everything you don't want: disease, stress, etc. Breathe deeply and watch everything drain out that trap door. When you feel it is complete, visualize closing the door. You can find a recording of the Trap Door tool at www.TheBEINGZone.com/tools.

Tool #58: Releasing Statements

Say the following statements out loud.

- I release all that doesn't serve me or the greater good.
- I forgive and release all who have wronged me and others.
- I release anger, conflict, and hatred and am free to be me.
- I release old blocks and beliefs that no longer serve me or others.
- I release stuckness and illness in my body.

Tool #59: Take an Epsom Salt Bath with Oils

A healing soak in Epsom Salt will help remove built up lactic acid, bringing relief to sore muscles and further aiding in relaxation to help release stress and negativity. I suggest setting an intention while you're soaking to release all negativity and enhance the cleansing of your body and aura. You could also think about adding an essential oil. Lavender is very calming, another great oil to use is frankincense, it's known as being super powerful at removing negative energy from the body, aura, and environment.

Journaling Time

YOUR PLAN FOR STEP "E" OF THE DAILY B.E.I.NG.
PRACTICE JOURNALING EXERCISE #103:
Write Your E Step into your *BEING Journal* or notebook.

> · Review the above practices as well as all the other energy tools you
> learned in Chapter 7, and journal about which ones you will begin
> to use on a daily basis. If you plan to use your cell phone Notepad
> like I do, add these notes there also.

Step #3 - I: State Your Intentions

"You must be the change you wish to see in the world."
—Mahatma Gandhi

"I for INTENTIONS" Overview

This step is about setting your intention for the day, every day!
Stating your intentions for each of the 5 Sphere areas is an effective way to get started and get your life into balance.

Remember, what you focus on becomes your reality. You must
say what you want, and intentions allow you to do just that. Integrating gratitude statements with your intention statements will
build a higher vibration. Manifesting your intentions requires
being in that high vibration state of receiving. In the book *The
Power of Thanks*, authors Eric Mosley and Derek Irvine state
"Gratitude magnifies the spirit and promotes well-being. In good
times and bad, authentic appreciation creates perspective, literally
stepping back from the distractions of the moment and affirm-
ing something more lasting than passing circumstance."[119] There
are multiple exercises throughout this book for creating intention statements and mantras for balancing all 5 Spheres of your
life's activities. Start with the generic options outlined below and
build it from there to meet your daily needs.

Clear Intentions

This isn't about dictating the outcome; it is about giving a very broad statement (I gratefully intend to live my life with ease and grace) and then allowing the Universe to help define what that means.

5 Sample Intention Statements:

1. **Career & Achievement**: I am grateful that I remain in good energy and well-balanced in my work-life and professional growth.
2. **Health & Wellness**: I am thankful I can eat healthy, exercise, and spend time Grounding daily.
3. **Relationships**: I am blessed to be able to spend quality time doing fun things with friends and family.
4. **Spirituality**: I am grateful for the opportunity to connect with Source daily and seek guidance.
5. **Happiness-Boosting Activities**: I am thankful I am able to do one Happiness-Boosting activity each day.

Additional General Intention Statements:

- I am grateful I am inspired, happy, and healthy today and every day.
- I am blessed that I am able to create and maintain harmony and balance in every day.
- I am thankful I am able to spend my time and energy on things that benefit the greater good of all.

Tool #60: Grateful Statements

Gratitude brings you more happiness and more of what you appreciate.[120] It attracts more of what you desire. The universal law of attraction says that you will attract into your life the things you think about and focus on.

Example Grateful Statements:

· I am grateful for what each day brings to me so that I can learn and grow.
· I am grateful for the blue skies and warm sun.
· I am thankful for the birds singing.
· I am grateful for the beauty and power of our Earth.

Tool #61: Life-Affirming Activities

Choose two to five Happiness-Boosting activities and develop a plan to make them a regular part of your life. Just think about what fills you up! I recommend scheduling them on your calendar until they become a habit or way of life. For instance, I do art projects and incorporate hiking or walking into every day.

Tool #62: Reconnecting with Your Soul

There is a recording at www.TheBEINGZone.com/tools that moves you into a place of healing your soul. It is about loving yourself unconditionally and spreading it out to the world to increase energy. It is an ancient technique often called Soul Retrieval used by Shamans across the globe.

Tool #63: Daily Mantra

How we speak to ourselves matters. Your daily mantra incorporates the word or words that really outline who you are and what you stand for. For example, a few of my favorites include "Just *BE*" or "Breathe." They tie back to my intentions and affirmations but are quick ways to say it. One of the best ways to start to reprogram your thinking is repetitively state or chant your personal mantras.

Journaling Time

YOUR "I" STEP IN YOUR DAILY B.E.I.NG.

PRACTICE JOURNALING EXERCISE #104:

Pull out your notebook or *BEING Journal* to make notes in.

- Your intentions are the most likely things to continue to change in your daily practice. Write the ones that are most appropriate for you today and just know as you achieve things, you will be updating these to keep you moving forward.

- Don't forget to build your gratefulness into this, on the front end to help make the intention happen and on the hind end after you have achieved it.

Step #4 - N: Affirm Your True North, AKA Purpose

"What you seek is seeking you."
—Rumi

"N for TRUE NORTH" Overview

In this step you want to come up with an affirmation having to do specifically with your True North. Below are three exercises for daily affirmations of your life's purpose and of your commitment to letting that purpose unfold in your life. Your True North is your orienting point that helps you stay on track in life, like your own personal compass, keeping you pointed in the right direction. This is the step where you align with what is most important to you, state your affirmations in a positive way, and visualize as if it's already happened.

New Tools for Affirming Your True North

Tool #64: Reading Your True North

Write down your True North/Purpose, as you defined it in Chapter 6. This becomes your compass for your daily life. If you know where you are going, it is easier to get there. If your True North/Purpose is what you are focused on daily, you will know what things to do or which direction to turn. Every morning read these and feel into your True North statement as part of your morning practice. Repetition creates the belief within your mind, body, and spirit, and that is what causes it to become a reality.

Tool #65: Visualize Your Goals

The power of visualization is instrumental in turning dreams into reality for anyone. There are specific exercises in Chapter 8 that will assist you in strengthening your visualization skills. The key is to visualize the steps along the way and see success at each level instead of focusing on the final outcome. According to scientific studies, it is seeing success at each step in the process that wins the race.[121] Instead of visualizing yourself on the podium winning medals, you want to visualize every step of the race seeing success and knowing intimately how it feels to run at the perfect pace.

Tool #66: True North Affirmations

The first step to making positive changes in your life is to overcome your negative thoughts and limiting belief systems. The best way to change these patterns is to reprogram the mental energy you are sending out into the Universe through positive affirmations, targeted toward your desired results. The following sample affirmations are all based on "I am" statements and can be built into daily habits.

In Chapter 6, you were given the tools to uncover your True North/Life's Purpose through the exercises. You will find some basic affirmations in the information below about general practices. Feel free to add your specifics to the words.

Example Affirmation Statements:

- I am grounded in all things in my life.
- I am open and flexible to continued growth and learning.
- I honor the power of Source within me and listen and follow the guidance.

- I am love; I am. I am peace; I am. I am happiness; I am.
- I am meant to make a difference in this world for the greater good of all. I will contribute what I am meant to.
- I affirm I trust the process and will let go of things allowing them to unfold in front of me.
- I affirm that I am on Earth to help to transform our world into a better place full of love.

Journaling Time

YOUR "N" STEP IN YOUR DAILY B.E.I.NG.

PRACTICE JOURNALING EXERCISE #105:

Document in your *BEING Journal* or notebook.

- Decide on your purpose and build your affirmation statements and visualizations of it happening into your daily work and add to your notepad.

Step #5 - G: Ask for Universal GUIDANCE

"Silence is the language of god; all else is poor translation."
—Rumi

"G for Guidance" Overview

This is about asking for guidance every day. You are one with the Universe. When you surrender to the signs you receive and believe

in the wisdom bestowed upon you, you learn to co-create miracles with the Universe.

Once you are in your *BEING Zone* state, relaxed and calm, ask
Source to be there with you and guide you. The next step is to ask
Source specific questions that you would like answers to. Then sit
and wait to see what comes to you. If your mind goes back to a
busy state, just stop and breathe and quiet it down again. Then
re-ask your question and stay in that quiet space so you can get
answers. Then trust what comes to you. Just remember, when you
are first starting your practice, you may not even realize you are
receiving messages. In time, it will become stronger and easier to
hear the messages and know they are real.

I offer three tools for acknowledging a power higher than you
and staying open to the guidance you receive. Select the tools
which resonate with you the most and incorporate them into your
daily practice. Feel free to expand on these as much as you wish
as it only increases your connection.

Tool #67: Morning Prayer

Thank you, Source (replace with the word you like), for
deciding for me where you would have me go. Thank you for
guiding me on what you would have me do, and what you would
have me say and to whom. What does the emerging world need
from me now? How may I best serve?

Tool #68: I Am Statements

Say each of the I am statements below out loud and feel
into it. Who or what am I? I am statements are a type of affirma-

tion. I am love; I am. I am happiness; I am. I am peace; I am. I am the divine, I am. I am you; you are me. I am, I will, I have. I am that I am. In me is all of heaven. In heaven is all of me. We are one.

Tool #69: Divine Source Request

Today, Divine Source, show me the way. I am open to all messages and signs. I will listen from deep inside and hold your guidance with reverence. I will move as if there is a force of love and light waiting to aid me in every area of my life, big and small. Use me, whatever I can give, for the highest good of all. Just let me be helpful and contribute what I am meant to, in this world. I know at a deep level that everything is unfolding just precisely as it is meant to, and I completely trust the process and have let go. It is not about my list of desires, but about witnessing my own birth.

Journaling Time

YOUR "G" STEP OF YOUR DAILY B.E.I.NG.

PRACTICE JOURNALING EXERCISE #106:

Open your *BEING Journal* or notebook and begin to write.

· Capture the exact words and sentences you will say and feel into as part of your daily practice for connecting with Source. When you sit with those words and are quiet, you will begin to get guidance.

Summary of the 5 Daily B.E.I.N.G. STEPS

Having a daily practice is a game-changer for you. You set yourself up for success by putting these 5 Daily B.E.I.N.G. Steps into your day. The key to happiness is consistency in *The BEING Zone*. If you are able to be in a present and calm place, then you can deal with most any situation in a thoughtful and happy manner. Most people I know tend to jump out of bed and hit the ground running, which does not bode well for shifting out of the *DOING Zone* and into *The BEING Zone*. I encourage you to create a personalized plan so that it can become a reality in your life. You have the opportunity to build on the foundational 5 Daily B.E.I.N.G. Steps to create your own B.E.I.N.G. Plan. When I spoke to my clients about what keeps them balanced, overwhelmingly it was the daily practice that leveled up their lives.

There is a cheat sheet included below to make this easier for you to write your B.E.I.N.G. Steps. You can also find this PDF at www.TheBEINGZone.com/tools.

You have to know where you are going to get there. The 5 B.E.I.N.G. Steps bring meaning and clarity of direction in your life. Consistently doing your daily practice results in a conscious, healthy, vibrant, and balanced life.

The 5 Daily B.E.I.N.G. Steps:

Step #1 - **B**: Move into Your *BEING Zone*

Step #2 - **E**: Change Your **Energy**

Step #3 - **I**: State Your **Intentions**

Step #4 - **N**: Affirm Your True **North**, AKA Purpose.

Step #5 - **G**: Ask for Universal **Guidance**

CUSTOMIZE YOUR 5 DAILY B.E.I.N.G. STEPS

If you have chosen ways to customize the daily practice, write them into each section below to have a game plan moving forward. Feel free to update and change this as many times as you want.

Step #1: B: Move into Your *BEING* Zone

1. Breathing Step: (Which Tool?)_____

2. Meditation or Relaxation Step: (Which Tool?)_____

Step #2: E: Change Your **Energy**

1. Remove Stuck Energy: (Which tool will you use?)_____

2. Bring in Good Energy: (Which tool will you use?)_____

Step #3: I: State your **Intentions**

1. Write up to three Intention Statements with a gratefulness approach:

    a. _____

    b. _____

    c. _____

Step #4: N: Affirm Your True **North,** AKA Purpose

1. Write up to two Affirmations following guidelines:

    a. _____

    b. _____

Step #5: G: Ask for Universal **Guidance**

1. Choose what words you would like to use for guidance and write below.

    a. _____

Key Messages

· Doing or not doing the B.E.I.N.G. steps daily can make the difference between a good day and a bad day.

· You want to make your 5 Daily B.E.I.N.G. Steps as natural as brushing your teeth.

· Create a practice that fits you and your lifestyle, so it becomes a habit.

· Take time to plan your daily practice today!

> **This Chapter's Gifts: The daily practice needed to transform your life for good.** Watch as your life changes day by day as you incorporate these activities into your life.

Your Happiness is a Choice.

*T*HERE IS AN old saying that the teacher will appear when the student is ready. The tools I've presented in this book are magical when you discipline yourself to use them daily, but I know that not everyone is prepared to do so. As I said in the beginning, not all my clients have been ready to change their lives, but everyone who has committed to going through *The BEING Zone* healing system and built the 5 Daily B.E.I.N.G Steps practice into their life has.

If you are ready, commit today to your daily practice. Who doesn't have time for 10 minutes a day when it can transform your life into one you love? What will you do? Are you ready? It's in your hands, and you are worth it. Don't forget every day is an opportunity for change; one little step at a time, you can transform yourself and the world around you. The tools and techniques are in the book or on my website. A one-on-one session is always an option. If you make the commitment and have the discipline, your life will transform. What will you choose?

Acknowledgments

I AM INDEBTED TO so many people who helped me make this book a reality. From Sarah Hansen, who gave me the courage to consider writing a book, to Annie Willis, who introduced me to Patricia King, who gave me great clarity on who I am and what I should be talking about in the book and life. Kudos to Patricia, who is a brilliant conceptual and developmental editor who made sense out of a tremendous amount of information. I will always be appreciative of being selected by Bruce Lipton and his team to attend the Sundance Ceremony in Alberta, Canada. Thanks to the Cree Tribe teachings, I greatly increased my understanding of how everything is interconnected. I value the time I have spent with Bruce and his family at different events and am awed by their authenticity and generosity. I was fortunate enough to meet March Twisdale at Sundance who generously introduced me to Beth Jusino, who helped me finalize the book and bring it to fruition. Her gifts in writing, editing, and publishing field are unmatched. I have been honored to work with over 1000 clients and been allowed to help guide them in a life-changing way and able to share their stories in this book.

I cherish all the brilliant minds I have learned from over the years that helped me understand the scientific and spiritual concepts that made me stronger as a coach, speaker, and author. I thank Wayne Dyer, Bruce Lipton, Joe Dispenza, Carolyn Myss, Louise Haye, Dr. Bernie Siegel, Dr. Andrew Weil, Mike Dooley, Anita Moorjani, and others for writing books, speaking, and sharing their knowledge. Most importantly, if it wasn't for David Morelli's and his Enwaken Coaches Program, I may not be doing what I do or writing this book. I am forever grateful for having the opportunity to learn from him as it took my life to a whole new level.

I am honored to have a fantastic support team who believes in me and what I am writing about that have dedicated many hours to helping proof, edit, comment, and add insight to what is written in this book. I can't thank Amanda Stovall enough. She co-authored The *BEING Journal* which is a companion book to *The BEING Zone* and is my new partner in crime for launching *The BEING Zone System* Certification program to the world. She has gone through the process and completely and totally revamped her own life and is now a certified Life Coach who is helping transform others' lives. She is one of the most naturally intuitive and positive, uplifting people I know. She has spent hours reading, providing feedback and research as needed to take this book to a higher level. Her contributions have been invaluable. Amanda is a talented artist and her illustrations grace the book and I smile each time I see one of our little stickmen.

I can't ignore all the value John Browning has provided by reading the book, going through the exercises from more of a novice standpoint to point out when something doesn't work or doesn't make sense. He has spent hours reading the book, testing the exercises, and providing valuable input. He gave us invaluable input on web design, and I cannot say enough about our logo's and the beautiful book covers he designed as a testament to his brilliant marketing and design mind. He is a true gift to this world. James Garcia was a true technical wizard bringing *The BEING Zone* website to life.

My son Brady thinks out of the box and challenges status quo. He is a lot like me where he doesn't see what is but what can be. He has a gift of knowing what people with connect with and has been instrumental in challenging me to think differently the marketing realm. My son Bryan is very analytical by nature but believes in what I teach and has been successful in transforming his own life to a better place following many of these beliefs over the years and always provides great support to me technically and personally.

Last but not least, I have to thank my husband, Mark, for his tremendous love, support and patience over the years as I have built my business and his belief in my ability to write a book that can make a difference and change lives.

About the Author

MARLA WILLIAMS IS not your average life, career, or business coach. She is a pioneering visionary who has experienced tremendous success as a key leader in helping create a culture that grew a $12-million-dollar company into a global leader in the industry, that later sold to a Fortune 500 and became a $2.3-billion-dollar corporation. She intuitively knew she was meant to do more in this world and went on to create her own legacy by building her own successful coaching business. Her extensive leadership experience includes strategic planning, human resource management, project management, marketing, and business ownership, making her uniquely able to understand and address issues across a wide variety of people, teams, and organizations. She has been instrumental in helping develop and improve culture within a variety of organizations. Whether she is coaching or speaking, Marla customizes every experience as she realizes that no two people, groups, or companies are alike.

Marla's own life story of dealing with ongoing health issues as a result of pushing herself too hard and being in a continual stress-state were the impetus for this book. She found solutions and healed herself when the medical community didn't have answers for her. She has taken her hands-on experiences and put them into a system that can help others heal and transform their lives as she did by learning to operate in *The BEING Zone*. She knew by documenting her experiences and sharing the tools she learned along the way, she could make a big difference in the lives of others who are going through similar struggles.

Marla's gifts are her innovative spirit and her innate ability to know exactly what to focus on as she guides her clients and/or their teams/companies through personal transformations where they are creating their own legacy or creating game-changing cultures that exist long after they are gone. If you are an individual seeking better health or greater meaning in life, knowing you want to make a more significant difference, this is a book to read to take your life to a higher level.

Training and Certification:

I F YOU ARE a Coach, Psychologist, Therapist, or work in a related field where you work with clients to help them transform their lives, you will benefit from being trained and certified in *The BEING Zone System*. If you are interested and ready to become certified as a *BEING Zone* Practitioner, go to www. TheBEINGZone.com to find a class schedule or online class that meets your needs.

Tool Index

Endnotes

1   "Stress, the 'health epidemic of the 21st century'," HCA Today, April 30, 2019. https://hcatodayblog.com/2019/04/30/stress-the-health-epidemic-of-the-21st-century/

2   Richard Florida, "The Unhappy States of America," CityLab, March 20, 2018. https://www.citylab.com/life/2018/03/the-unhappy-states-of-america/555800/

3   Ann Pietranglo and Stephanie Watson, "The Effects of Stress on Your Body," Healthline, June 5, 2017. https://www.healthline.com/health/stress/effects-on-body#1

4   Dr. Joe Dispenza, *Evolve Your Brain* (Health Communications Inc, 2008) and *Breaking the Habit of Being Yourself*, (Hay House, 2013).

5   Jessica Firger, "Chronic Fatigue Syndrome Affects 1 in 50 Teens," Newsweek, January 26, 2016, https://www.newsweek.com/chronic-fatigue-syndrome-affects-1-50-teens-419365

6   Rui Chen et al., "Traditional Chinese Medicine for Chronic Fatigue Syndrome," Evidence-based Complementary and Alternative Medicine Volume 7, Issue 1 (2010): 3-10. https://www.ncbi.nlm.nih.gov/pmc/articles/PMC2816380/

7   Dr. Joe Dispenza, "Introduction to *Breaking the Habit of Being Yourself*," YouTube, November 30, 2012. https://www.youtube.com/watch?v=6lbnrRqBjgE

8   Ben Renner, "American Families Spend Just 37 Minutes of Quality Time Together Per Day, Study Find," StudyFinds, March 21, 2018. https://www.studyfinds.org/american-families-spend-37-minutes-quality-time/

9   "Understanding the Impact of Trauma," in *Trauma-Informed Care in Behav-
       ioral Health Services* (Rockville, MD: Substance Abuse and Mental Health
       Administration, 2014). https://www.ncbi.nlm.nih.gov/books/NBK207191/

10   "Psychiatric Aspects of Chronic Pain," in Pain and Disability: Clinical, Behav-
       ioral, and Public Policy Perspectives, ed. Osterweis M, Kleinman A, Mechanic
       D (Washington (DC): National Academies Press (US); 1987). https://www.
       ncbi.nlm.nih.gov/books/NBK219250/

11   Susanne Babbel MFT, PhD, "The Connections Between Emotional Stress,
       Trauma and Physical Pain," Psychology Today, April 8, 2010, https://www.psy-
       chologytoday.com/us/blog/somatic-psychology/201004/the-connections-be-
       tween-emotional-stress-trauma-and-physical-pain

12   Nancy Olson, "Three Ways That Handwriting With A Pen Positively Affects
       your Brain," Forbes, May 15, 2015, https://www.forbes.com/sites/nancyol-
       son/2016/05/15/three-ways-that-writing-with-a-pen-positively-affects-your-
       brain/#3ef427e95705

13   Dr. Claudia Aguirre, "Does writing by hand sharpen your creativity," Head-
       space, September 23, 2015, https://www.headspace.com/blog/2015/09/23/can-
       handwriting-sharpen-your-mind/

14   "CDC-Kaiser ACE Study," Centers for Disease Control and Prevention, April
       2, 2019, https://www.cdc.gov/violenceprevention/childabuseandneglect/ace-
       study/about.html

15   Kristen Selleck, Jeannie Newman, and Debra Gilmore, "Child Protection in
       Families Experiencing Domestic Violence," in Child Abuse and Neglect User
       Manual Series, Page 18, https://www.childwelfare.gov/pubPDFs/domesticvio-
       lence2018.pdf

16   "Scope of the Problem: Statistics," RAINN, https://www.rainn.org/statistics/
       scope-problem

17   Rachel E Morgan, PhD., and Grace Kena, "Criminal Victimizations, 2016:
       Revised," U.S. Department of Justice, Bureau of Justice Statistics, October
       2018. https://www.bjs.gov/content/pub/pdf/cv16.pdf

18   "How Common is PTSD in Adults?", PTSD: National Center for PTSD,
       U.S. Department of Veterans Affairs, https://www.ptsd.va.gov/understand/
       common/common_adults.asp

19   University of Gothenburg. "Intensive mobile phone use affects young people's
       sleep." ScienceDaily. www.sciencedaily.com/releases/2012/06/120611134233.
       htm (accessed April 1, 2020).

20   SWNS, "Americans check their phones 80 times a day: study," New York Post, November 8, 2017, https://nypost.com/2017/11/08/americans-check-their-phones-80-times-a-day-study/ "Americans Check Their Phones 96 Times a Day," Asurion, November 21, 2019, https://www.asurion.com/about/press-releases/americans-check-their-phones-96-times-a-day/

21   "Technology Addiction," Digital Responsibility, http://www.digitalresponsibility.org/technology-addiction

22   "Smartphone Addiction," HelpGuide, February 14, 2020, https://www.helpguide.org/articles/addictions/smartphone-addiction.htm

23   Gareth Cook, "Why We Are Wired to Connect," Scientific American, October 22, 2013, https://www.scientificamerican.com/article/why-we-are-wired-to-connect/

24   David E. Linden, "Neurofeedback and networks of depression," Dialogues in Clinical Neuroscience Volume 16, Issue No. 1(2014): 103-112. https://www.ncbi.nlm.nih.gov/pmc/articles/PMC3984886/

25   "New Cigna Study Reveals Loneliness at Epidemic Levels in America," Multivu, https://www.multivu.com/players/English/8294451-cigna-us-loneliness-survey/

26   Ruben Castaneda, "How Your Smartphone May Be Making You Unhappy," U.S. News & World Report, February 12, 2018, https://health.usnews.com/wellness/mind/articles/2018-02-12/how-your-smartphone-may-be-making-you-unhappy

27   Shelley Galasso Bonanno, MA, "Social Media's Impact on Relationships," PsychCentral, October 8, 2018, https://psychcentral.com/lib/social-medias-impact-on-relationships/

28   Kross E, Verduyn P, Demiralp E, Park J, Lee DS, Lin N, et al., "Facebook Use Predicts Declines in Subjective Well-Being in Young Adults" (University of Michigan, 2013). http://selfcontrol.psych.lsa.umich.edu/wp-content/uploads/2017/02/PLOS_Paper.pdf

29   James A. Roberts and Meredith E. David, "My life has become a major distraction from my cell phone: Partner phubbing and relationship satisfaction among romantic partners," Computers in Human Behavior Volume 54, January (2016): 134-141 https://www.sciencedirect.com/science/article/pii/S0747563215300704?via%3Dihub

30   Xingchao Wang, et al., "Partner phubbing and depression among married Chinese adults: The roles of relationship satisfaction and relationship length," Personality and Individual Differences, Volume 10 (May 2017): 12-17. https://www.researchgate.net/publication/312382860_Partner_phubbing_and_depression_among_married_Chinese_adults_The_roles_of_relationship_satisfaction_and_relationship_length

31 Kate Moran and Kim Flaherty, "Filling the Silence with Digital Noise," Nielsen Norman Group, https://www.nngroup.com/articles/filling-silence-digital-noise/

32 Timothy D. Wilson, et al., "Just think: The challenges of a disengaged mind," Science Magazine, Volume 345, Issue No. 6192 (2014): 75-77. https://science.sciencemag.org/content/345/6192/75

33 Dr. Daniel Goleman, Emotional Intelligence: Why It Can Matter More Than IQ (Bantam, 2005).

34 Ruben Castaneda, "How Your Smartphone May Be Making You Unhappy," U.S. News & World Report, February 12, 2018, https://health.usnews.com/wellness/mind/articles/2018-02-12/how-your-smartphone-may-be-making-you-unhappy

35 "Smartphone Addiction," HelpGuide, February 14, 2020, https://www.helpguide.org/articles/addictions/smartphone-addiction.htm

36 Erin Reid and Lakshmi Ramarajan, "Managing the High-Intensity Workplace," Harvard Business Review, June 2016, https://hbr.org/2016/06/managing-the-high-intensity-workplace

37 "Technology Creating Workaholics, Professor Says," The Oklahoman, January 22, 1992, https://oklahoman.com/article/2382558/technology-creating-workaholics-professor-says

38 Melissa A. Clark, PhD, "Workaholism: It's not just long hours on the job," American Psychological Association, April 2016, https://www.apa.org/science/about/psa/2016/04/workaholism

39 Janet Byron, "KP Research Radio: Epidemic of deaths due to heart failure underway in U.S.," October 29, 2019, https://spotlight.kaiserpermanente.org/epidemic-of-deaths-due-to-heart-failure/

40 Kavitha Chinnaiyan, MD, "Want To Beat Heart Disease? Deal With Your Emotional Issues," Mindbodygreen, February 5, 2020, https://www.mindbodygreen.com/0-12817/want-to-beat-heart-disease-deal-with-your-emotional-issues.html

41 Ning Xia and Huige Li, "Loneliness, Social Isolation, and Cardiovascular Health," Antioxidants & Redox Signaling Volume 28, Issue No. 9 (2018): 837-851. https://www.ncbi.nlm.nih.gov/pmc/articles/PMC5831910/

42 Alan Rozanski, et al., "Impact of Psychological Factors on the Pathogenesis of Cardiovascular Disease and Implications for Therapy," Circulation 99 (1999):2192-2217. https://www.ahajournals.org/doi/full/10.1161/01.cir.99.16.2192

43   "Brain Waves," ScienceDirect, April 22, 2020, https://www.sciencedirect.com/topics/agricultural-and-biological-sciences/brain-waves

44   Craig Gustafson, "Bruce Lipton, PhD: The Jump from Cell Culture to Consciousness," Integr Med (Encinitas) Volume 16, Issue No. 6 (2017): 44-50. https://www.ncbi.nlm.nih.gov/pmc/articles/PMC6438088/

45   Bret Stetka, "Changing Our DNA through Mind Control?", Scientific American, December 16, 2014, https://www.scientificamerican.com/article/changing-our-dna-through-mind-control/

46   "Anxiety and depression linked to increased cancer and death risk," NHS, January 26, 2017, https://www.nhs.uk/news/cancer/anxiety-and-depression-linked-to-increased-cancer-death-risk/

47   "What Is Tapping and How Does It Work?", Tapping Solution Foundation, April 3, 2020, https://www.tappingsolutionfoundation.org/howdoesitwork/

48   Craig Weiner, DC, and Alina Frank, "What is EFT?", EFT Tapping Training Institute, July 28, 2019, https://www.efttappingtraining.com/what-is-eft/

49   David Feinstein, "Acupoint Stimulation in Treating Psychological Disorders: Evidence of Efficacy, Review of General Psychology, August 20, 2012, https://yves-wauthier.com/wp-content/uploads/2014/06/acupoint-stimulation-feinstein.pdf

50   Connie Domino, The Law of Forgiveness: Tap in to the Positive Power of Forgiveness—and Attract Good Things to Your Life (Berkley, 2009).

51   Therese J. Borchard, "The Power of Forgiveness," PsychCentral, July 8, 2018, https://psychcentral.com/blog/the-power-of-forgiveness/

52   KA Lawler, et al., "A change of heart: cardiovascular correlates of forgiveness in response to interpersonal conflict," Journal of Behavioral Medicine Volume 26, Issue No. 5 (2003): 373-93. https://www.ncbi.nlm.nih.gov/pubmed/14593849

53   Kirsten Weir, "Forgiveness can improve mental and physical health," Monitor on Psychology Volume 48, Issue No. 1(2017): 30 https://www.apa.org/monitor/2017/01/ce-corner

54   Dr. Marc Sopher, "TMS – Information," date unknown, http://www.tms-mindbodymedicine.com/tmsinfo.html

55   Dr. John Sarno, The Divided Mind (New York: Harper Perennial, 2007).

56   Julia Belluz, "America's most famous back pain doctor said pain is in your head. Thousands think he's right," Vox, July 23, 2018, https://www.vox.com/science-and-health/2017/10/2/16338094/dr-john-sarno-healing-back-pain

57   All the Rage, directed by Michael Galinsky, Suki Hawley, and David Beilinson (2017: RumuR Inc.)

58   Mike Dooley, Choose Them Wisely: Thoughts Become Things (Portland, OR: Beyond Words, 2010).

59   Daniel E. Gustafson, Alta du Pont, Mark A. Whisman, and Akira Miyake, "Evidence for Transdiagnostic Repetitive Negative Thinking and Its Association with Rumination, Worry, and Depression and Anxiety Symptoms: A Commonality Analysis, Collabra: Psychology Volume 4, Issue No. 1(2018): 13. https://www.ncbi.nlm.nih.gov/pmc/articles/PMC6370308/

60   Edward R. Watkins, "Constructive and Unconstructive Repetitive Thought," Psychological Bulletin Volume 134, Issue No. 2(2008): 163-206. https://www.ncbi.nlm.nih.gov/pmc/articles/PMC2672052/

61   Daniel E. Gustafson, Alta du Pont, Mark A. Whisman, and Akira Miyake, "Evidence for Transdiagnostic Repetitive Negative Thinking and Its Association with Rumination, Worry, and Depression and Anxiety Symptoms: A Commonality Analysis, Collabra: Psychology Volume 4, Issue No. 1(2018): 13. https://www.ncbi.nlm.nih.gov/pmc/articles/PMC6370308/

62   University of Colorado at Boulder. "Your brain on imagination: It's a lot like reality, study shows." ScienceDaily. www.sciencedaily.com/releases/2018/12/181210144943.htm (accessed April 3, 2020).

63   Pablo Briñol, Margarita Gascó, Richard E. Petty, et al., "Treating Thoughts as Material Objects Can Increase or Decrease Their Impact on Evaluation," Psychological Science Volume 24, Issue No. 1(2013): 41-41. https://journals.sagepub.com/doi/abs/10.1177/0956797612449176

64   "Chapter 06: Energetic Communication," in Science of the Heart: exploring the role of the heart in human performance (HearthMath Research Center, 2001), https://www.heartmath.org/research/science-of-the-heart/energetic-communication/

65   "New Study Further Supports Intuition," Science of the Heart, October 2, 2010, https://www.heartmath.org/articles-of-the-heart/science-of-the-heart/new-study-further-supports-intuition/

66   "The Brain-Gut Connection," Johns Hopkins Medicine, April 03, 2020, https://www.hopkinsmedicine.org/health/wellness-and-prevention/the-brain-gut-connection

67   Richard E. Cytowic, MD, "The Pit in Your Stomach is Actually Your Second Brain," Psychology Today, January 17, 2017, https://www.psychologytoday.com/us/blog/the-fallible-mind/201701/the-pit-in-your-stomach-is-actually-your-second-brain

68   Megan Clapp, Nadia Aurora, Lindsey Herrera, et al., "Gut microbiota's effect on mental health: The gut-brain axis," Clinics and Practice Volume 15, Issue No. 4 (2017): 987. https://www.ncbi.nlm.nih.gov/pmc/articles/PMC5641835/

69   Adam Hadhazy, "Think Twice: How the Gut's "Second Brain" influences Mood and Well-Being," Scientific American, February 12, 2010, https://www.scientificamerican.com/article/gut-second-brain/

70   Marcia Reynolds, PsyD, "How to Use Your Intuition," Psychology Today, September 24, 2014, https://www.psychologytoday.com/us/blog/wander-woman/201409/how-use-your-intuition

71   Lisa Firestone, PhD, "The Healing Power of Gratitude," Psychology Today, November 19, 2015, https://www.psychologytoday.com/us/blog/compassion-matters/201511/the-healing-power-gratitude

72   Jeremy Dean, PhD, "Practicing Gratitude Can Increase Happiness by 25%," PSYBLOG (blog), September 2007, https://www.spring.org.uk/2007/09/practicing-gratitude-can-increase.php

73   Robert A. Emmons and Robin Stern, "Gratitude as a Psychotherapeutic Intervention," Journal Of Clinical Psychology: In Session Volume 69, Issue No. 8(2013): 846-855. http://ei.yale.edu/wp-content/uploads/2013/11/jclp22020.pdf

74   Nancy Digdon and Amy Koble, "Effects of Constructive Worry, Imagery Distraction, and Gratitude Interventions on Sleep Quality: A Pilot Trial," Applied Psychology: Health and Well-Being Volume 3, Issue No. 2(2011). https://onlinelibrary.wiley.com/doi/abs/10.1111/j.1758-0854.2011.01049.x

75   Frederick M. Winship, "Forbes memorialized as 'happiest millionaire'", UPI, March 1, 1990, https://www.upi.com/Archives/1990/03/01/Forbes-memorialized-as-happiest-millionaire/8383636267600/

76   Steve Taylor, PhD, "The Madness of Materialism," Psychology Today, March 10, 2012, https://www.psychologytoday.com/us/blog/out-the-darkness/201203/the-madness-materialism

77   Kathleen Doheny, "Working Yourself to Death: Long Hours Bring Risks," WebMD, July 16, 2018, https://www.webmd.com/balance/stress-management/news/20180716/working-yourself-to-death-long-hours-bring-risks

78   John Ross, MD, FIDSA, "Only the overworked die young," Harvard Health Blog (blog), Harvard Health Publishing, Harvard Medical School, December 14, 2015, https://www.health.harvard.edu/blog/only-the-overworked-die-young-20151214881

79   Lindsay Kolowich, "Why Overworking Is Bad For Your Health (And Who's to Blame)," Hubspot (blog), July 28, 2017, https://blog.hubspot.com/marketing/overwork-bad-health

80   "Understanding the stress response," Harvard Health Publishing, May 1, 2018, https://www.health.harvard.edu/staying-healthy/understanding-the-stress-response

81   Steven Sauter, et al., "Stress...At Work," DHHS (NIOSH) Publication No. 99-101, CDC, https://www.cdc.gov/niosh/docs/99-101/pdfs/99-101.pdf

82   Lieke ten Brummelhuis and Nancy P. Rothbard, "Workaholic Differs from Working Long Hours—and Why That Matters for Your Health," Harvard Business Review, March 22, 2018, https://hbr.org/2018/03/how-being-a-workaholic-differs-from-working-long-hours-and-why-that-matters-for-your-health

83   Dr. Joe Dispenza, "The Art of Change," Dr. Joe Dispenza (blog), April 3, 2020, https://drjoedispenza.net/blog/the-art-of-change/

84   Lisa Ryan and Suzanne Dziurawiec, "Materialism and Its Relationship to Life Satisfaction," Social Indicators Research Volume 55 (2001): 185-197. https://link.springer.com/article/10.1023/A:1011002123169

85   Karyn Twaronite, Global generations: A global study on work-life challenges across generations, (EY, 2015), https://www.ey.com/Publication/vwLUAssets/Global_generations_study/$FILE/EY-global-generations-a-global-study-on-work-life-challenges-across-generations.pdf

86   "Who's Feeling Rushed?", Pew Research Center, February 28, 2006, https://www.pewsocialtrends.org/2006/02/28/whos-feeling-rushed/

87   Kris Gunnars, "Nine ways that processed foods are harming people," Medical News Today, August 1, 2017, https://www.medicalnewstoday.com/articles/318630

88   The Magic Pill, directed by Robert Tate, September 7, 2017, https://g.co/kgs/XCBF4P

89   Len Wisneski, MP, FACP, and Lucy Anderson, MSW, "The Scientific Basis of Integrative Medicine," Evidence-Based Complementary and Alternative Medicine Volume 2, Issue No. 2(2005): 257-259, https://www.ncbi.nlm.nih.gov/pmc/articles/PMC1142191/

90   Bruce H. Lipton, PhD, The Biology of Belief 10th Anniversary Edition (Hay House, 2016).

91   Tina Schomburg, "How to Heal Your Body by Using the Frequency of Life," Medium (blog), October 23, 2014, https://medium.com/meducated-org/how-to-heal-your-body-by-using-the-frequency-of-life-9307af550fbb

92   Dr. Joe Dispenza, *Breaking the Habit of Being Yourself*, (Hay House, 2013).

93   Dr. Richard Gerber, Vibrational Medicine Handbook, (Bear & Company, 2001).

94   Graham C.L. Davey, PhD, "The Psychological Effects of TV News," Psychology Today, June 19, 2012, https://www.psychologytoday.com/us/blog/why-we-worry/201206/the-psychological-effects-tv-news

95   Dr, Lissa Rankin, Mind Over Medicine: Scientific Proof That You Can Heal Yourself (Hay House, 2014).

96   A Mohagheghzadeh, P Faridi, M Shams-Ardakani, Y Ghasemi, "Medicinal smokes," Journal of Ethnopharmacology Volume 108, Issue No. 2(2006): 161-184, https://www.ncbi.nlm.nih.gov/pubmed/17030480

97   "This is Actual Science. Crystals at the Earth's Core Power its Magnetic Field," Universe Today, February 27, 2017, https://www.universetoday.com/133791/actual-science-crystals-earths-core-power-magnetic-field/

98   The Earthing Movie, directed by Josh and Rebecca Tickell (2019), Online. https://www.groundology.co.uk/videos?show=the-earthing-movie

99   "First-Ever Study: Grounding Patients with Hypertension Improves Blood Pressure," PR Newswire, March 06, 2019, https://www.prnewswire.com/news-releases/first-ever-study-grounding-patients-with-hypertension-improves-blood-pressure-300807799.html

100   Dr. Josh Axe, "Earthing: 5 Ways It Can Help You Fight Disease," DrAxe.com, August 23, 2019, https://draxe.com/health/earthing/

101   Dr. Laura Koniver, "Grounding FAQs," Intuition Physician, https://www.intuition-physician.com/grounding-faqs/

102   "Energy Flows Where Attention Goes - Focus & Energy: Tony Robbins," TobyRobbins.com, August 21, 2019, https://www.tonyrobbins.com/career-business/where-focus-goes-energy-flows/

103   Len Wisneski, MP, FACP, and Lucy Anderson, MSW, "The Scientific Basis of Integrative Medicine," Evidence-Based Complementary and Alternative Medicine Volume 2, Issue No. 2(2005): 257-259, https://www.ncbi.nlm.nih.gov/pmc/articles/PMC1142191/

104   "The Pineal Gland and The Third Eye Chakra," Gaia, February 26, 2020, https://www.gaia.com/article/pineal-third-eye-chakra

105   Deborah King, "The Secret to Connecting with God," Heal Your Life, May 97, 2014, https://www.healyourlife.com/the-secret-to-connecting-with-god

106   Anne Marie Helmenstine, PhD, "How Many Atoms Are There in a Human Cell?" ThoughtCo. https://www.thoughtco.com/how-many-atoms-in-human-cell-603882 (accessed May 14, 2020).

107 Lily Feinn, "Binge-Watching Television May Make Us Depressed, According To New Study," Bustle, March 7, 2016, https://www.bustle.com/articles/146333-binge-watching-television-may-make-us-depressed-according-to-new-study

108 Melanie Curtin, "This 75-Year Harvard Study Found the 1 Secret to Leading a Fulfilling Life," Inc., February 27, 2017, https://www.inc.com/melanie-curtin/want-a-life-of-fulfillment-a-75-year-harvard-study-says-to-prioritize-this-one-t.html

109 John Sharry, "The importance of relationships and belonging," The Irish Times, March 4, 2018, https://www.irishtimes.com/life-and-style/health-family/parenting/the-importance-of-relationships-and-belonging-1.3405948

110 Lukasz M. Konopka, "Where art meets neuroscience: a new horizon of art therapy," Croatian Medical Journal Volume 55, Issue No. 1(2014): 73-74. https://www.ncbi.nlm.nih.gov/pmc/articles/PMC3944420/

111 Vanessa Van Edwards, "The Benefits of Music: How the Science of Music Can Help You," Science of People, February 24, 2020, https://www.scienceofpeople.com/benefits-music/

112 Laura Ferreri, Ernest Mas-Herrero, Robert J. Zatorre, et al., "Dopamine modulates the reward experiences elicited by music," Proceedings of the National Academy of Sciences Volume 116, Issue No. 9(2019): 3793-3798. https://www.pnas.org/content/116/9/3793

113 Stacey Colino, "The Health Benefits of Expressive Writing," U.S. News & World Report, August 31, 2016, https://health.usnews.com/wellness/articles/2016-08-31/the-health-benefits-of-expressive-writing

114 Sheldon Cohen and Thomas Ashby Wills, "Stress, Social Support, and the Buffering Hypothesis," Psychological Bulletin Volume 98, Issue No. 2(1985): 310-357. http://lchc.ucsd.edu/MCA/Mail/xmcamail.2012_11.dir/pdfYukIL-vXsL0.pdf

115 Maria-Victoria Zunzunegui, Beatriz E. Alvarado, Teodoro Del Ser, and Angel Otero, "Social Networks, Social Integration, and Social Engagement Determine Cognitive Decline in Community-Dwelling Spanish Older Adults," The Journal of Gerontology Series B: Psychological Sciences and Social Sciences Volume 58, Issue No. 2(2003): S93-S100. https://www.ncbi.nlm.nih.gov/pmc/articles/PMC3833829/

116 John Sharry, "The importance of relationships and belonging," The Irish Times, March 4, 2018, https://www.irishtimes.com/life-and-style/health-family/parenting/the-importance-of-relationships-and-belonging-1.3405948

117 "If You Feel Thankful, Write It Down. It's Good For Your Health," NPR, December 24, 2018, https://www.npr.org/sections/health-shots/2018/12/24/678232331/if-you-feel-thankful-write-it-down-its-good-for-your-health

118 Ephrat Livini, "Blue Mind science proves the health benefits of being by water," Quartz, August 5, 2018, https://qz.com/1347904/blue-mind-science-proves-the-health-benefits-of-being-by-water/

119 Peter Economy, "14 Scientifically Proved Ways Gratitude Can Bring You Success and Happiness," Inc., November 03, 2016, https://www.inc.com/peter-economy/14-powerfully-beneficial-effects-of-gratitude.html

120 "Giving thanks can make you happier," Healthbeat (blog), Harvard Health Publishing, accessed April 5, 2020, https://www.health.harvard.edu/healthbeat/giving-thanks-can-make-you-happier

121 Lien B. Pham and Shelley E. Taylor, "From Thought to Action: Effects of Process-Versus Outcome-Based Mental Stimulations on Performance," Personality and Social Psychology Bulletin Volume 25, Issue No. 2(1999): 250-260. https://journals.sagepub.com/doi/abs/10.1177/0146167299025002010

Made in the USA
Coppell, TX
25 September 2020

38778068R00218